ISBN 978-1-4234-3932-5

7777 W. BLUEMOUND RD. P.O. BOX 13819 MILWAUKEE, WI 53213

Visit Hal Leonard Online at
www.halleonard.com

Are You Gonna Be My Girl

Words and Music by Nic Cester and Cameron Muncey

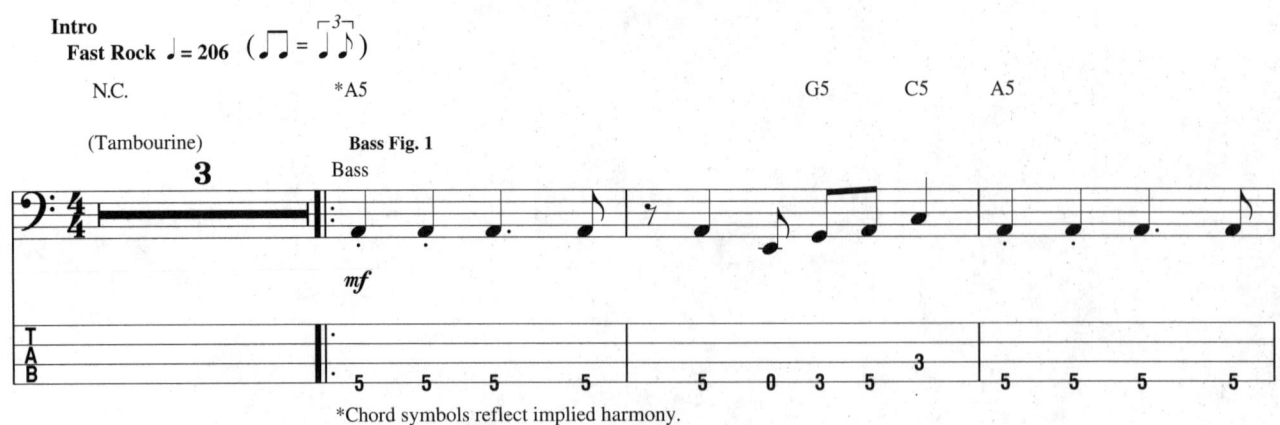

*Chord symbols reflect implied harmony.

Bass: w/ Bass Fig. 1 (1st 7 meas.)

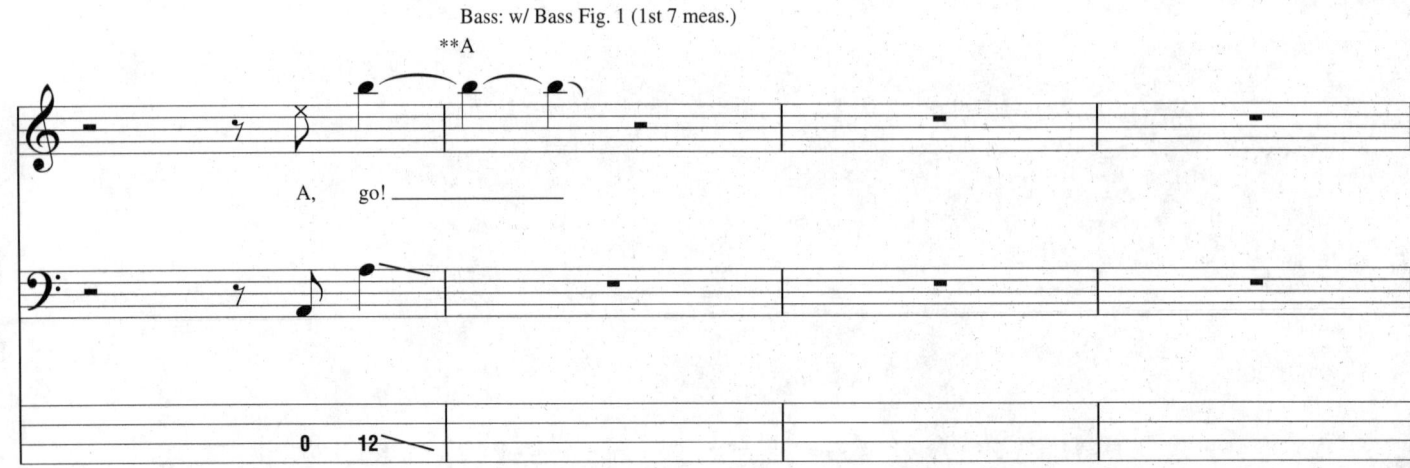

**Chord symbols reflect overall harmony.

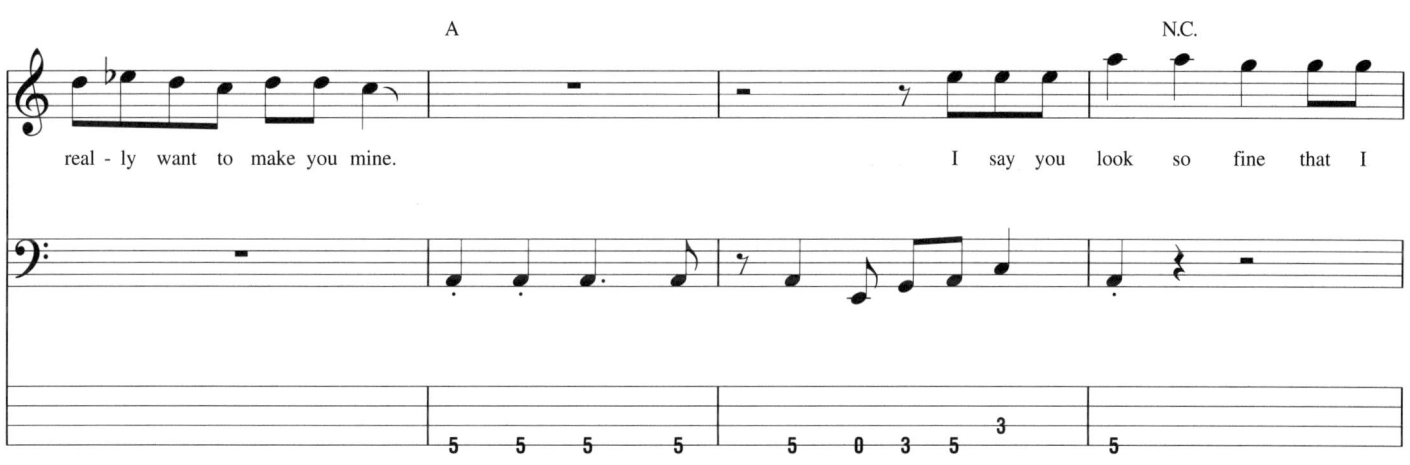

_____ and get your kicks. Now you don't need mon-ey { when you look like that, do you, hon - ey? }
{ with a face like that, do ya? _____ }

Bass: w/ Bass Fig. 1 (last 4 meas.)

Pre-Chorus

Big _____ black boots, long _____ brown hair. _____

Bass Fig. 2

End Bass Fig. 2

Bass: w/ Bass Fig. 2

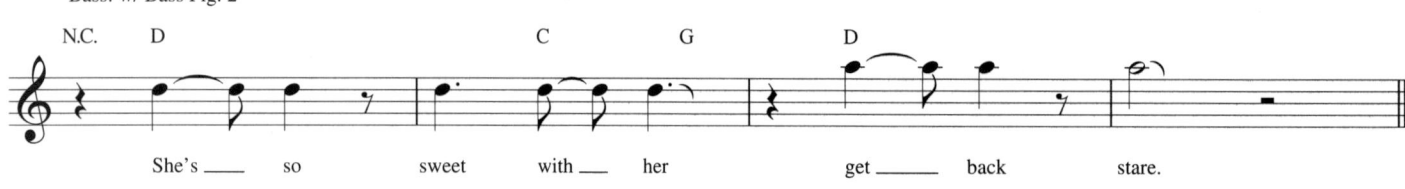

She's _____ so sweet with _____ her get _____ back stare.

Chorus

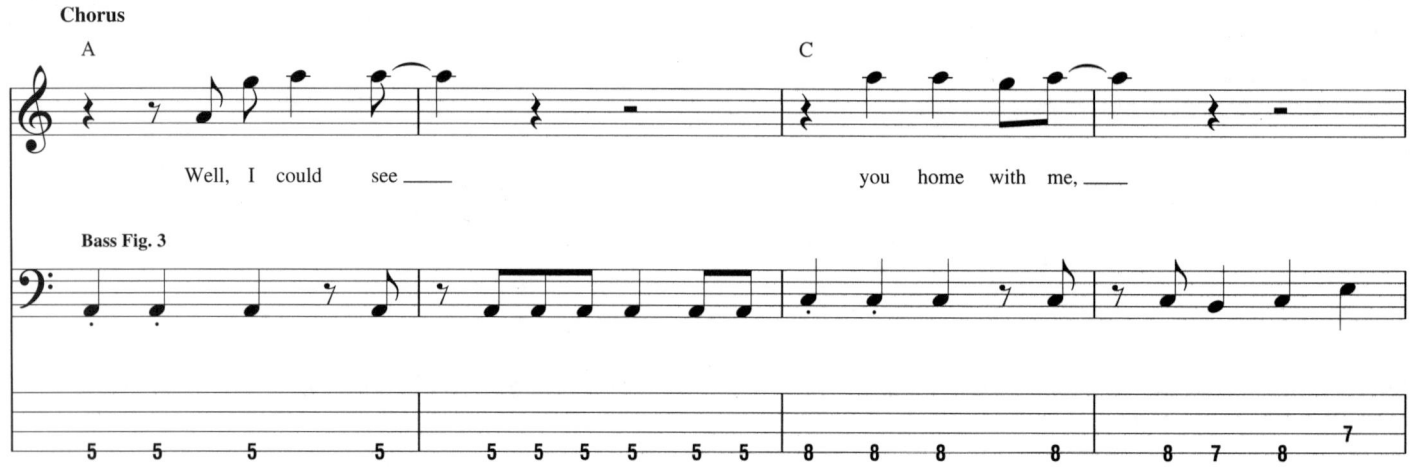

Well, I could see _____ you home with me, _____

Bass Fig. 3

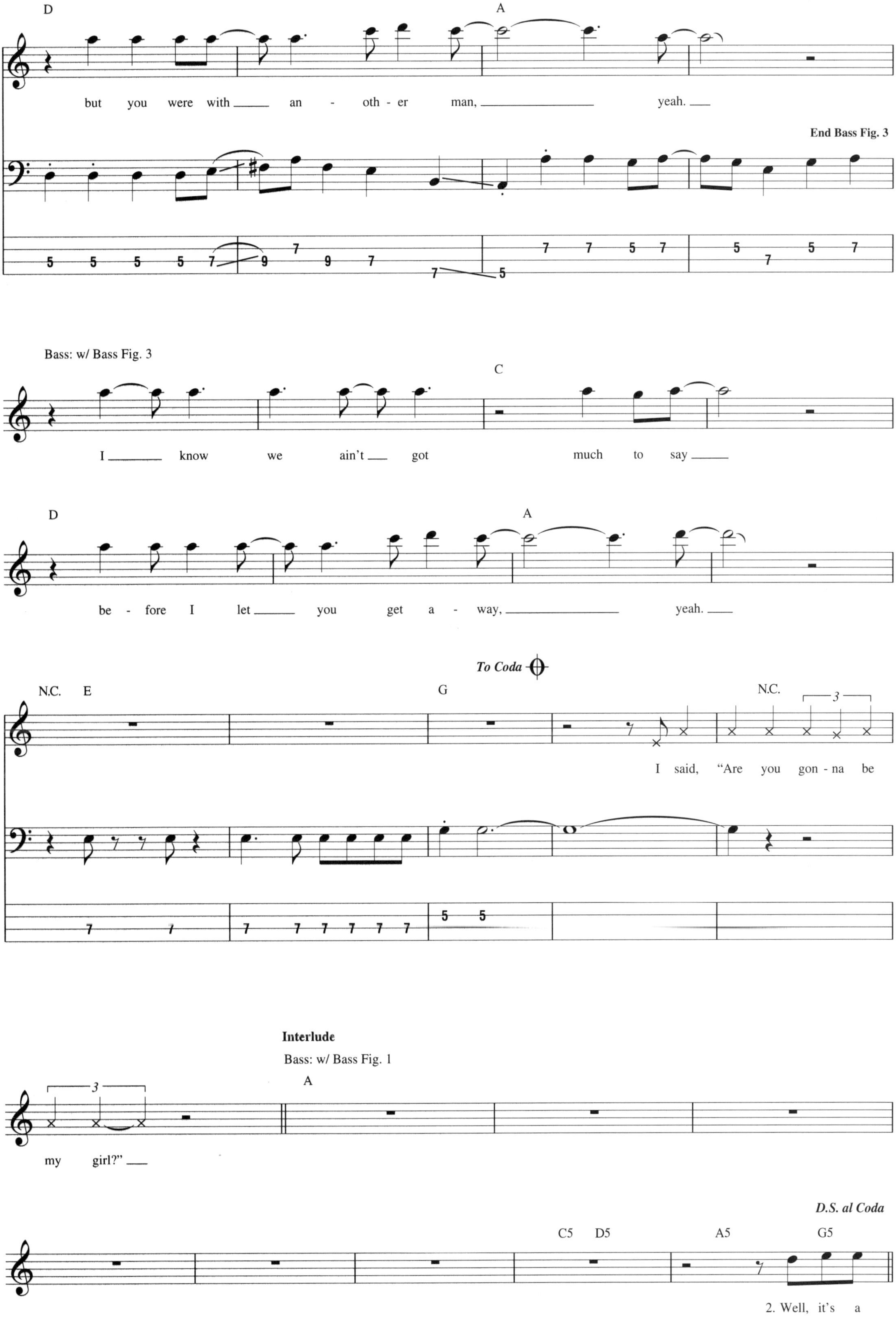

D

but you were with _____ an - oth - er man, _____ yeah. _____

End Bass Fig. 3

Bass: w/ Bass Fig. 3

I _____ know we ain't _____ got much to say _____

D

be - fore I let _____ you get a - way, _____ yeah. _____

To Coda ⊕

N.C. **E**

I said, "Are you gon - na be

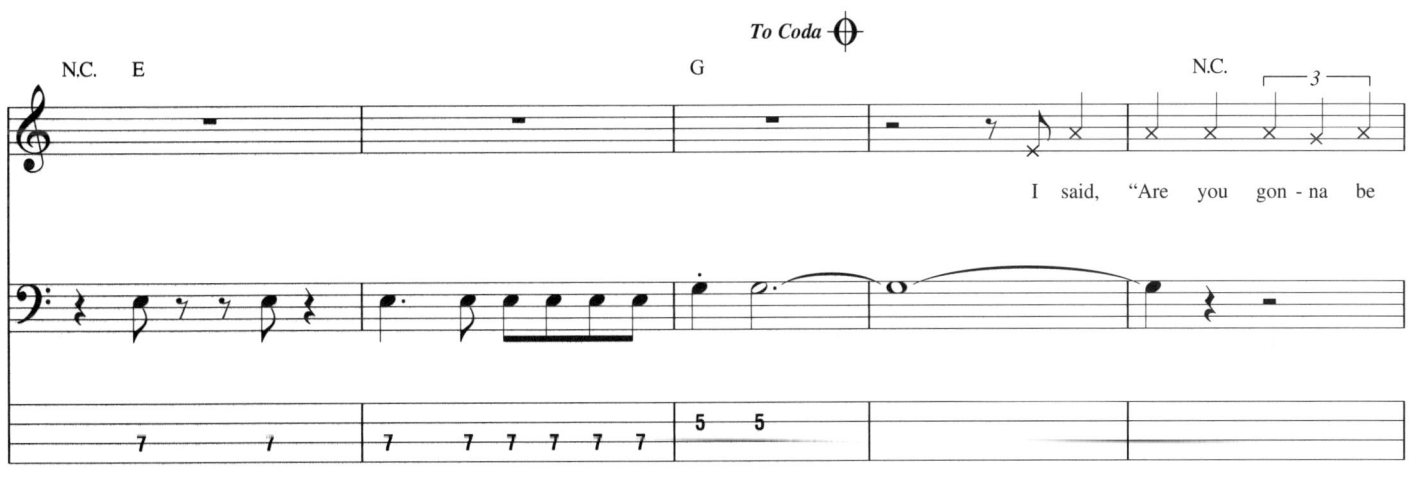

Interlude

Bass: w/ Bass Fig. 1

my girl?" _____

D.S. al Coda

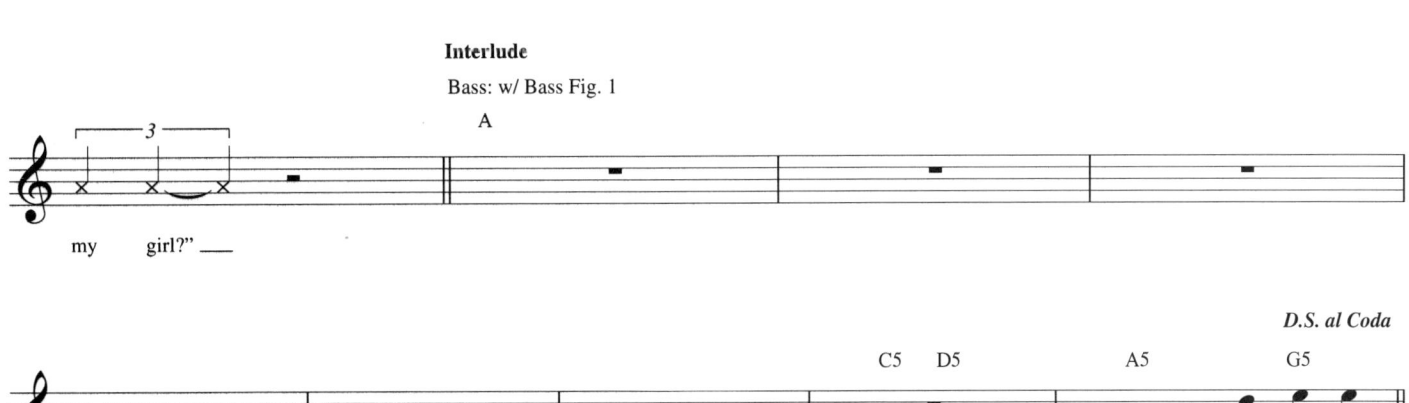

2. Well, it's a

⊕ Coda

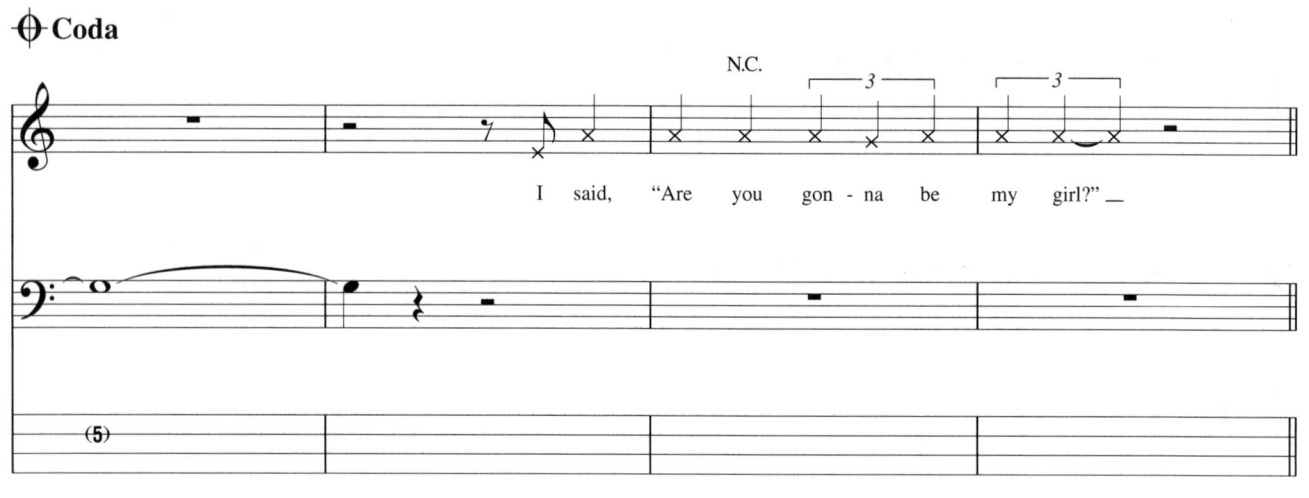

N.C.

I said, "Are you gon-na be my girl?" —

Interlude

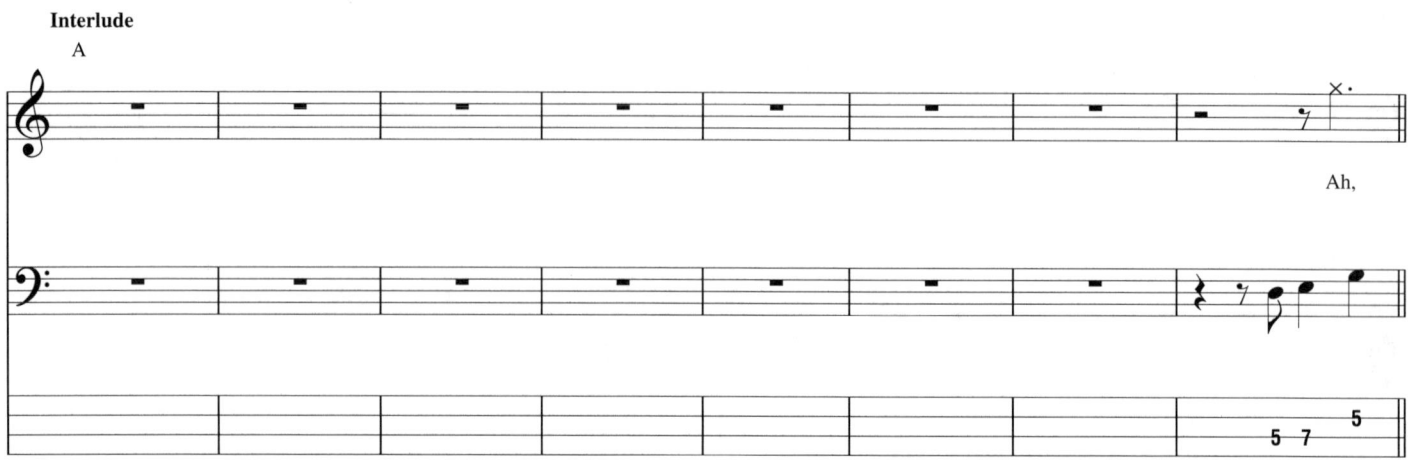

Ah,

Guitar Solo

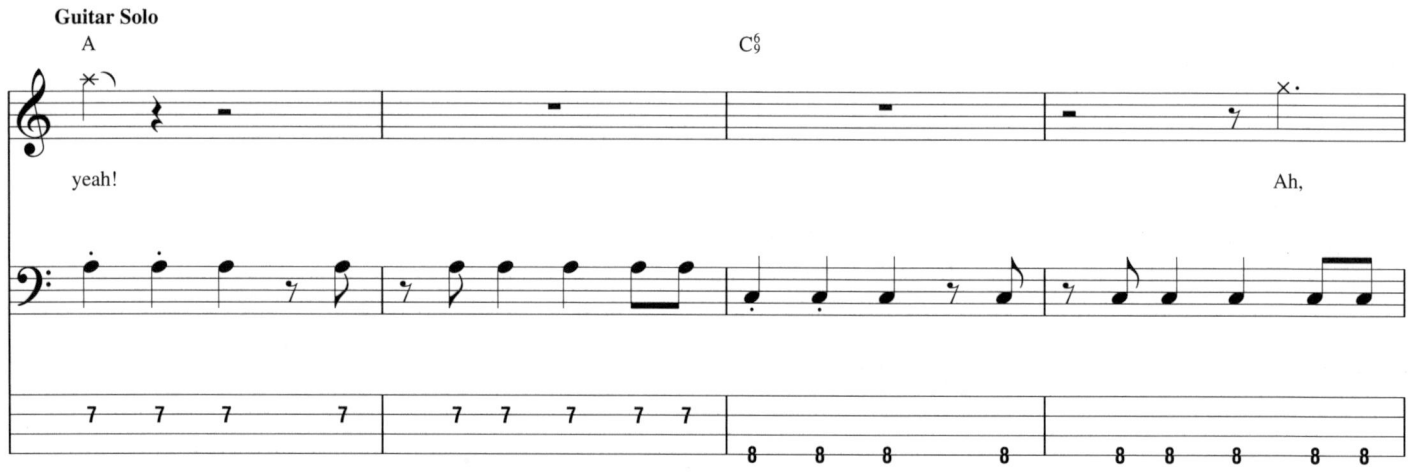

yeah!

Ah,

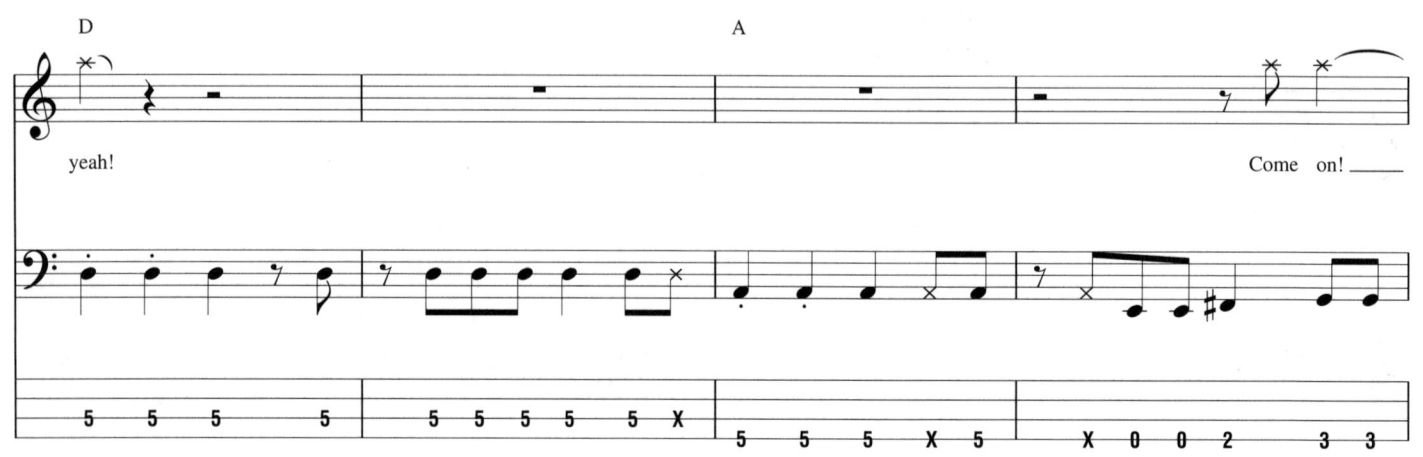

yeah!

Come on! ____

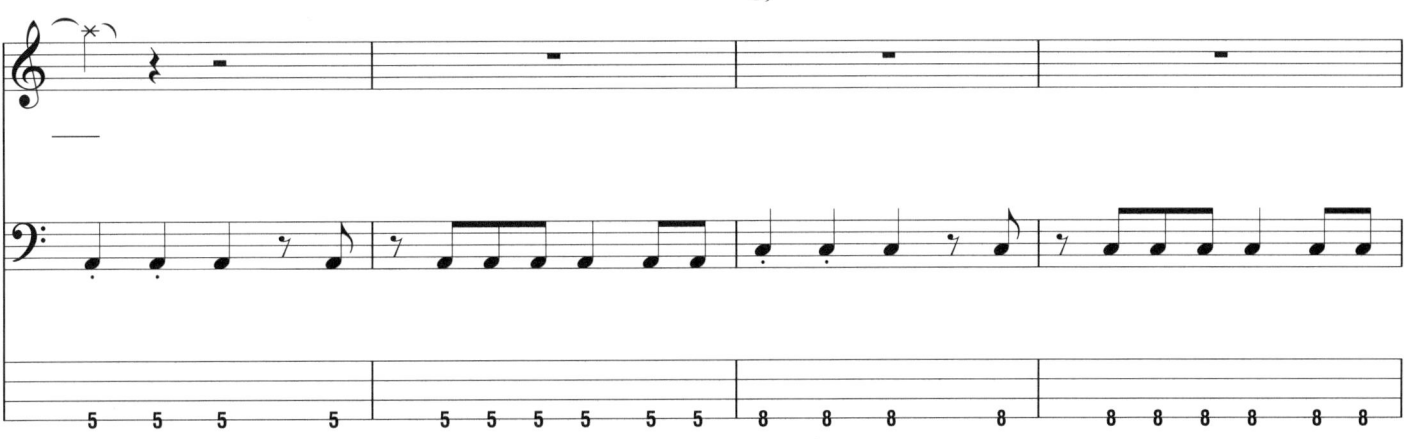

Chorus

Bass: w/ Bass Fig. 3 (2 times)

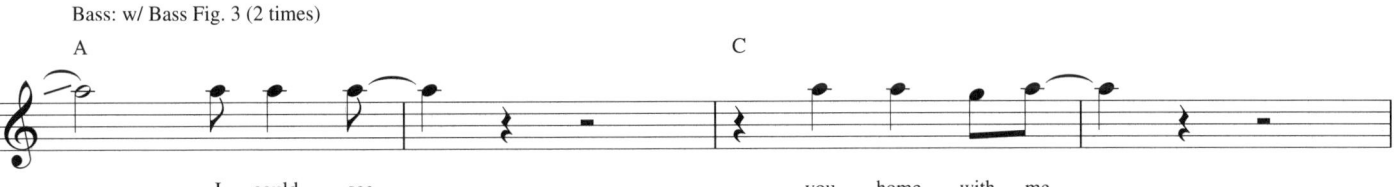

I could see _____ you home with me, _____

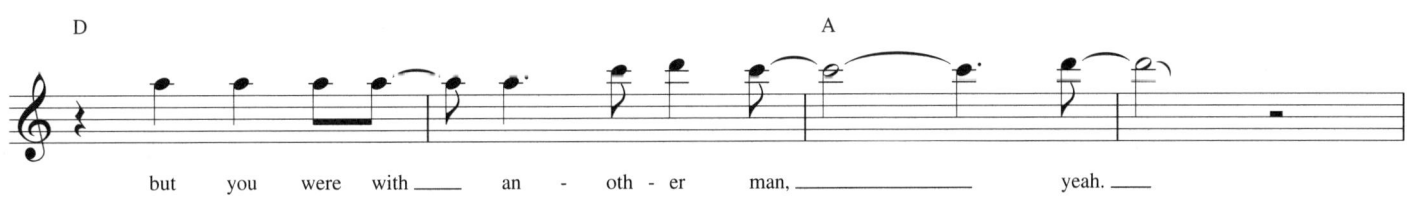

but you were with _____ an - oth - er man, _____ yeah. _____

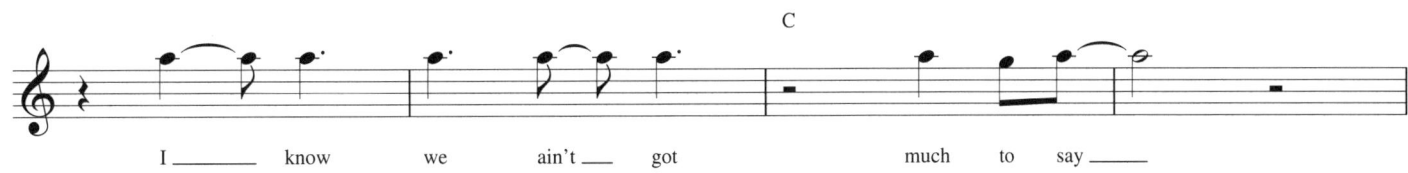

I _____ know we ain't _____ got much to say _____

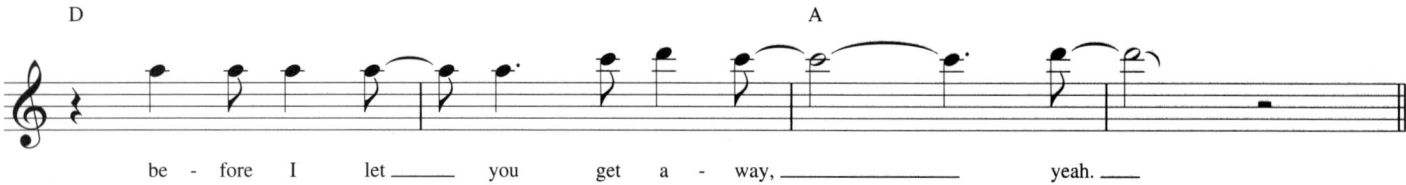

be - fore I let ____ you get a - way, _____ yeah. ____

Outro

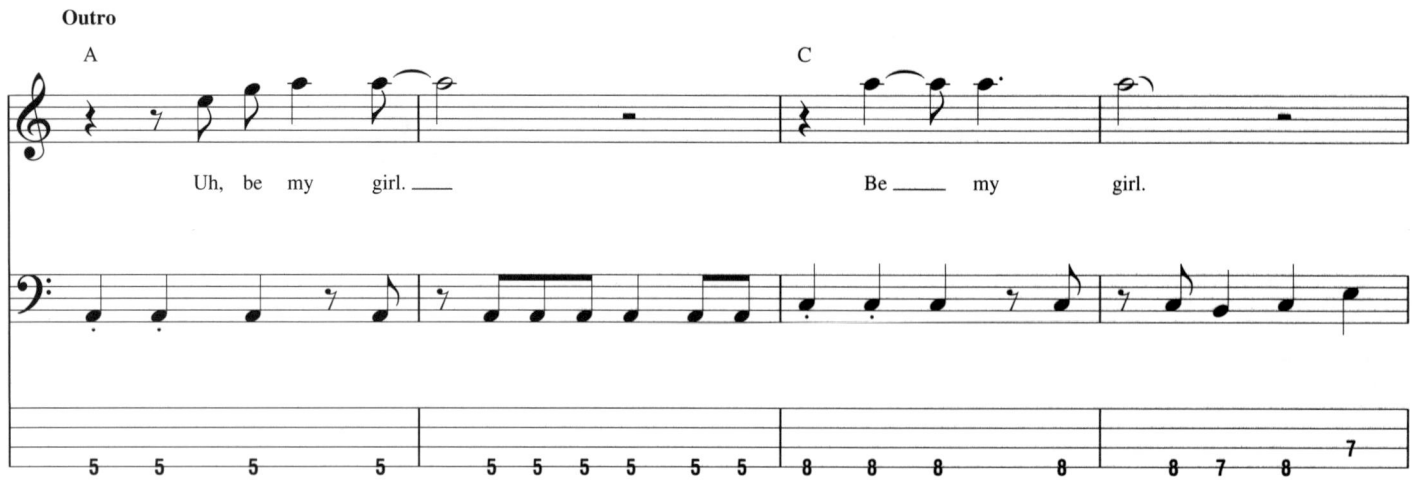

Uh, be my girl. ____   Be ____ my   girl.

Are   you   gon - na   be ____ my   girl? _____

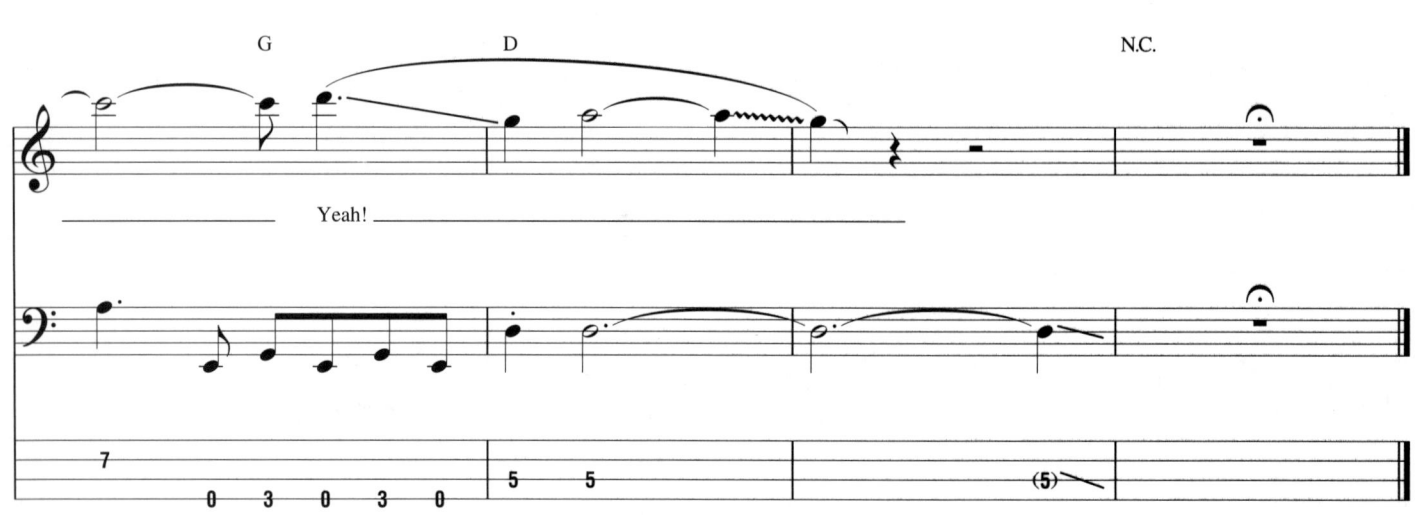

_____ Yeah! ____

Black Hole Sun

Words and Music by Chris Cornell

*Drop D Tuning:
(low to high) D-A-D-G

Intro
Slow Rock ♩ = 53

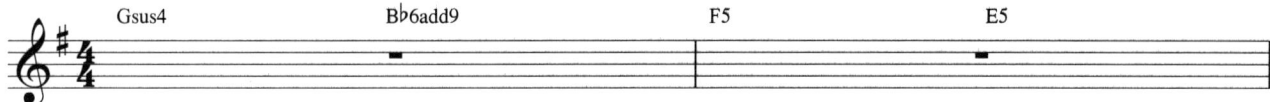

*Recording sounds 1/4 step sharp.

Verse

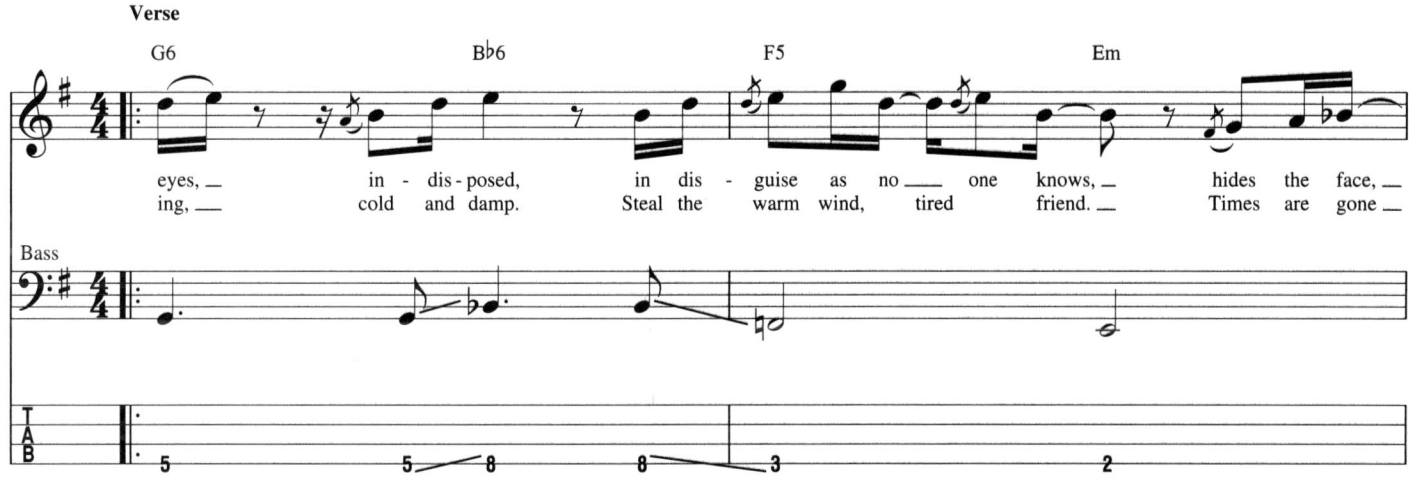

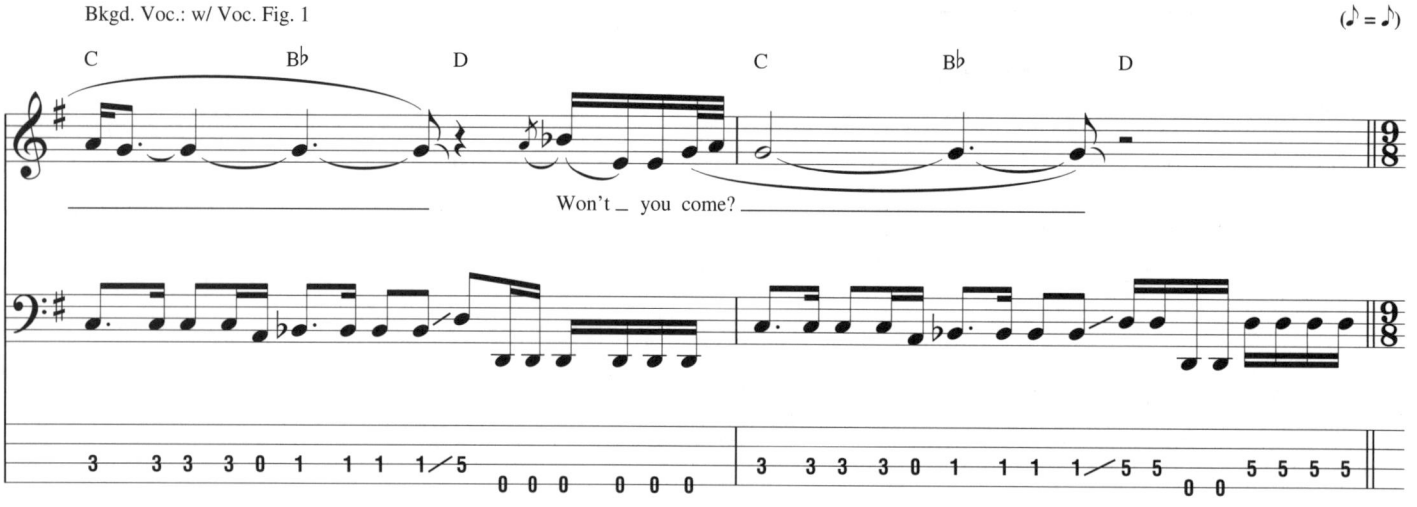

Guitar Solo

Verse

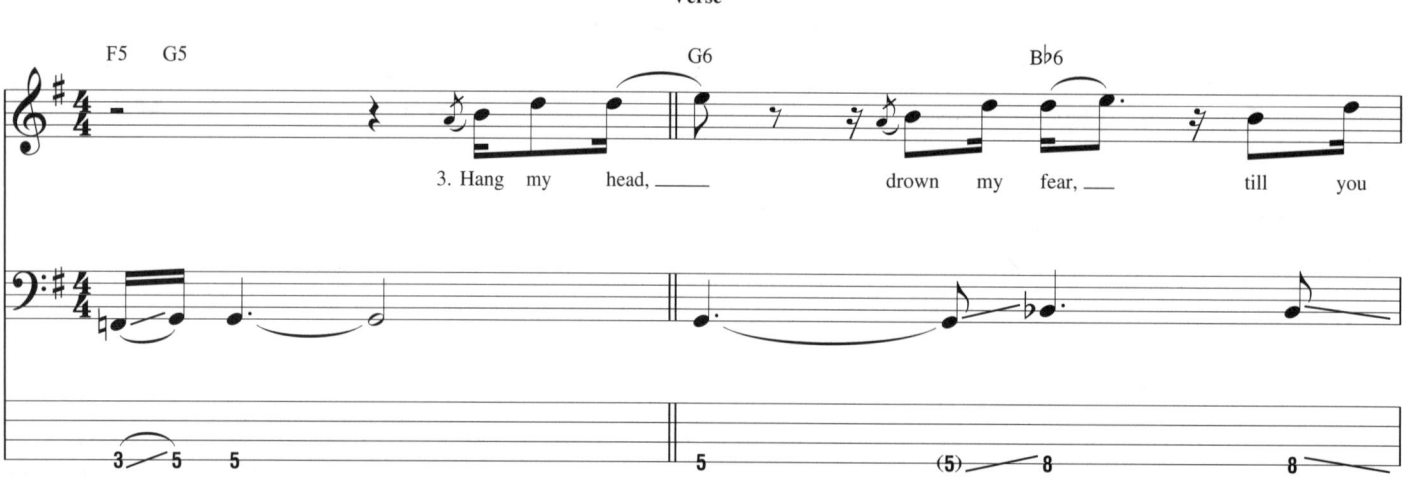

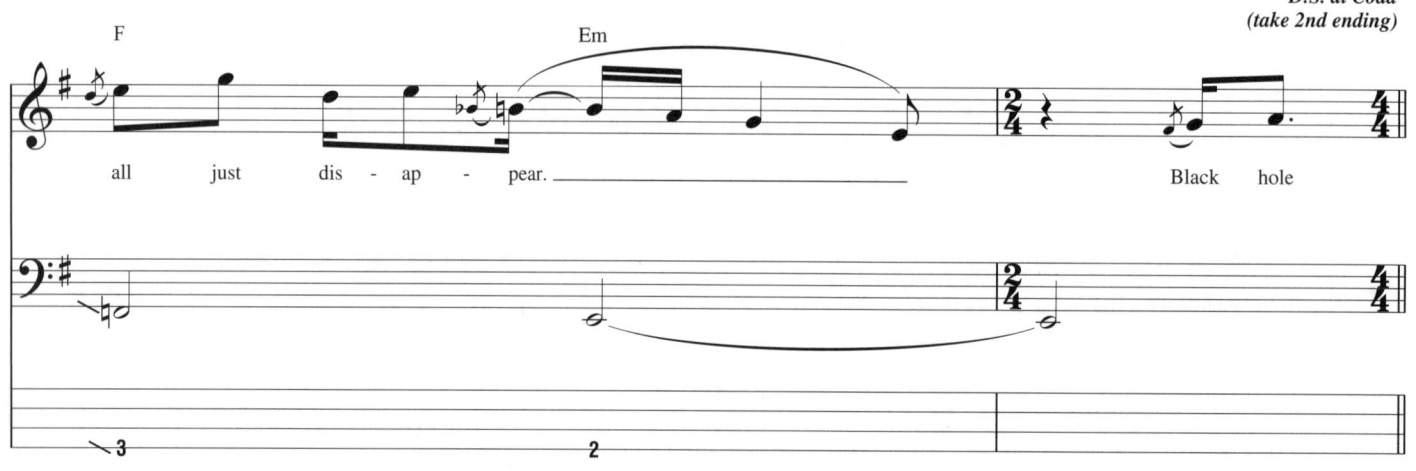

Coda

Creep

Words and Music by Albert Hammond, Mike Hazlewood, Thomas Yorke, Richard Greenwood, Philip Selway, Colin Greenwood and Edward O'Brian

*Chord symbols reflect overall harmony.

1. When you were here ___ be - fore, ___

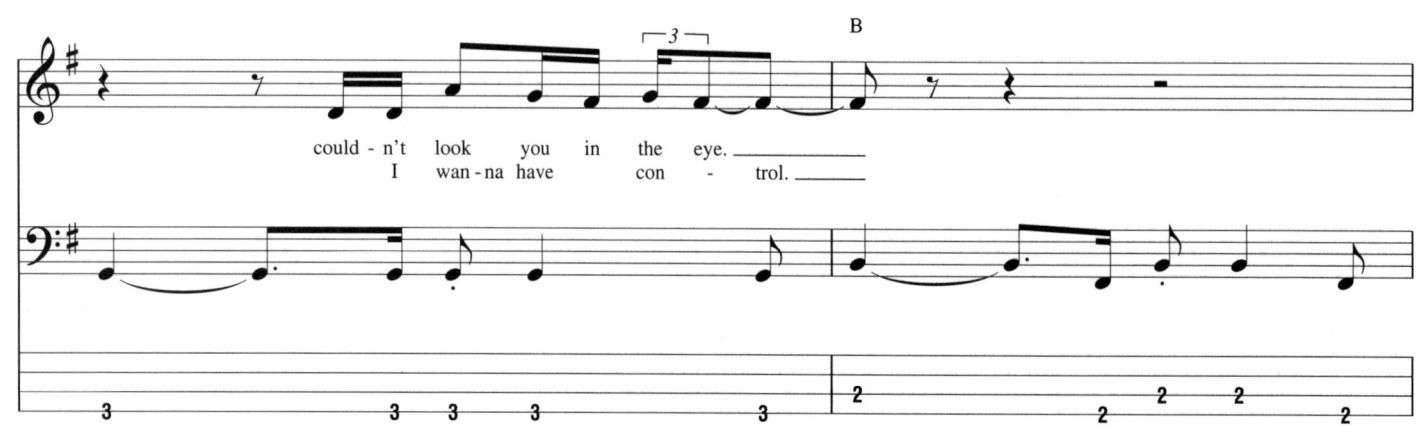

could - n't look you in the eye. ___
I wan - na have con - trol. ___

You're so fuck - ing spe - cial,
I wish I was spe - cial,

Chorus

2nd time, Bass: w/ Bass Fill 1

but I'm a ____ creep. I'm a ____ weird -

- o. ____ What the hell ___ am I do - ing here? __

Bass Fill 1

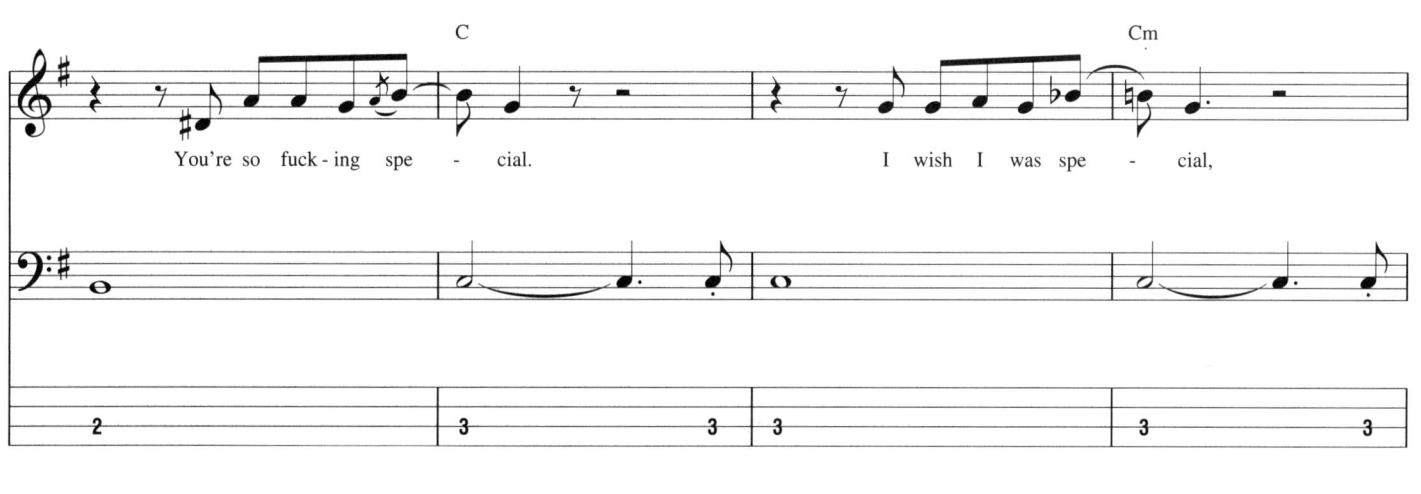

You're so fuck-ing spe - cial. I wish I was spe - cial,

Outro-Chorus

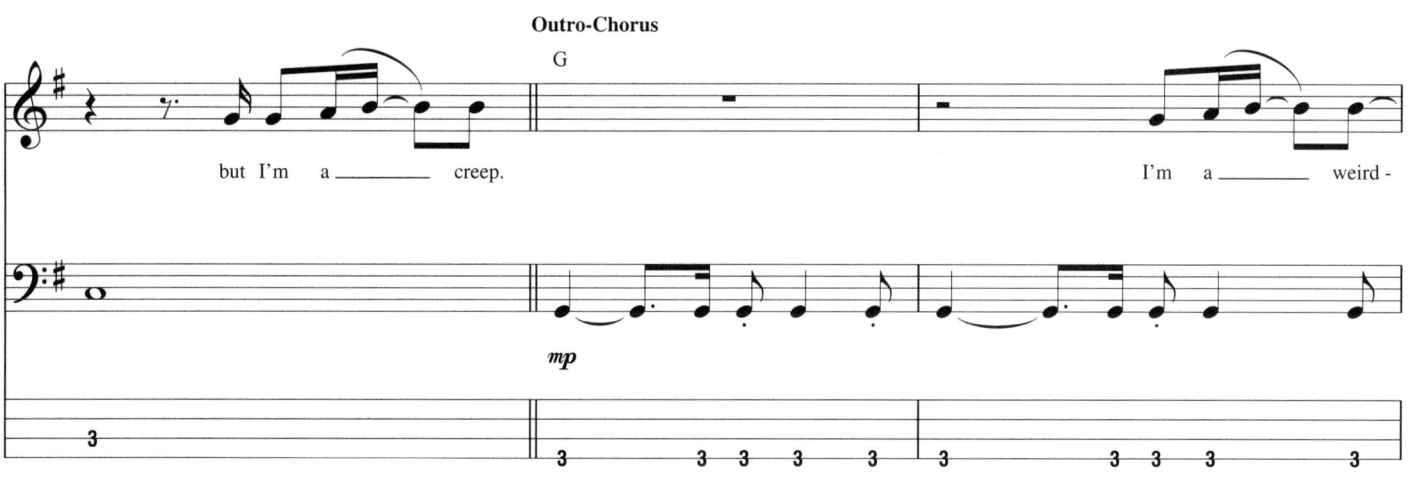

but I'm a _____ creep. I'm a _____ weird -

- o. _____ What the hell am I do-ing here? __

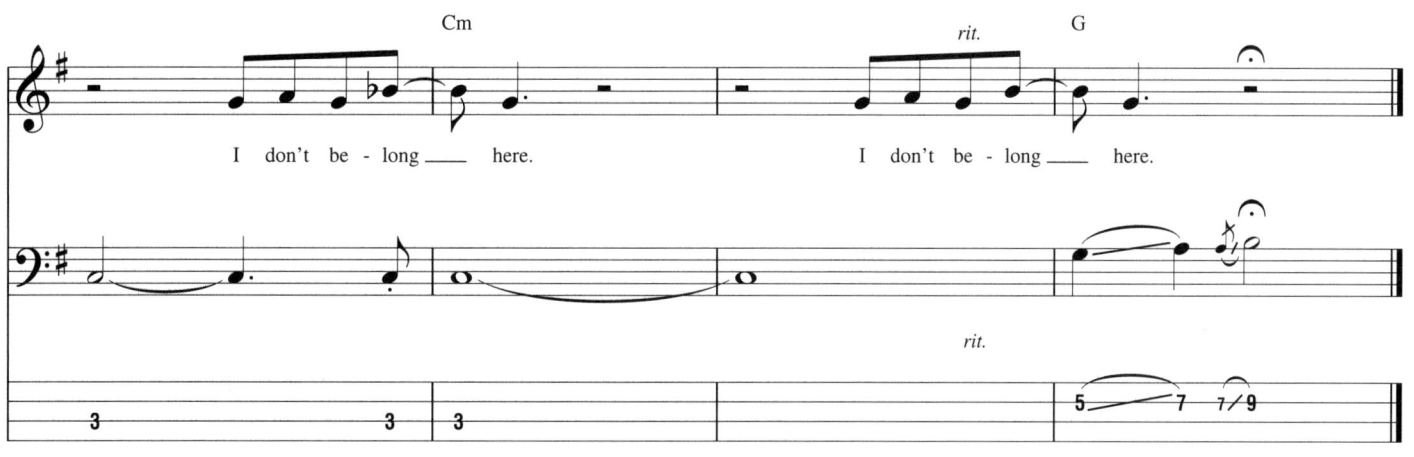

I don't be - long _____ here. I don't be - long _____ here.

Dani California

Words and Music by Anthony Kiedis, Flea, John Frusciante and Chad Smith

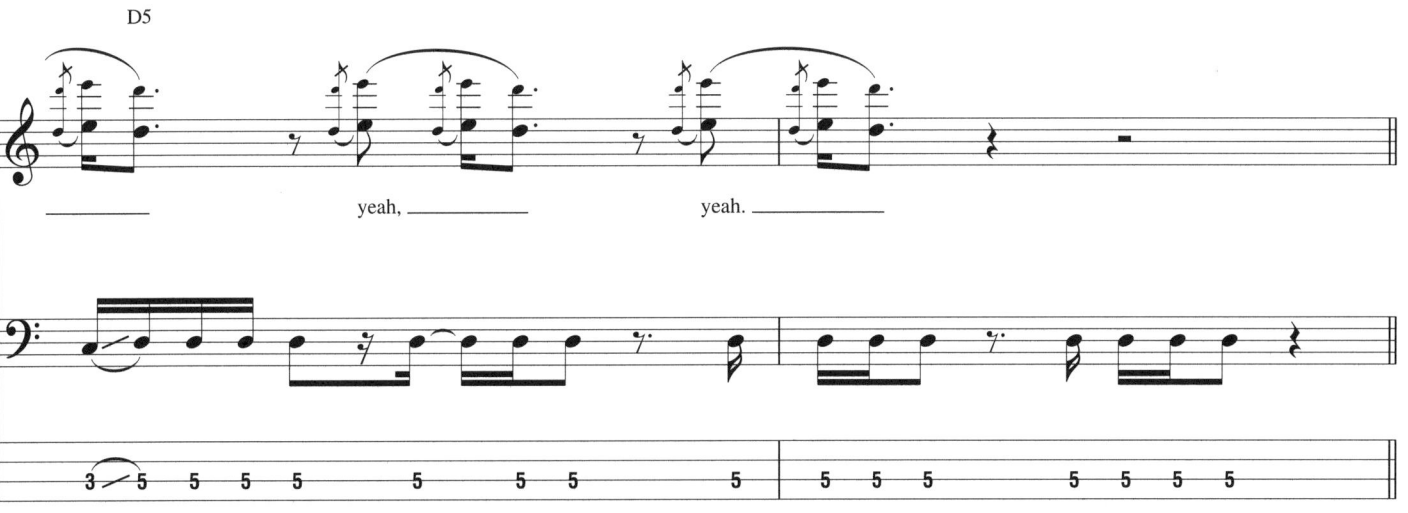

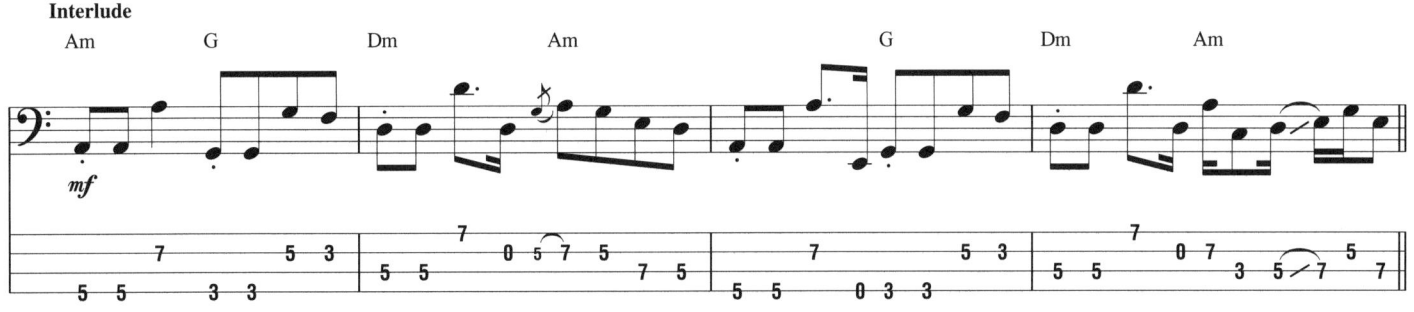

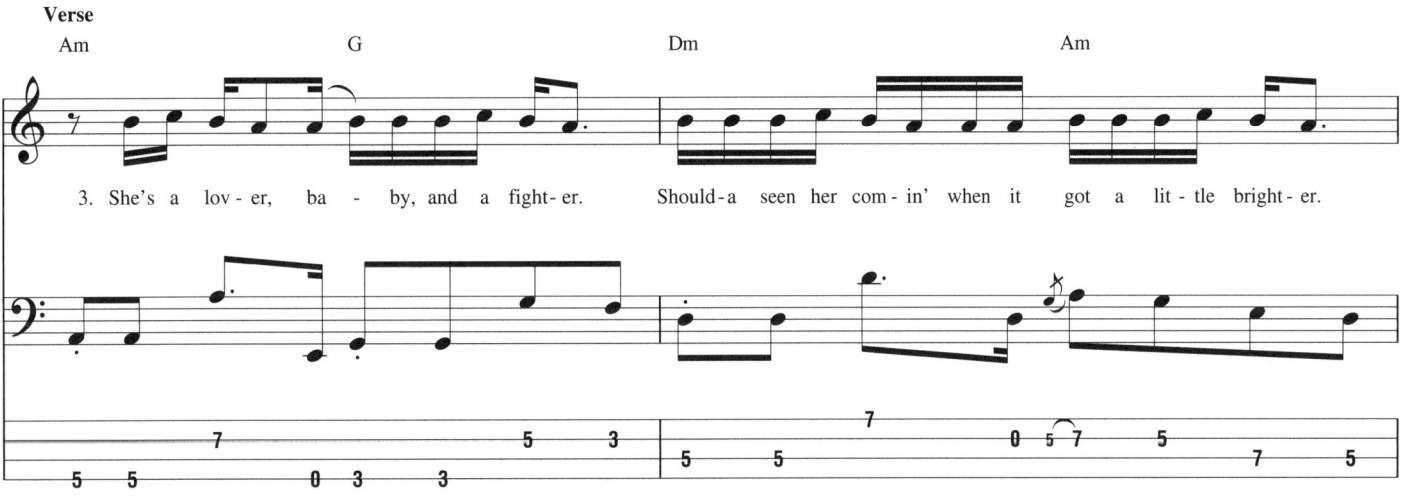

3. She's a lov-er, ba - by, and a fight-er. Should-a seen her com-in' when it got a lit - tle bright-er.

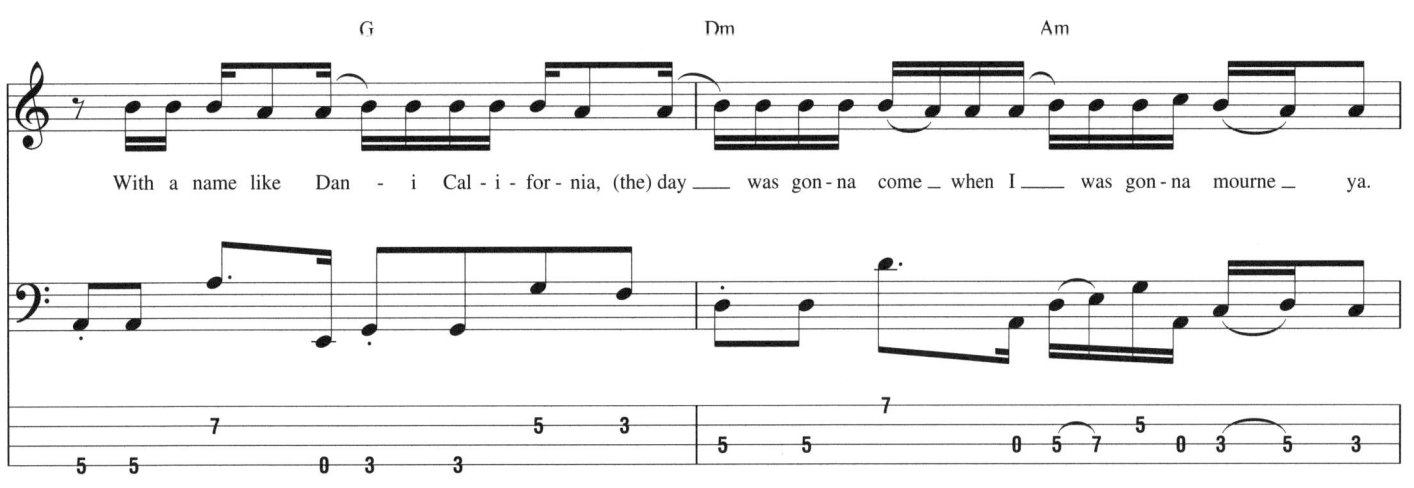

With a name like Dan - i Cal-i-for-nia, (the) day ___ was gon-na come ___ when I ___ was gon-na mourne ___ ya.

A lit- tle load- ed, she was steal- in' an- oth - er breath.

I love my ba- by to death. _____ Cal - i - for -

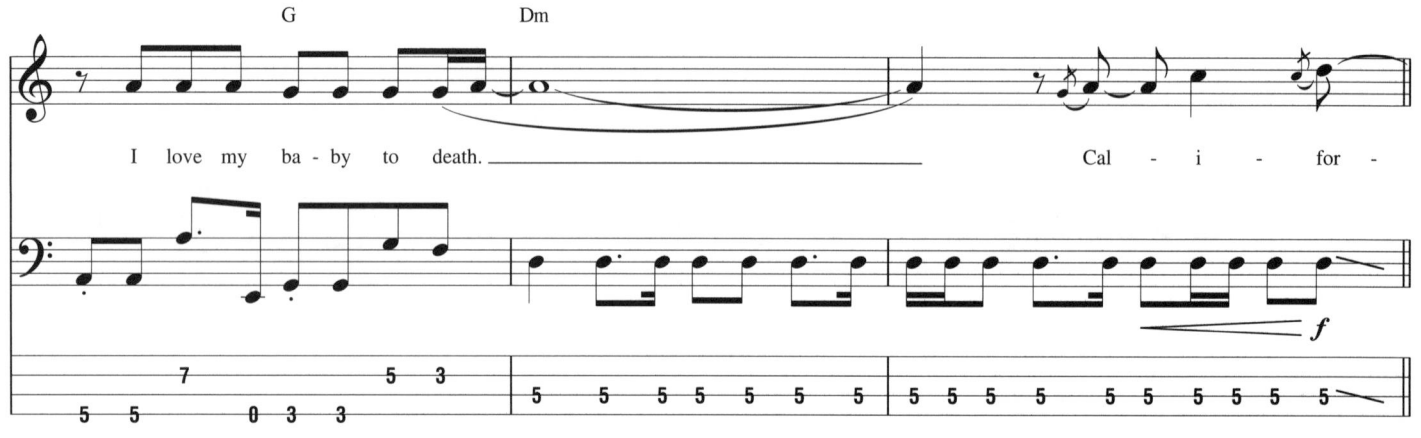

Chorus
Bass: w/ Bass Fig. 1 (3 1/2 times)

- nia, rest ___ in peace. ___ Si - mul- ta - ne -ous ___ re - lease. ___ Cal - i - for -

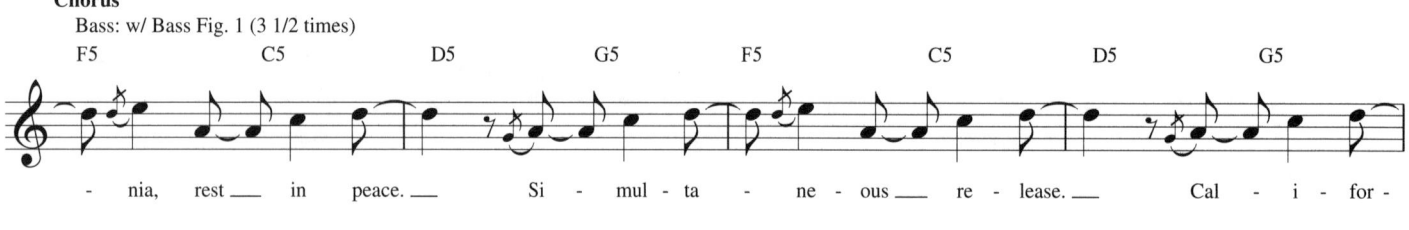

- nia, show ___ your teeth. ___ She's ___ my priest -ess, I'm ___ your priest,

yeah, _____ yeah. ___

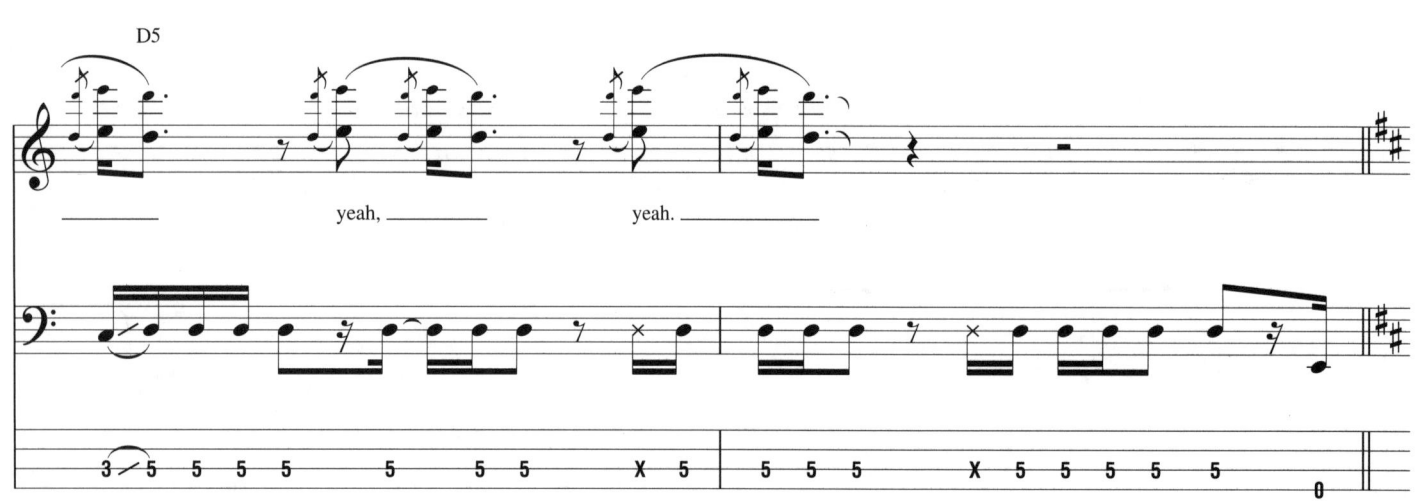

-nia, show ___ your teeth. ___ She's ___ my priest-ess, I'm ___ your priest, ___
Dum, de, dum, ___ da.)

___ yeah, ___ yeah. ___

Outro-Guitar Solo

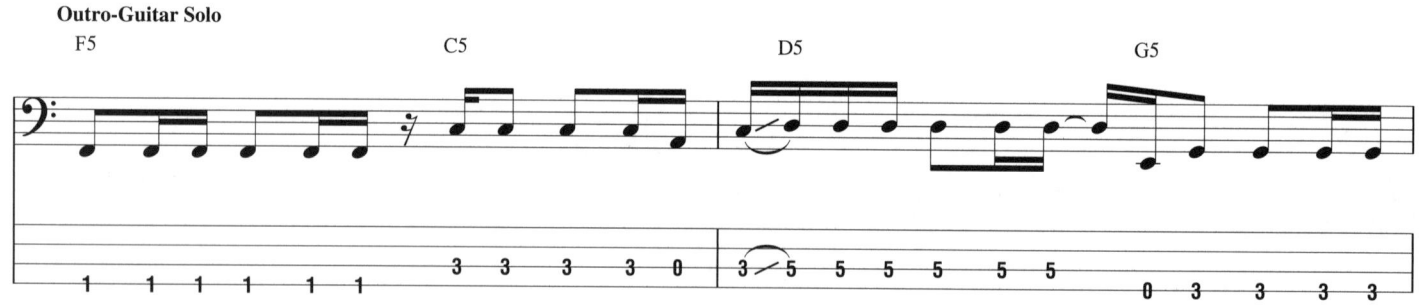

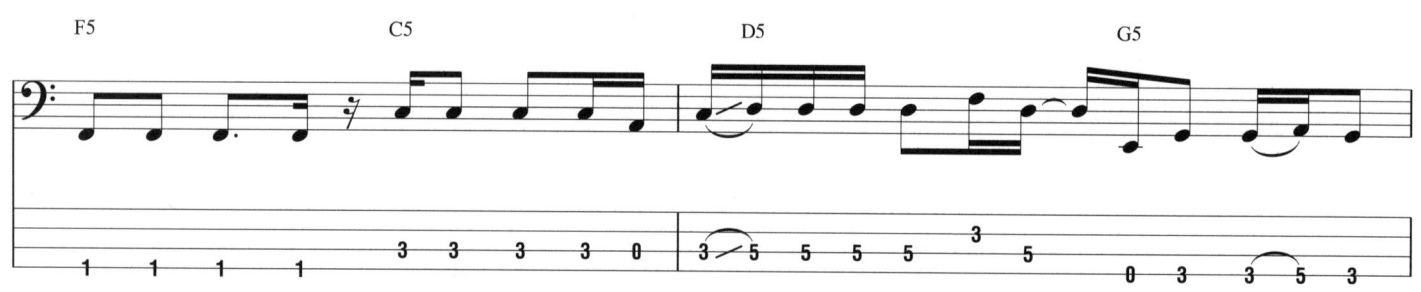

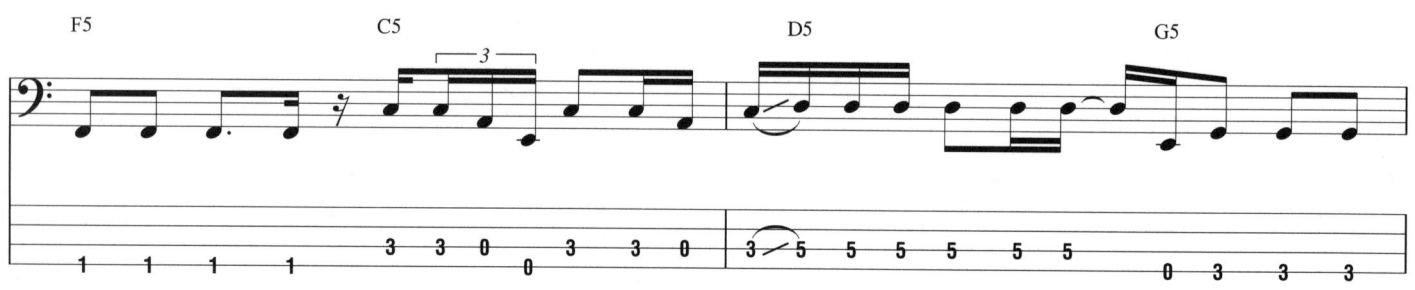

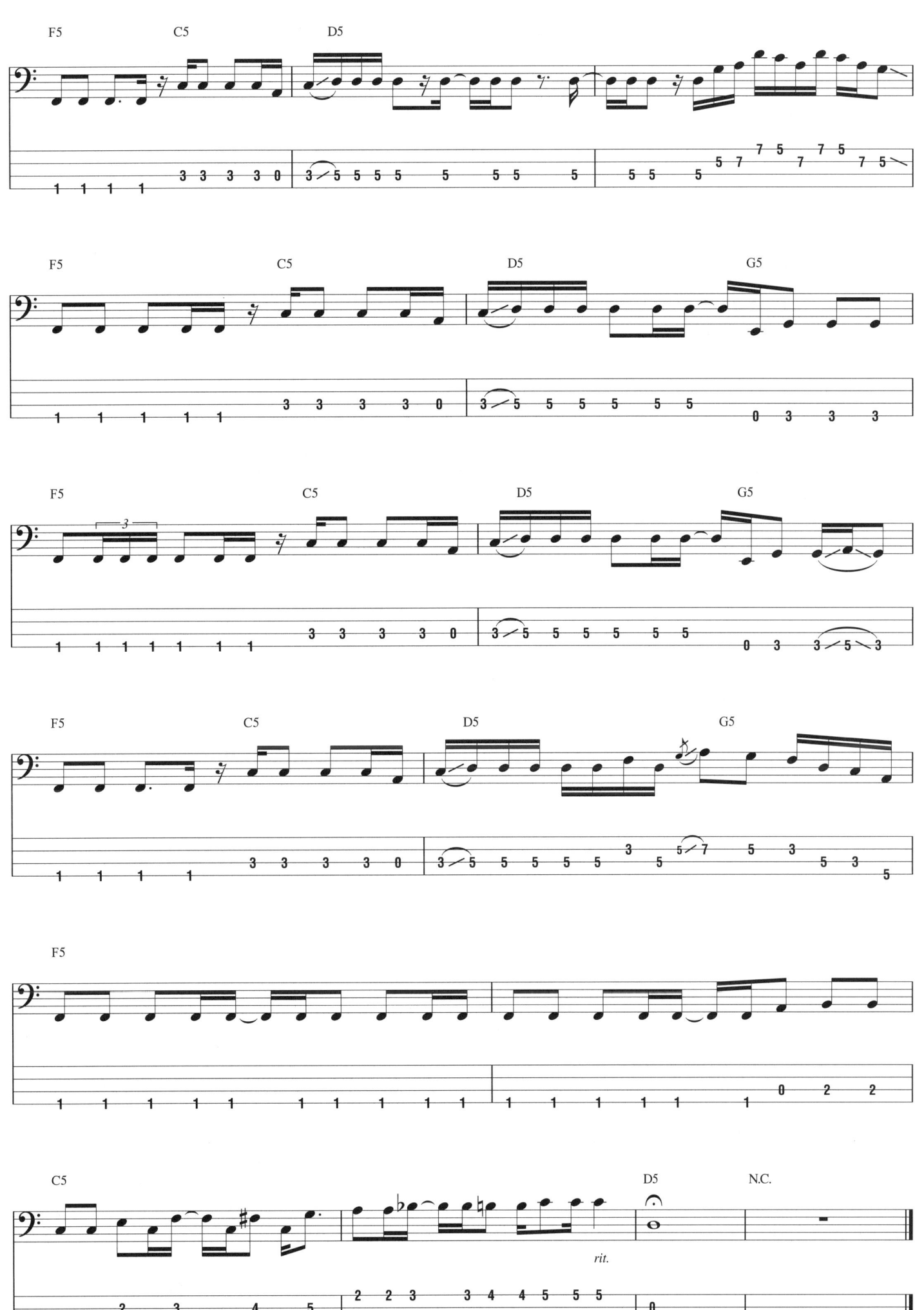

Detroit Rock City

Words and Music by Paul Stanley and Bob Ezrin

* Chord symbols derived from gtr.

feel so good, I'm so a - live. _
Oh my God! No time to turn. _

To Coda ⊕

Hear my song _ play-in' on the ra - di - o. _____ It goes: ___
got to laugh _ 'cause I know I'm gon-na die! _____ Why? ___

Get up! _

Chorus

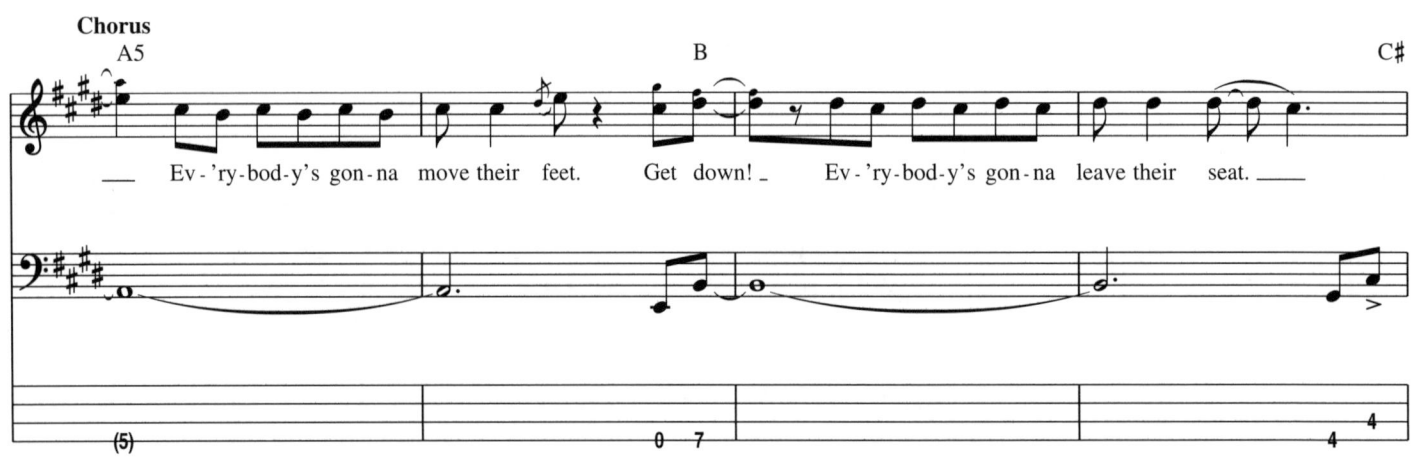

_ Ev-'ry-bod-y's gon-na move their feet. Get down! _ Ev-'ry-bod-y's gon-na leave their seat. ____

Interlude

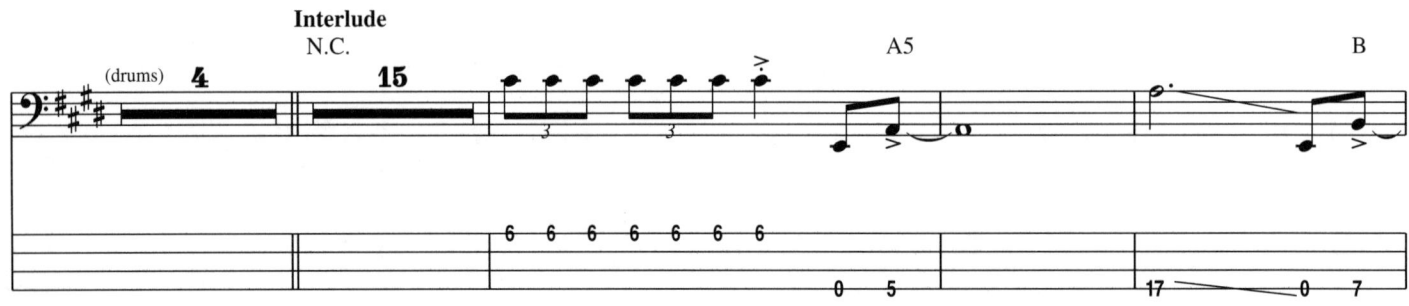

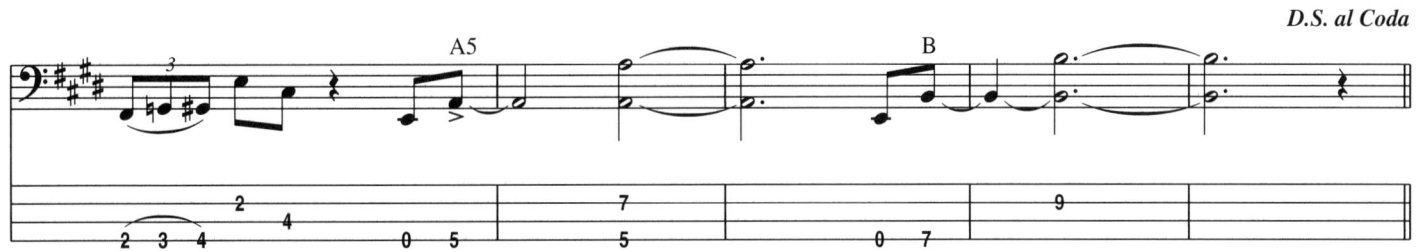

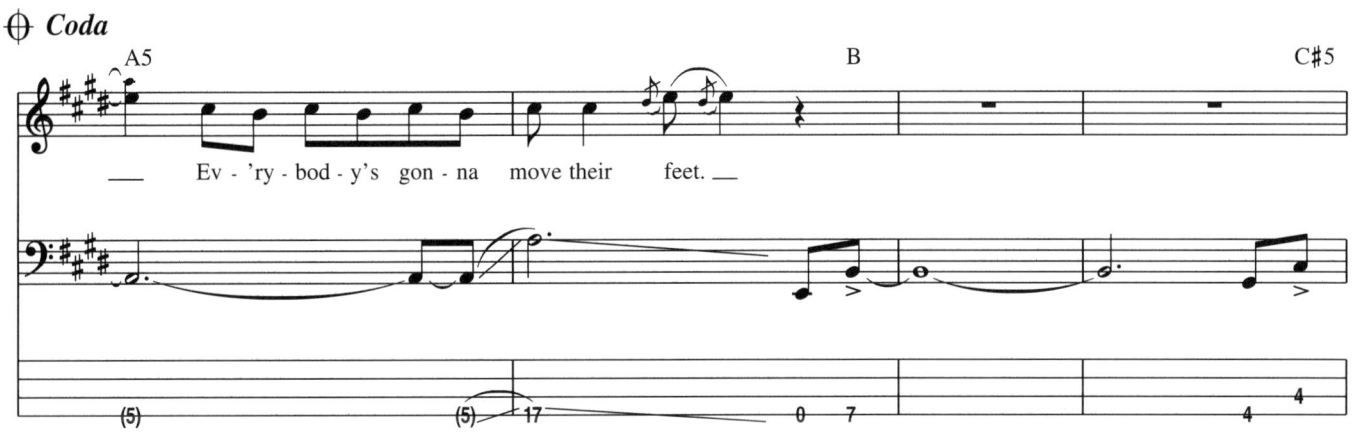

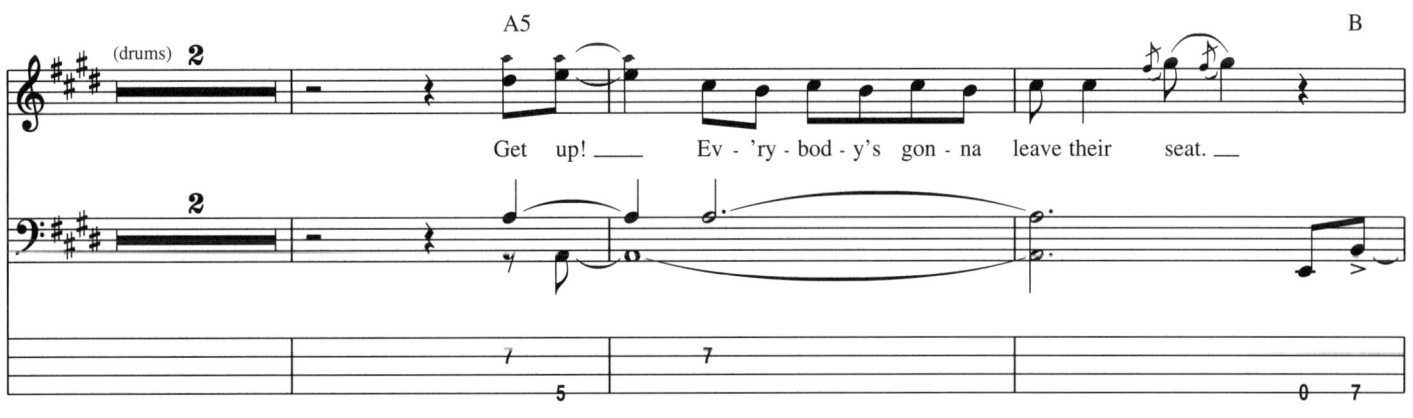

Don't Fear the Reaper

Words and Music by Donald Roeser

*Chord symbols reflect implied harmony.

Interlude
A5 G F G A5 G F G
La, la, la, la, la.
A5 G5 F G A5 G5 F5 G5
La, la, la, la, la.
A5 G5 F G A5
Bass tacet
Fm G7
Fm G7

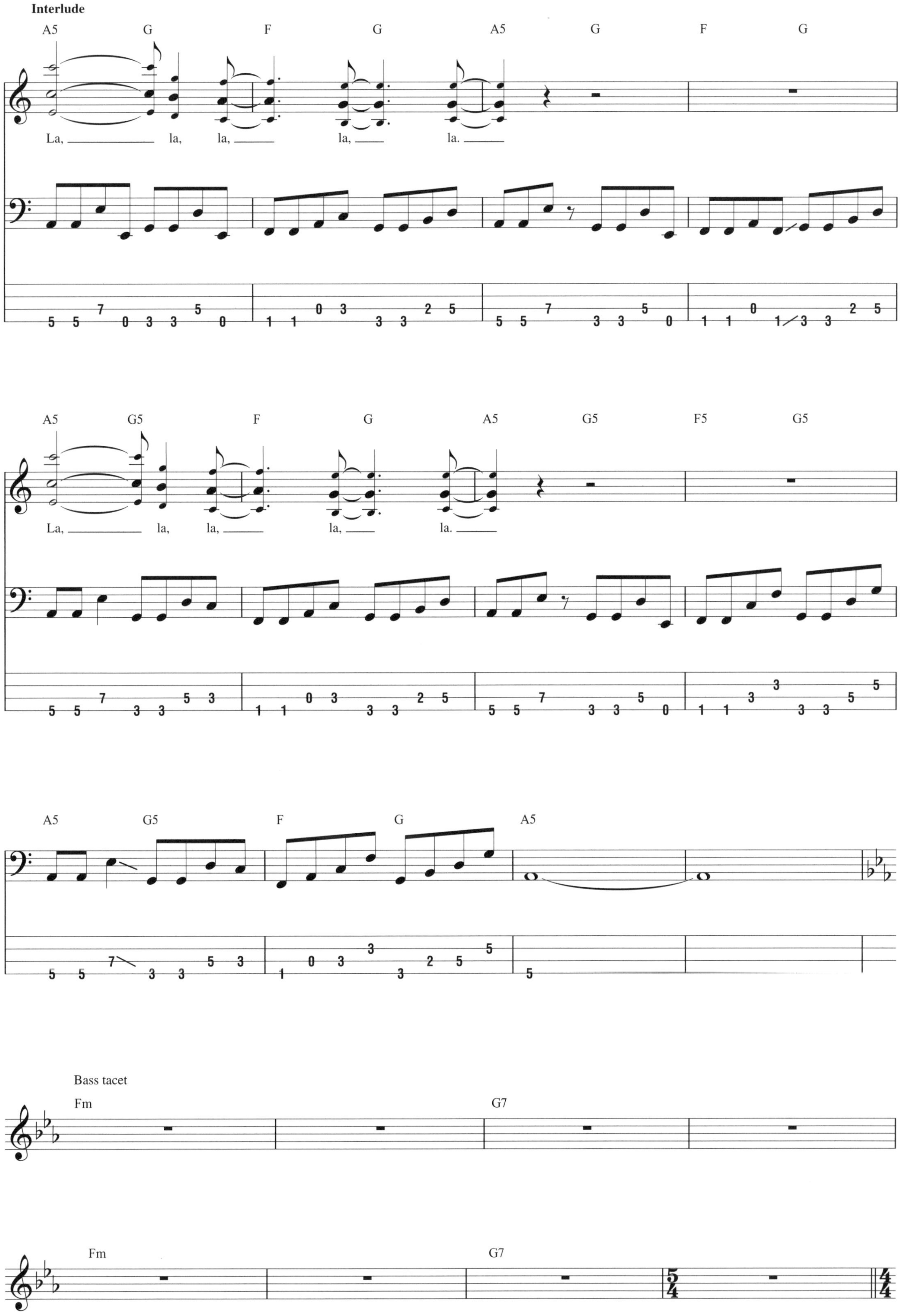

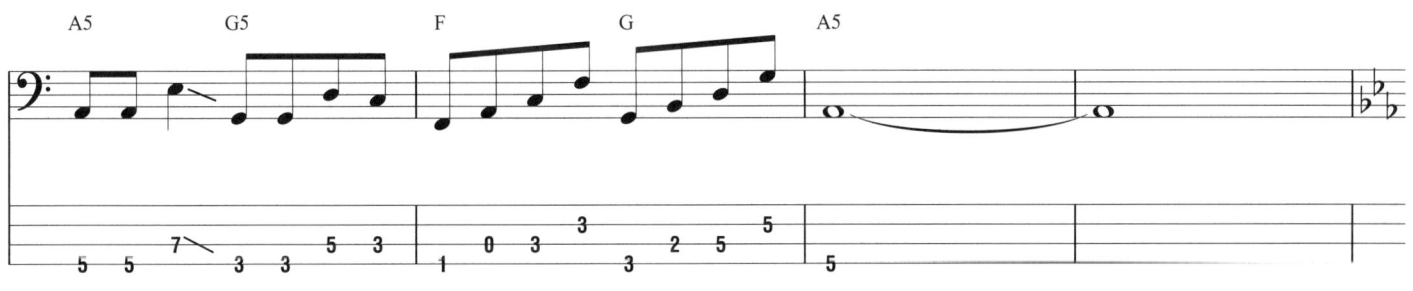

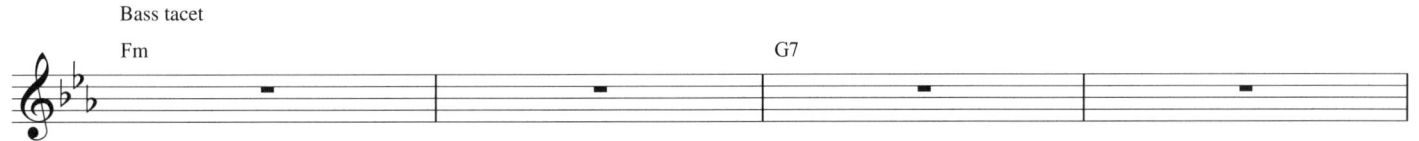

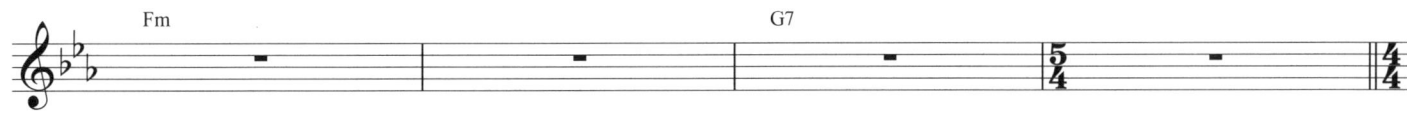

Guitar Solo

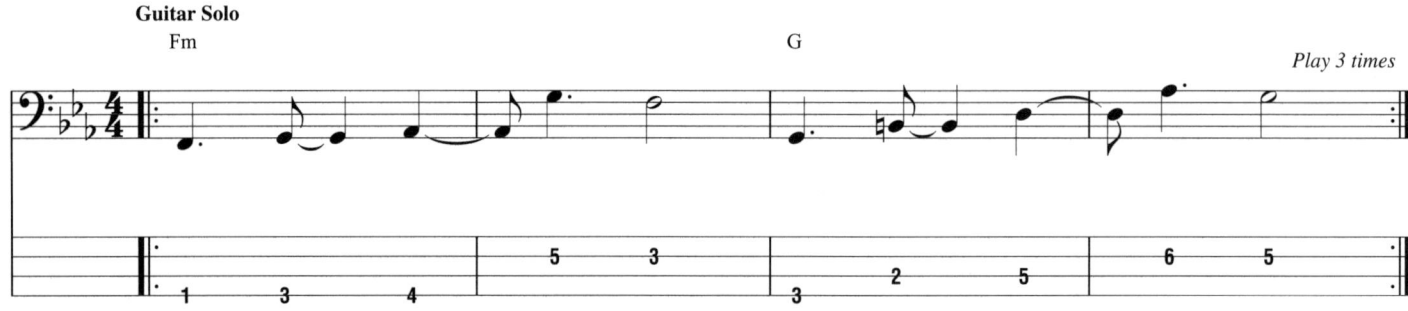

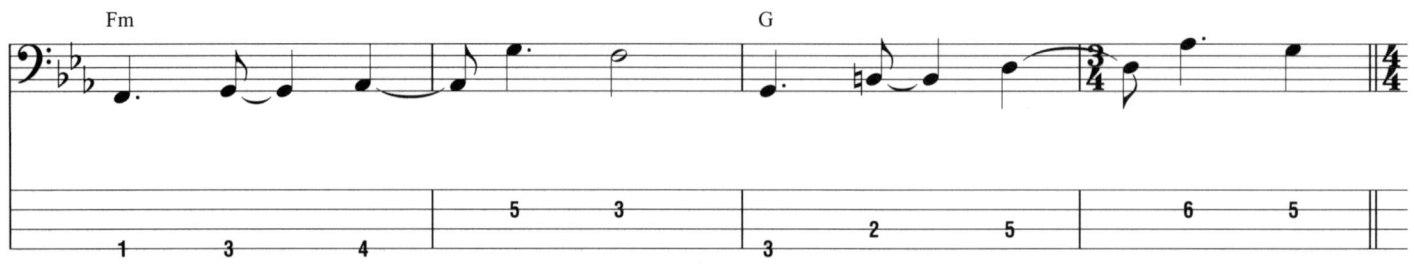

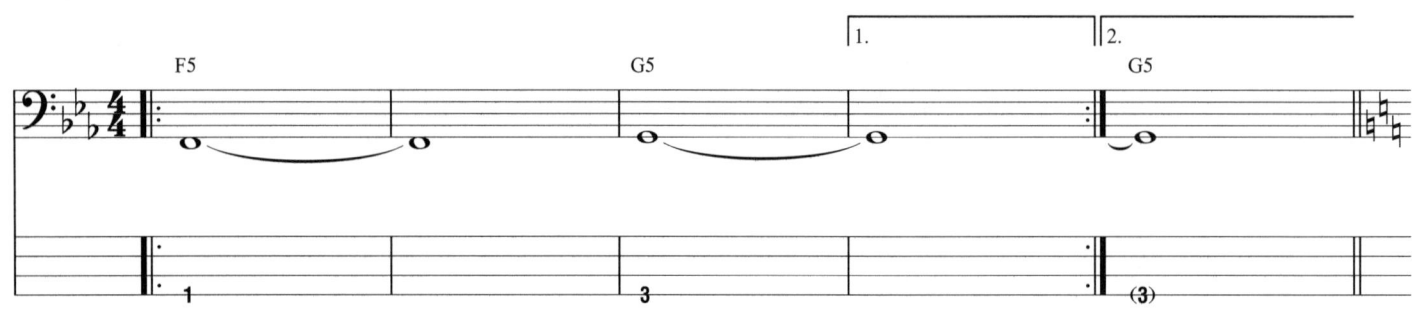

Interlude

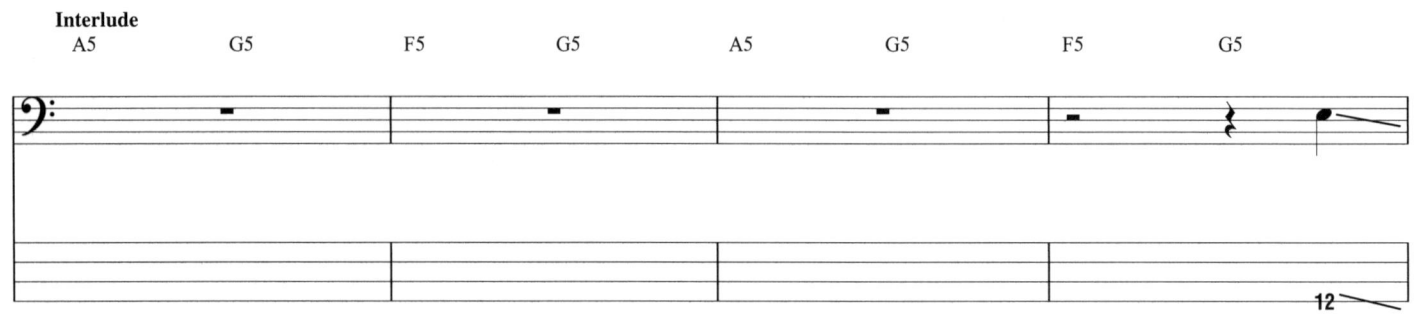

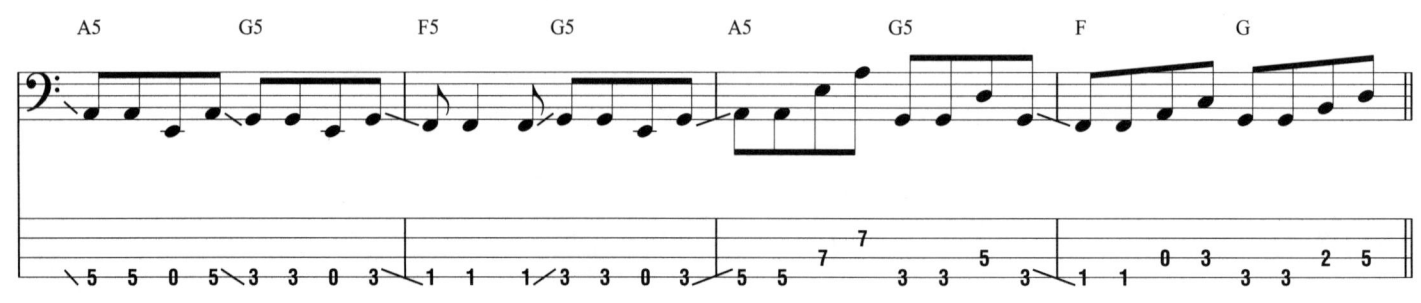

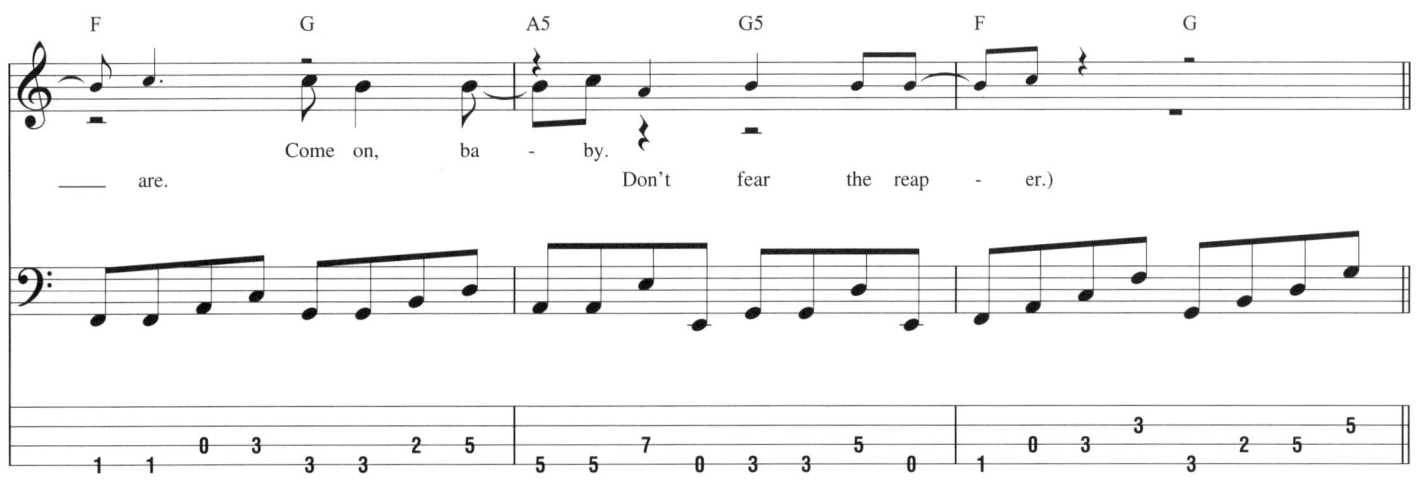

Come on, ba - by.
____ are. Don't fear the reap - er.)

Outro

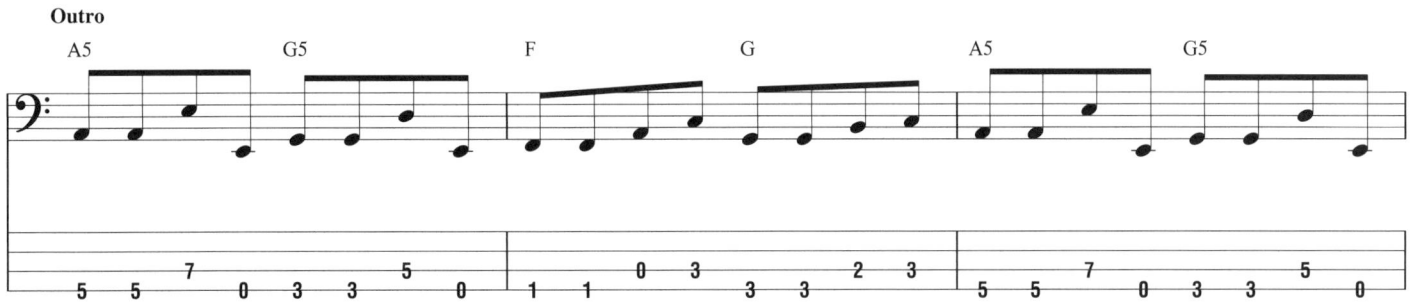

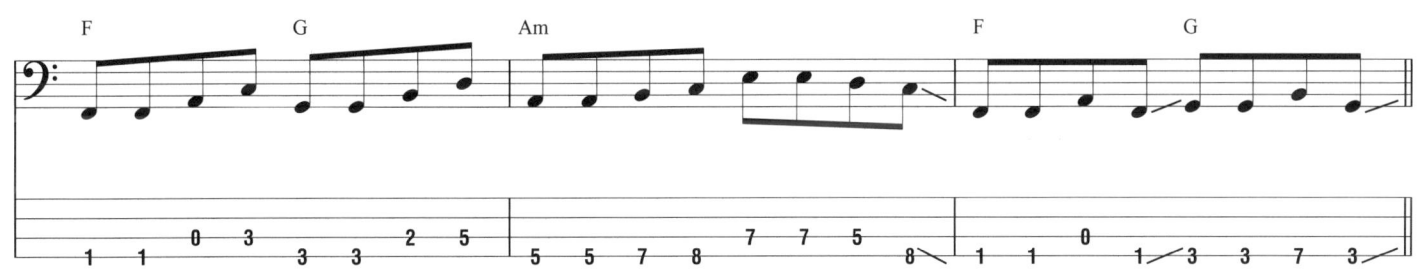

Play 4 times

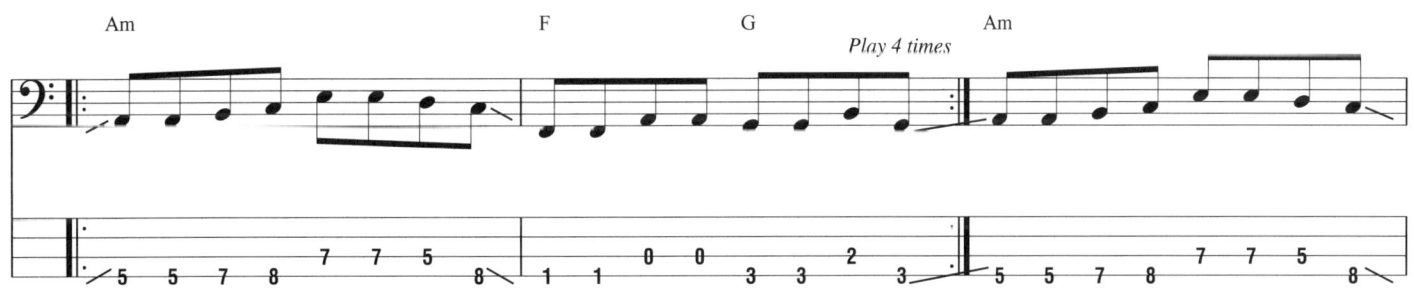

Play 4 times and fade

Green Grass and High Tides

Words and Music by Hugh Thomasson Jr.

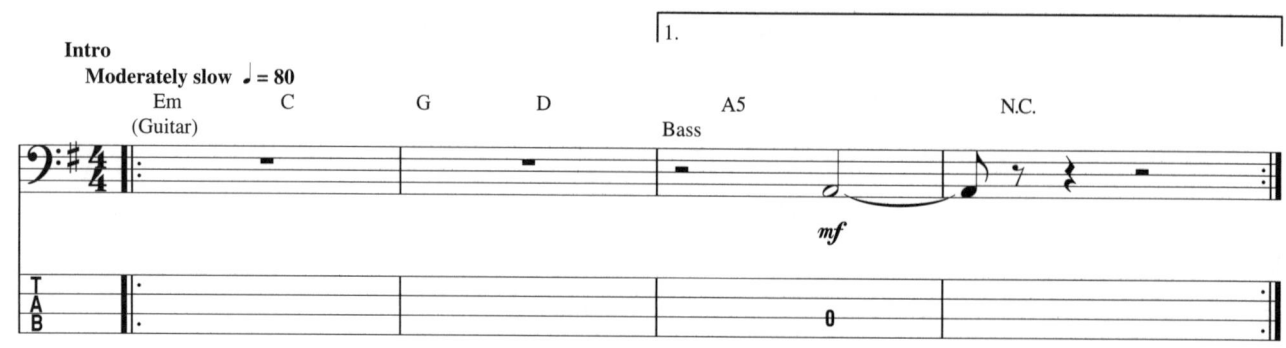

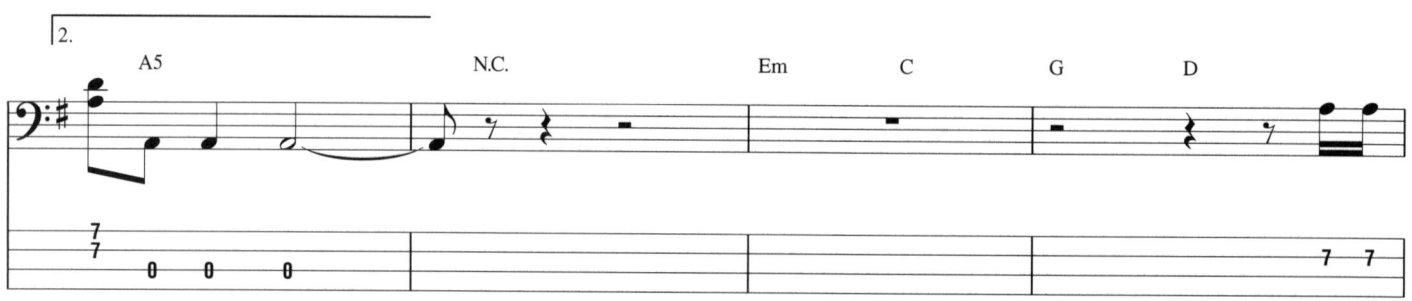

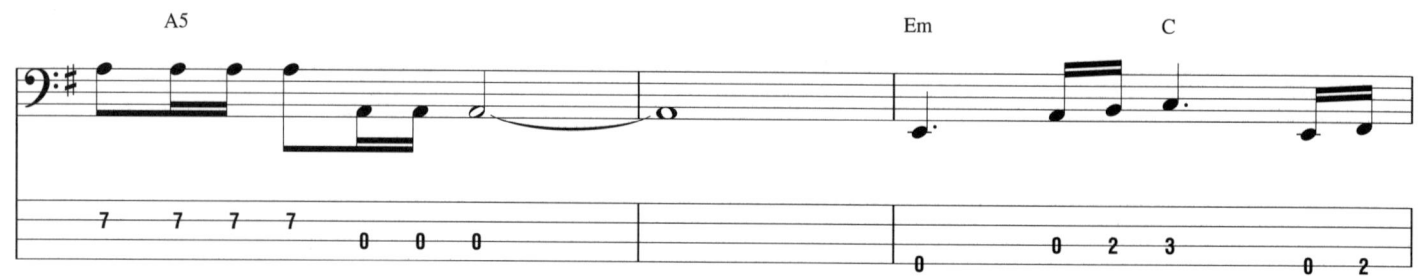

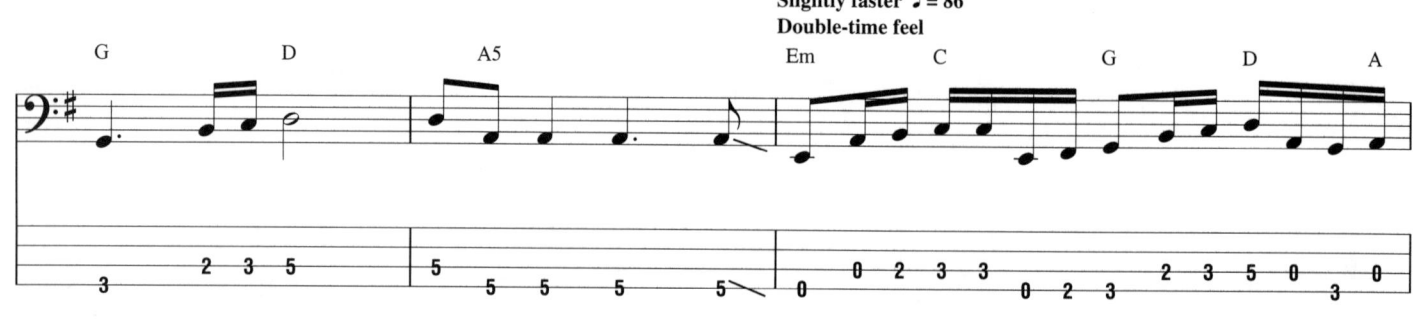

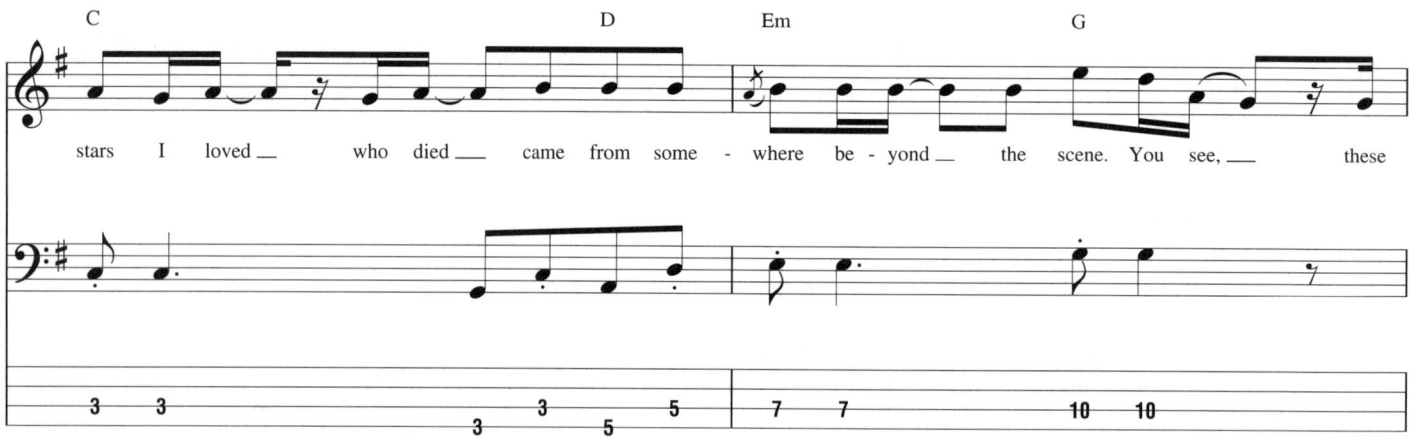

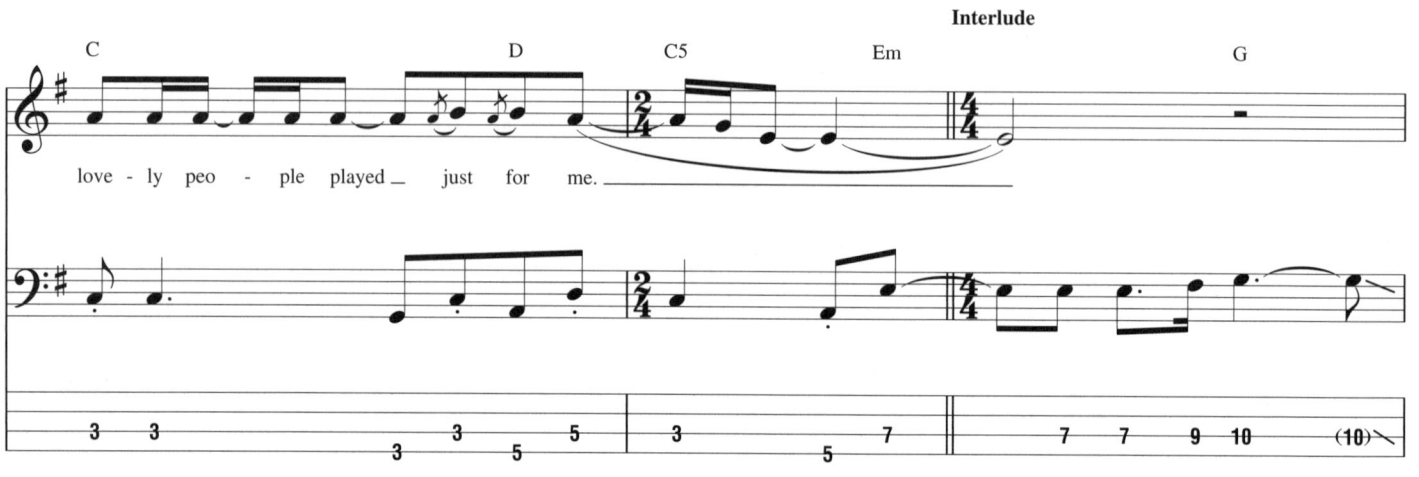

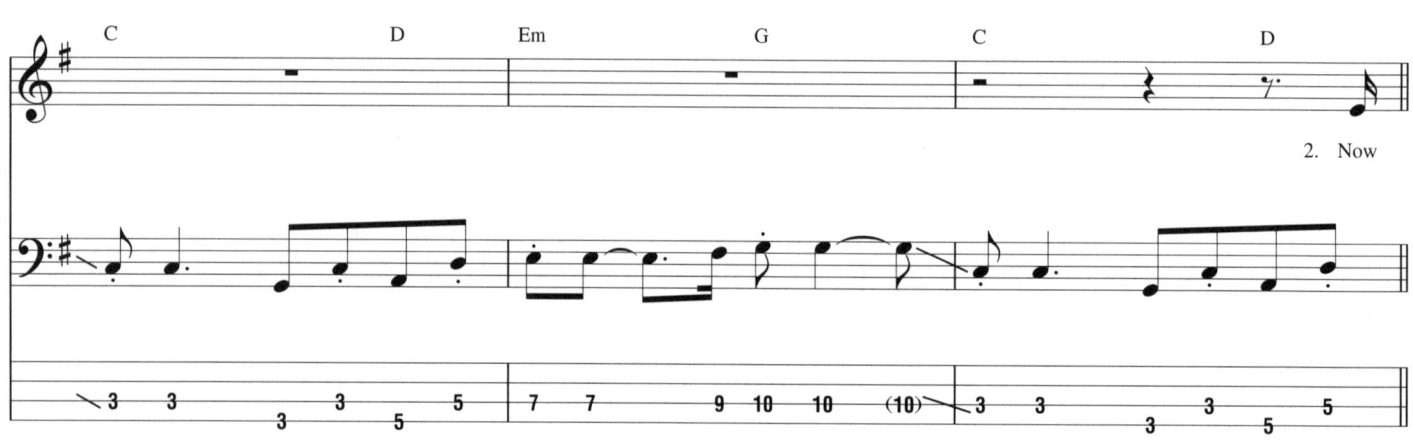

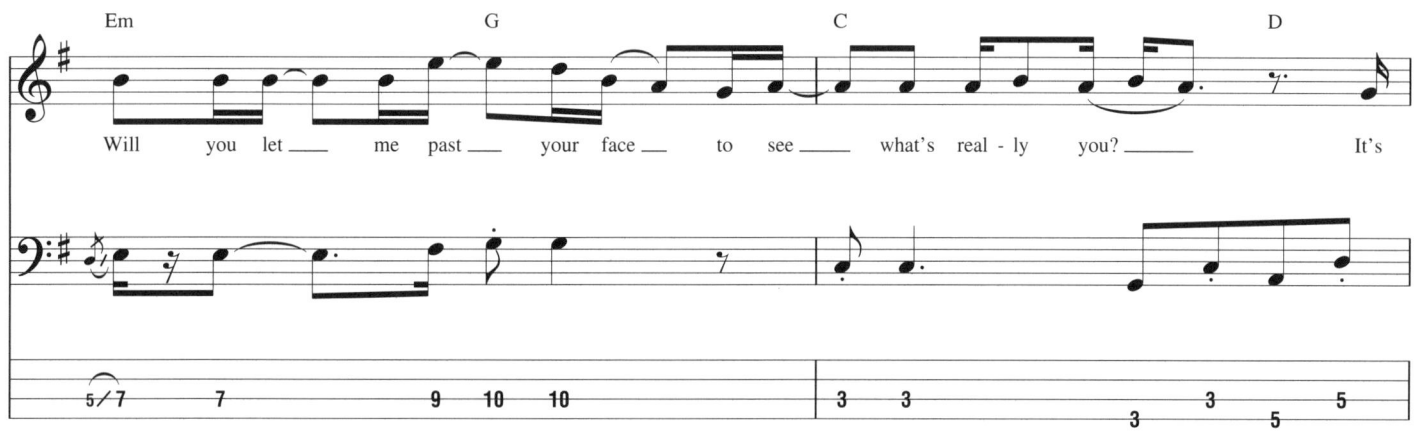

Will you let __ me past __ your face __ to see __ what's real - ly you? _____ It's

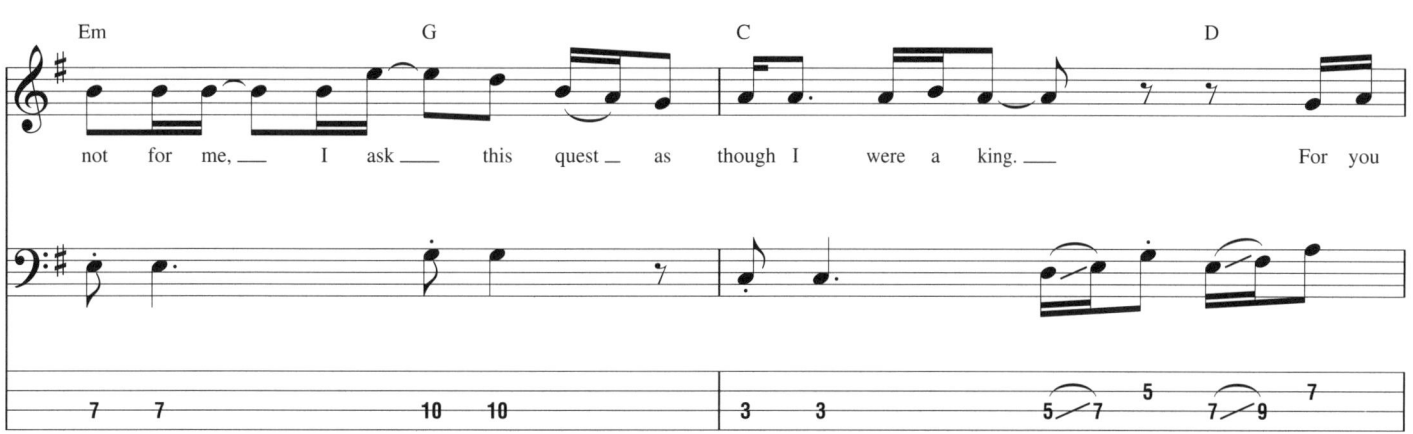

not for me, __ I ask __ this quest __ as though I were a king. __ For you

have to love, __ be - lieve, __ and feel __ be - fore __ the burst __ of tam - bou - rines _____

Chorus

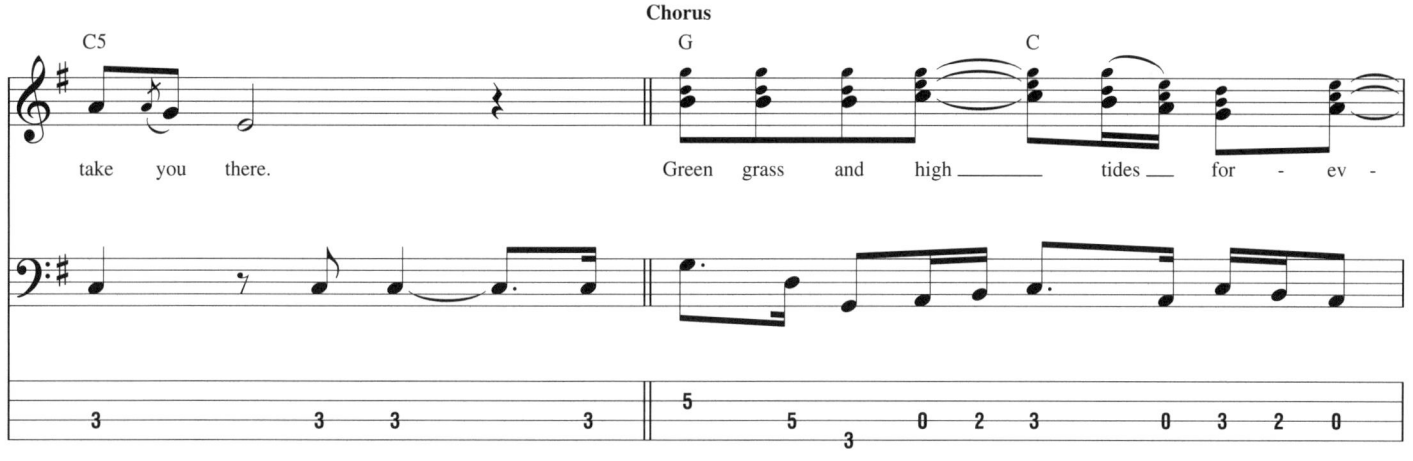

take you there. Green grass and high _____ tides __ for - ev -

*Sing 1st time only.

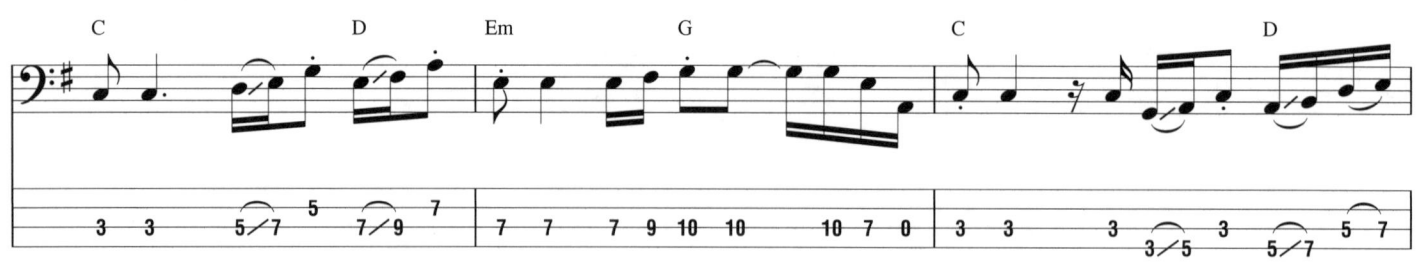
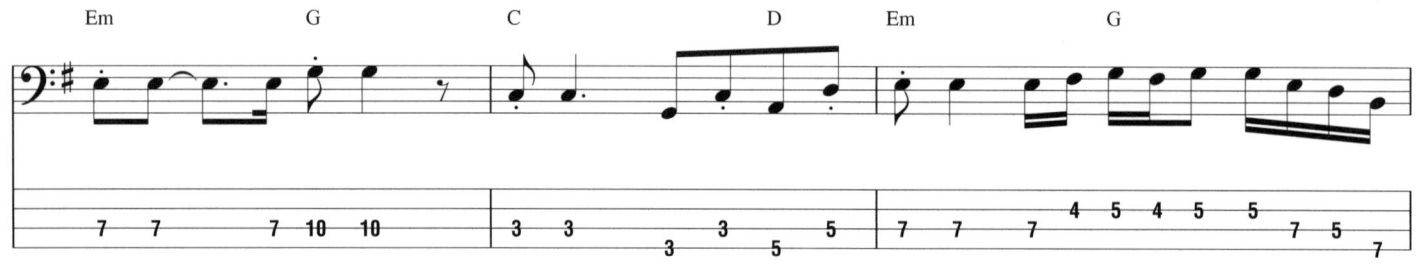

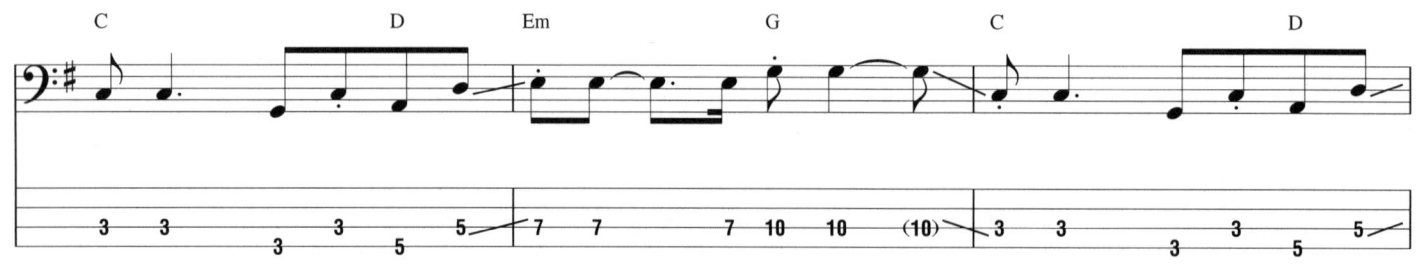
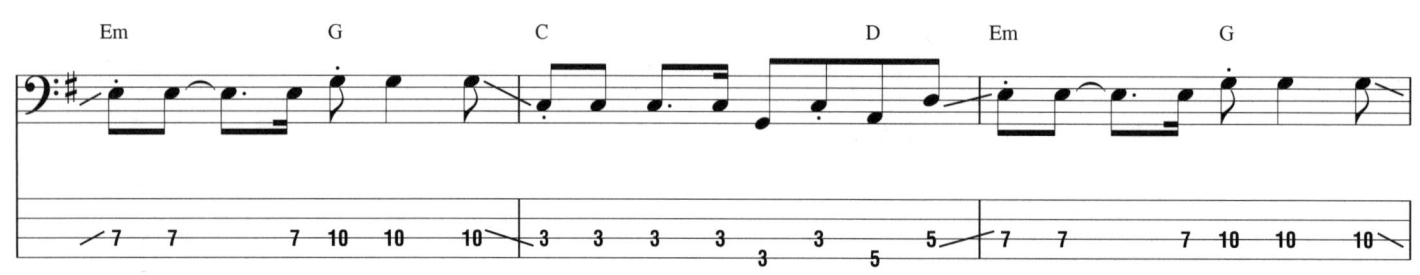

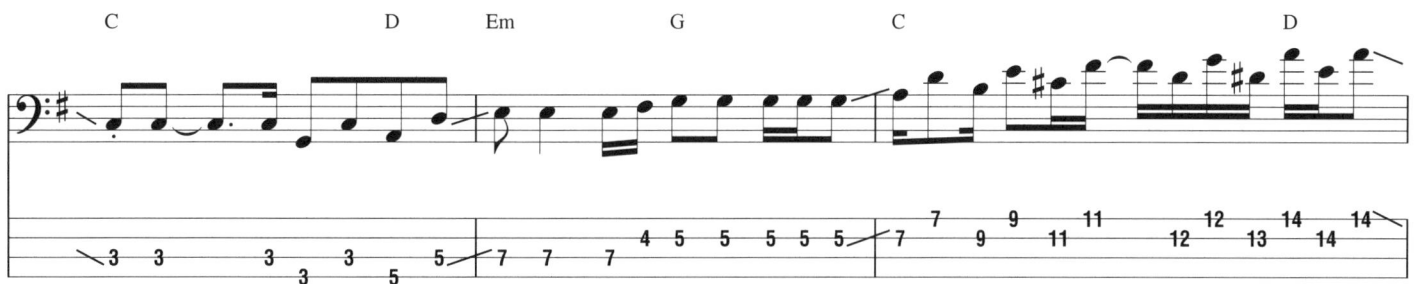

Verse

3. Those who don't __ be - lieve __ me find __ your souls __ and set __ them free.

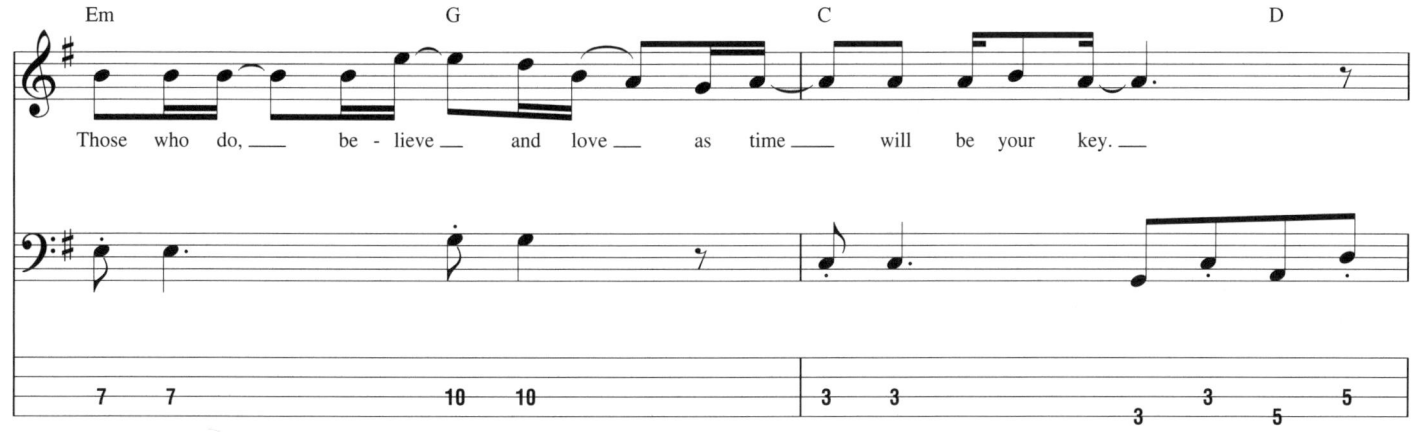

Those who do, __ be - lieve __ and love __ as time __ will be your key. __

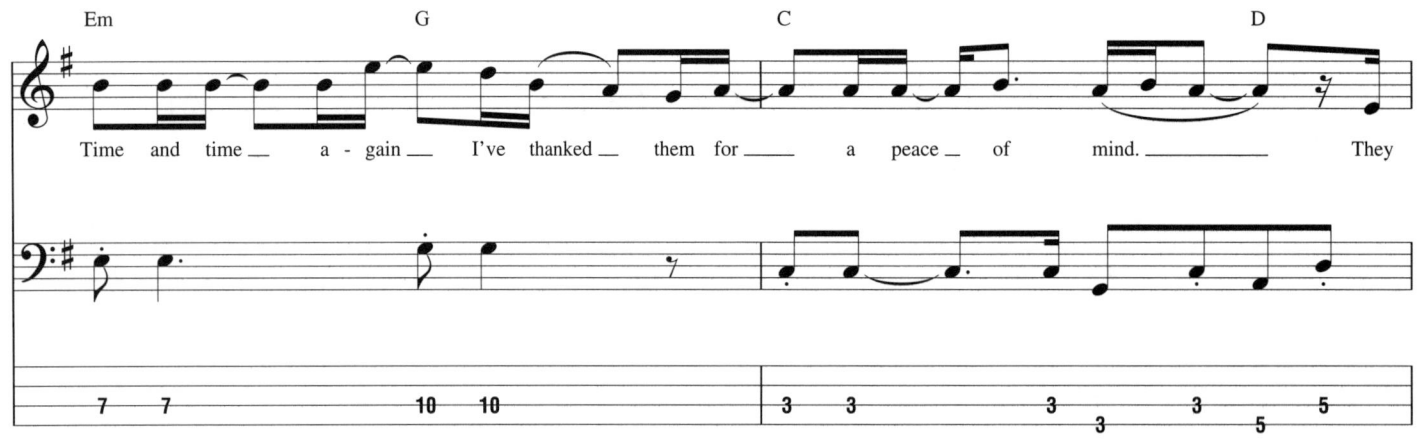

Time and time a-gain I've thanked them for a peace of mind. They

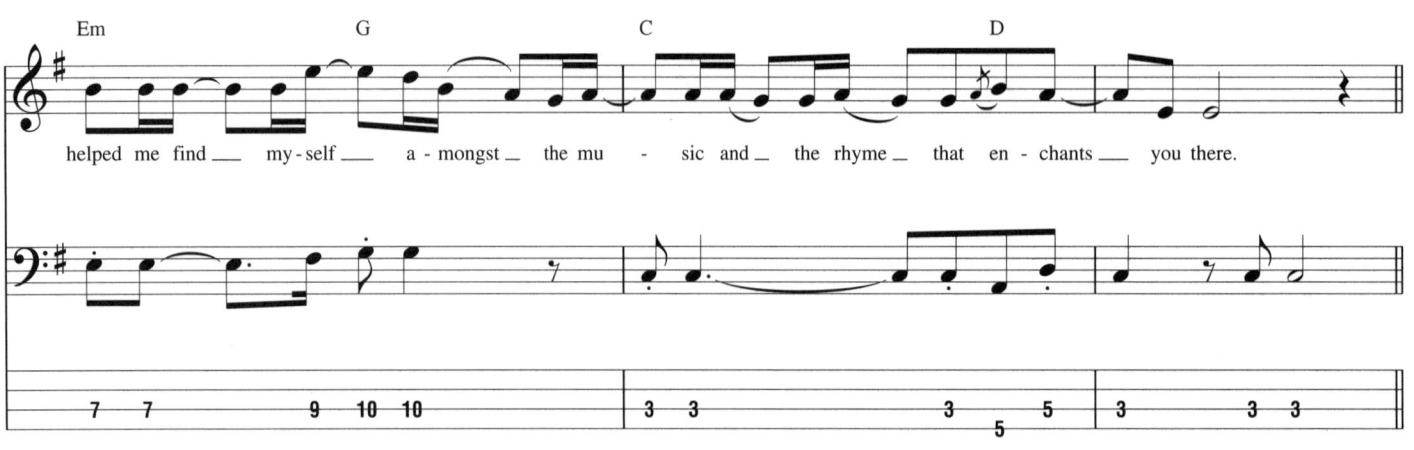

helped me find my-self a-mongst the mu - sic and the rhyme that en - chants you there.

Chorus

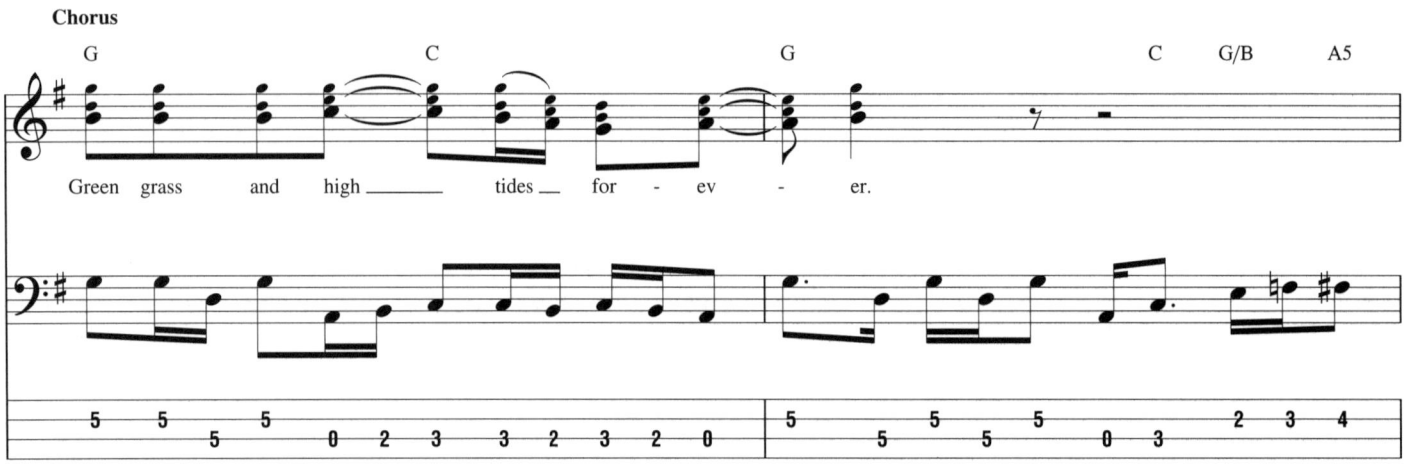

Green grass and high tides for - ev - er.

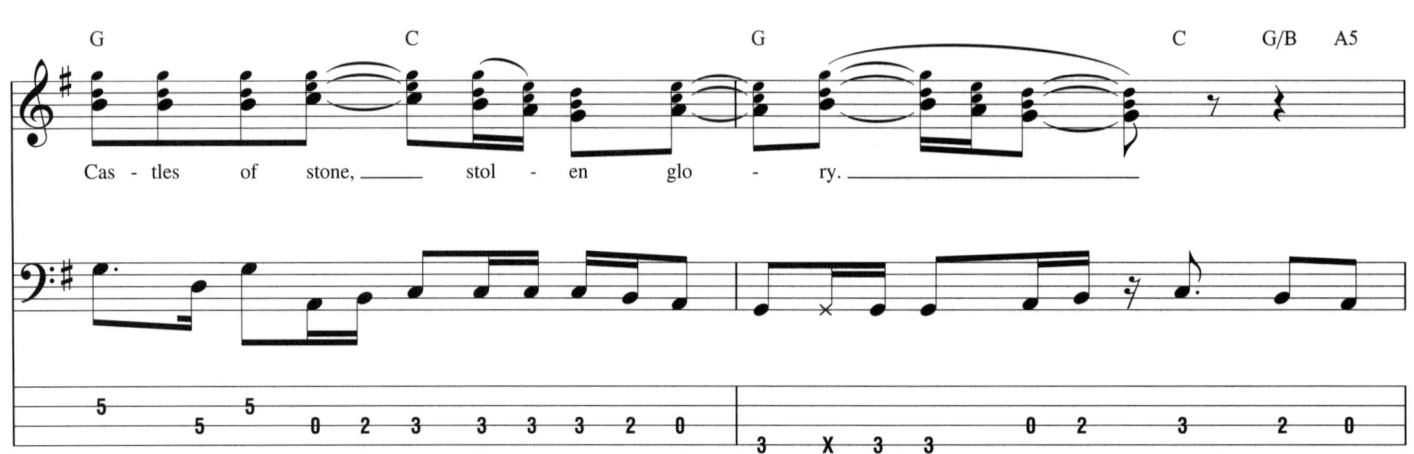

Cas - tles of stone, stol - en glo - ry.

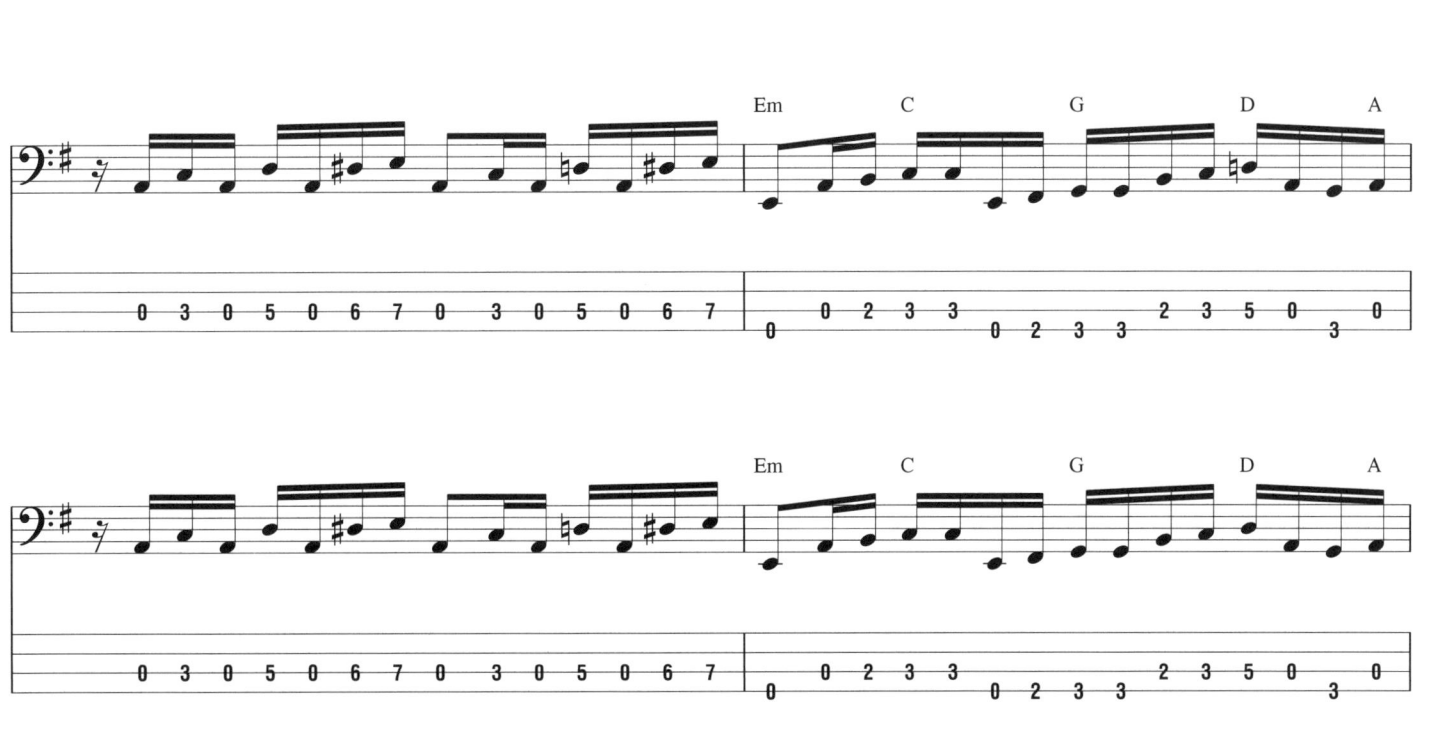

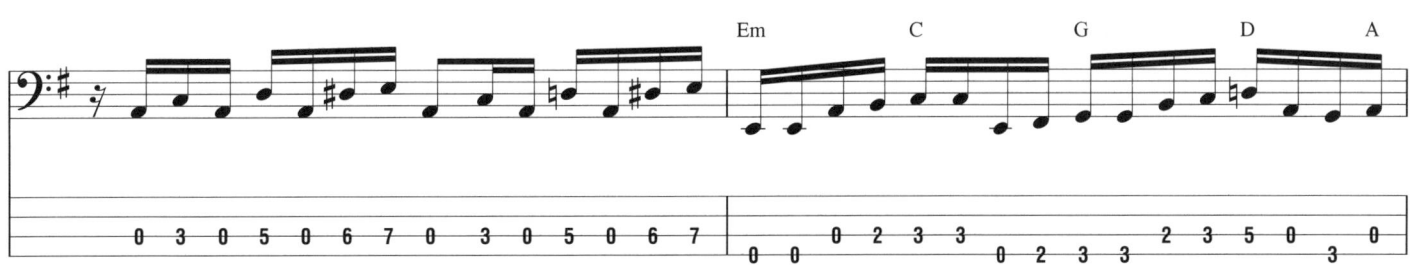

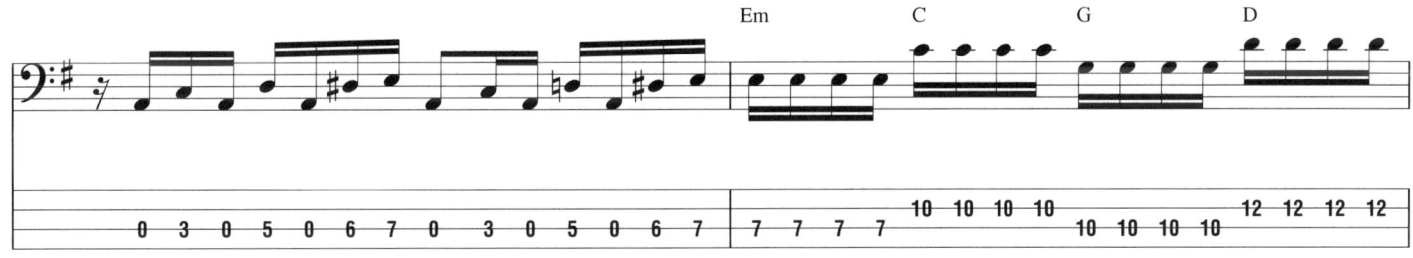

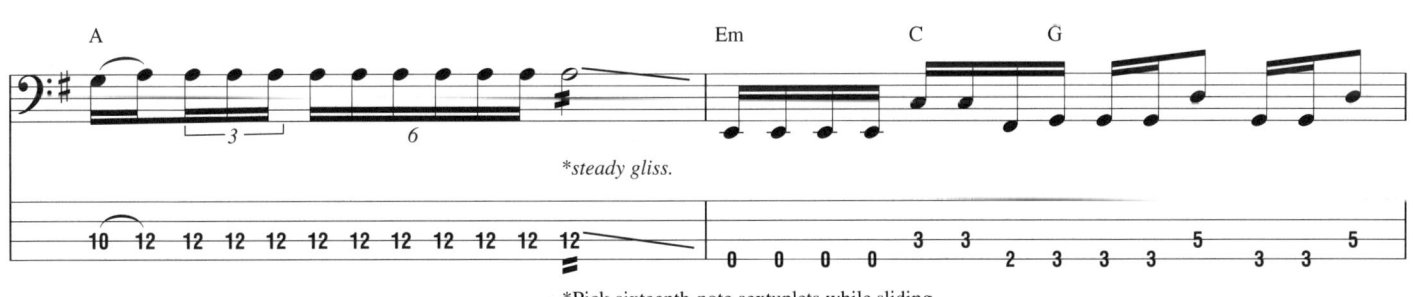

steady gliss.

*Pick sixteenth-note sextuplets while sliding.

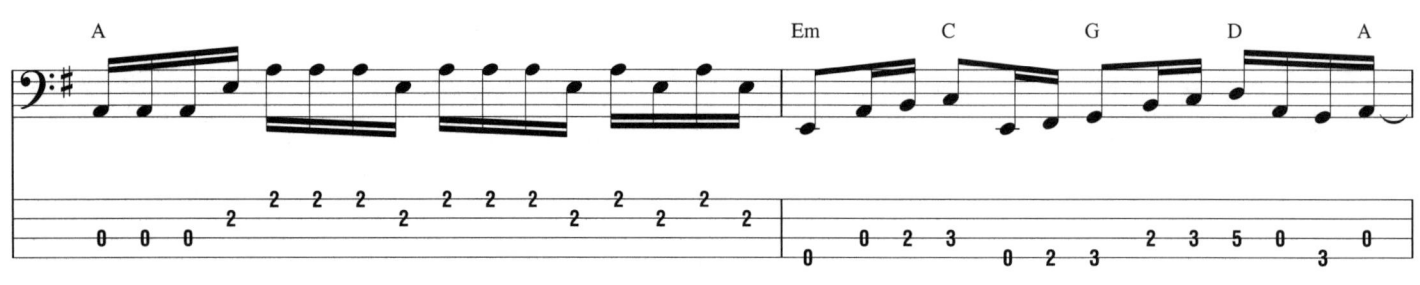
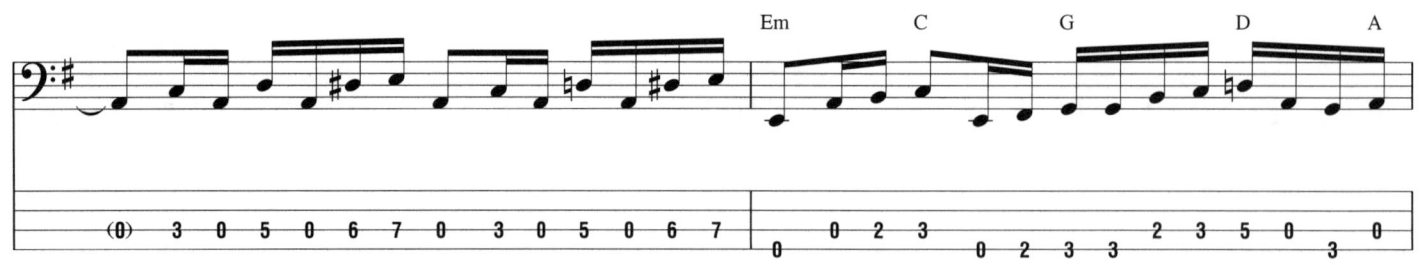

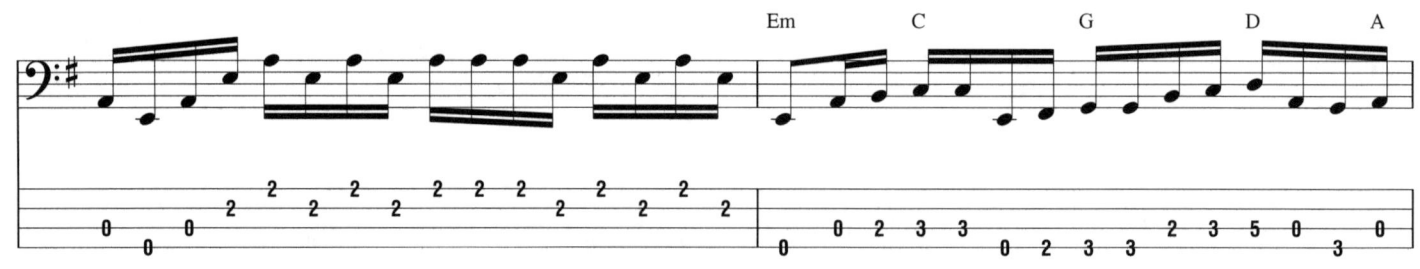
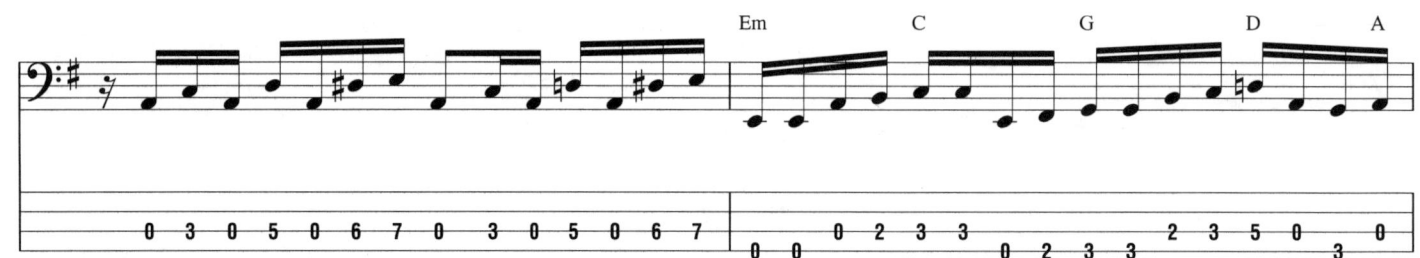

58

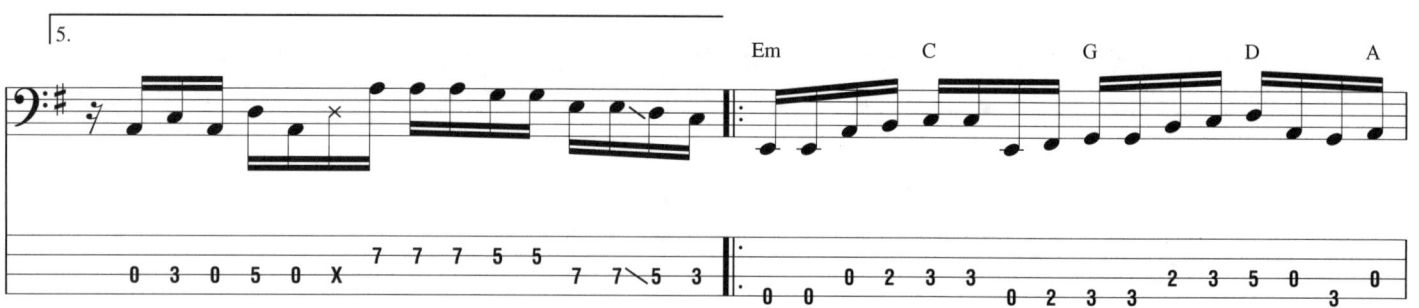

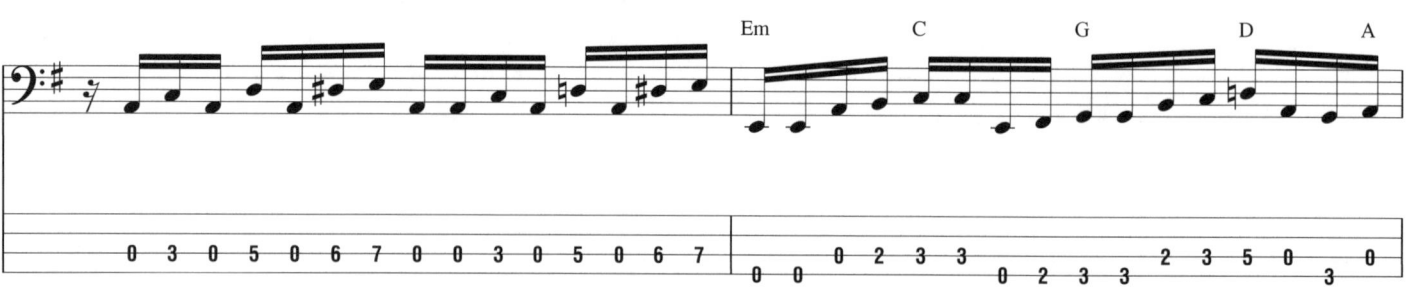

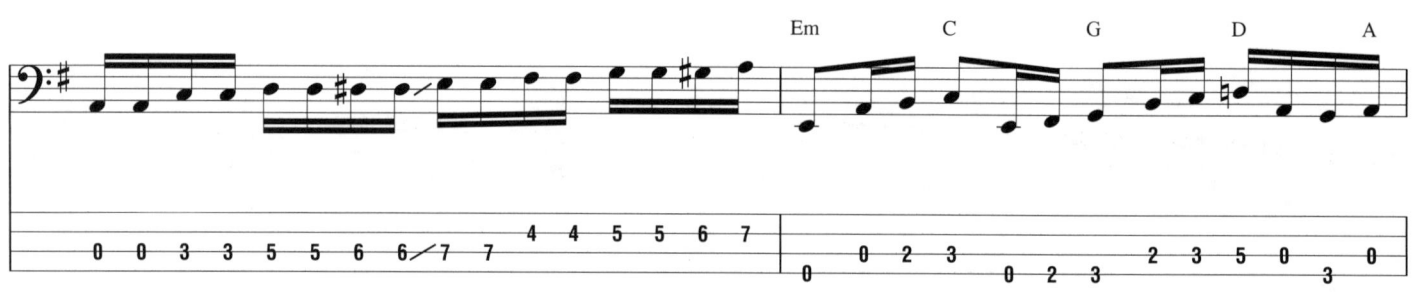

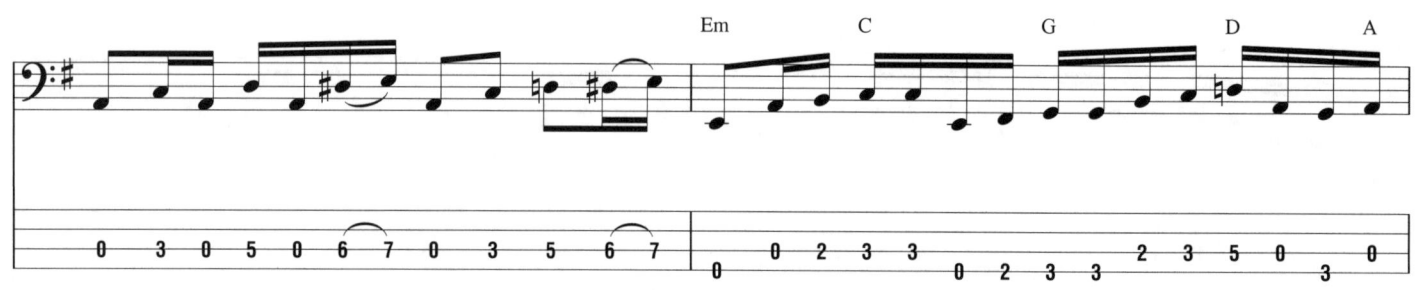

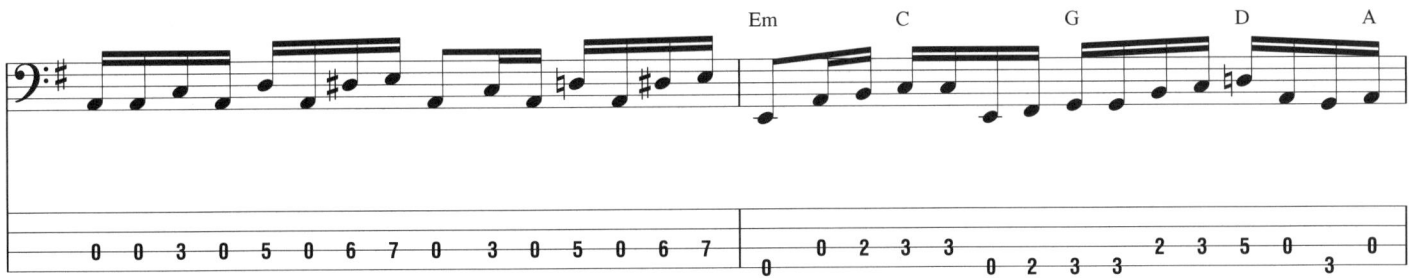

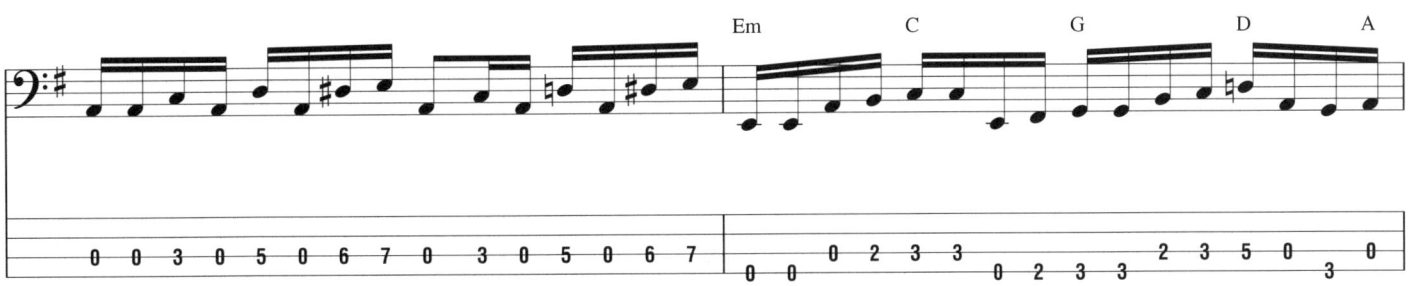

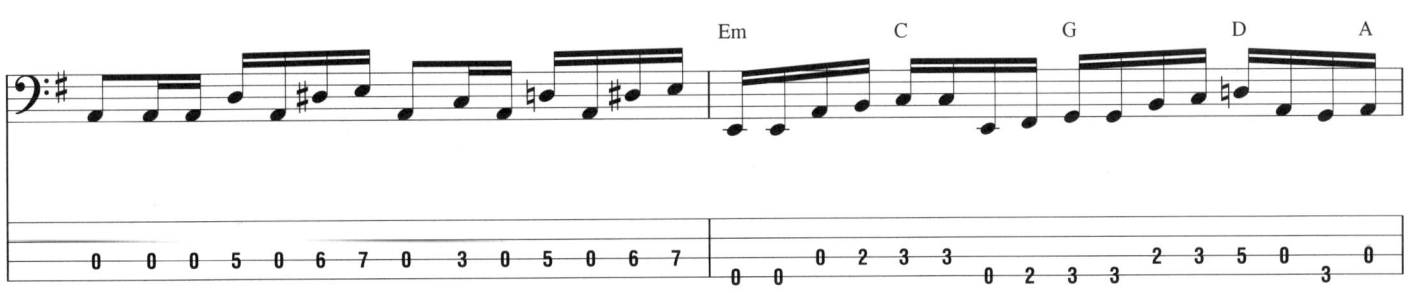

*Pick sixteenth-note sextuplets while sliding.

Highway Star

Words and Music by Ritchie Blackmore, Ian Gillan, Roger Glover, Jon Lord and Ian Paice

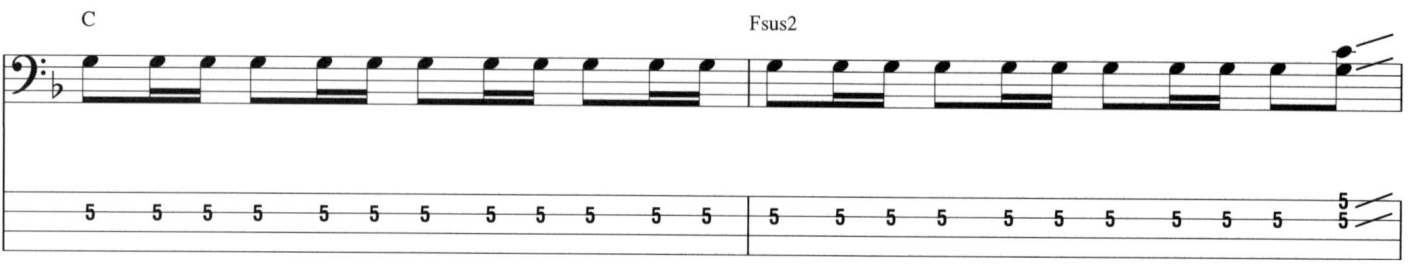

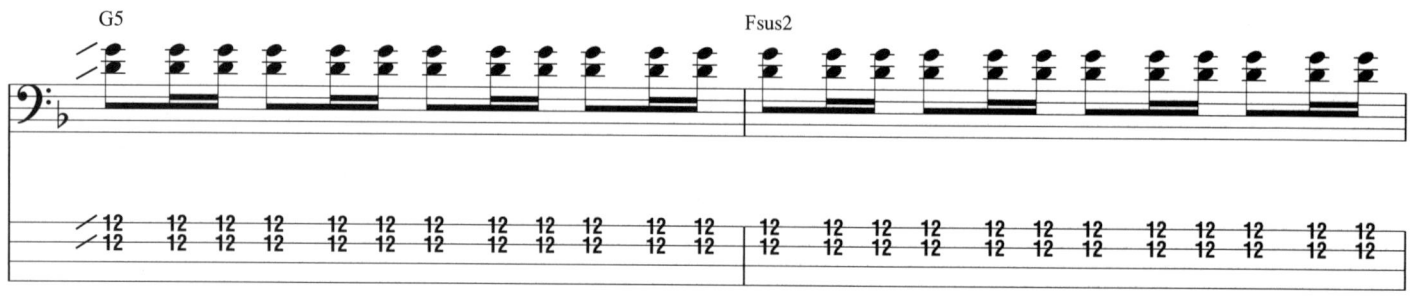

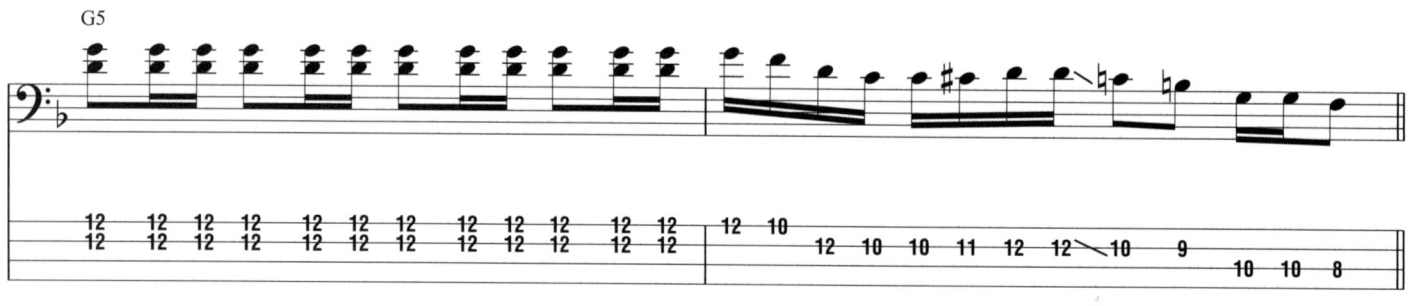

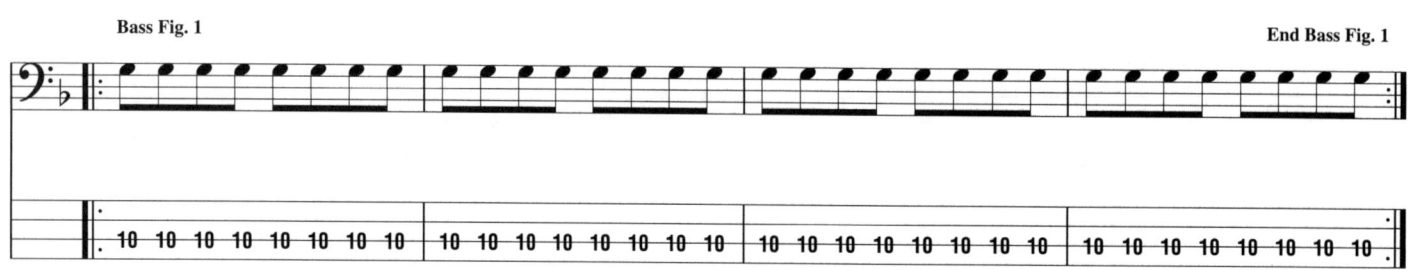

Ah. _____

(Ah. _____)

(Ah.) _____

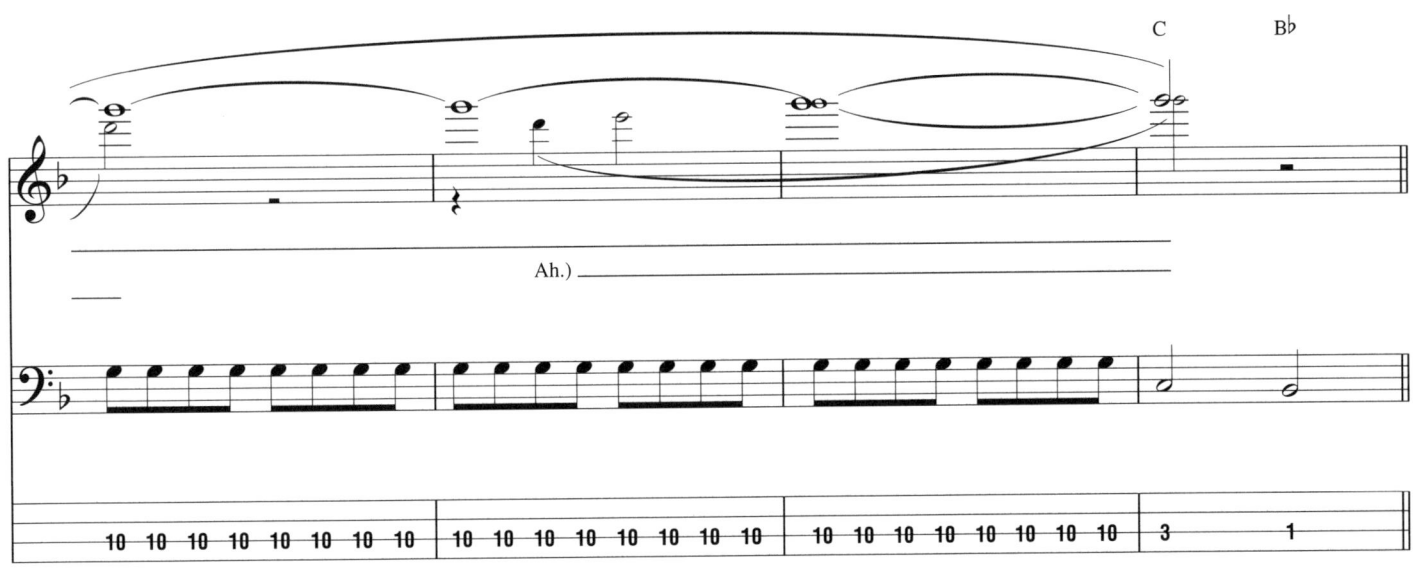

Ah.) _____

§ **Verse**

2nd & 3rd times, Bass: w/ Bass Fill 1
4th time, Bass: w/ Bass Fill 4

F5 G5

1., 4. No - bod - y gon - na take my car, ___ I'm gon - na race it to the ground. _____
2. No - bod - y gon - na take my girl, ___ I'm gon - na keep her to the end. _____
3. No - bod - y gon - na take my head, ___ I got speed in - side my brain. _____

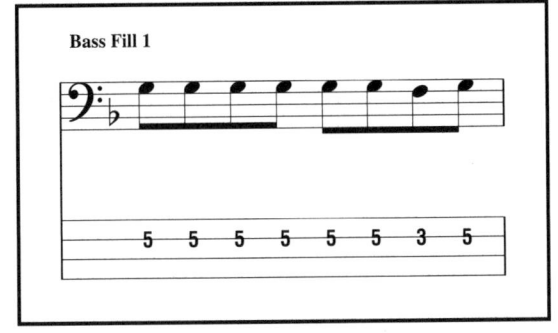

Bass Fill 1

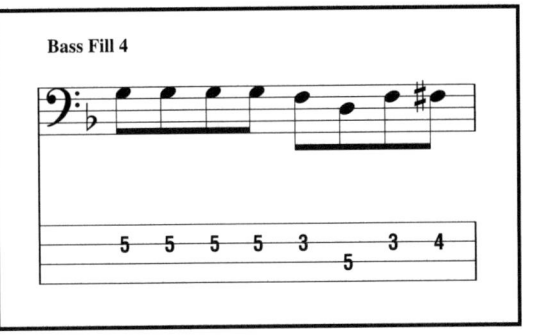

Bass Fill 4

A, no - bod - y gon - na beat my car, __ it's gon - na break the speed of sound. _____
A, no - bod - y gon - na have my girl, __ she stays close on ev -'ry bend. __ _____
A, no - bod - y gon - na steal my head, __ now that I'm on the road a - gain. __ _____

Ooh, _____ it's a kill - in' ma - chine, __ it's got, a, ev -'ry - thing. __
Ooh, _____ she's a kill - in' ma - chine, __ she's got, a, ev -'ry - thing. __
Ooh, _____ I'm in heav - en a - gain, __ I got, a, ev -'ry - thing. __

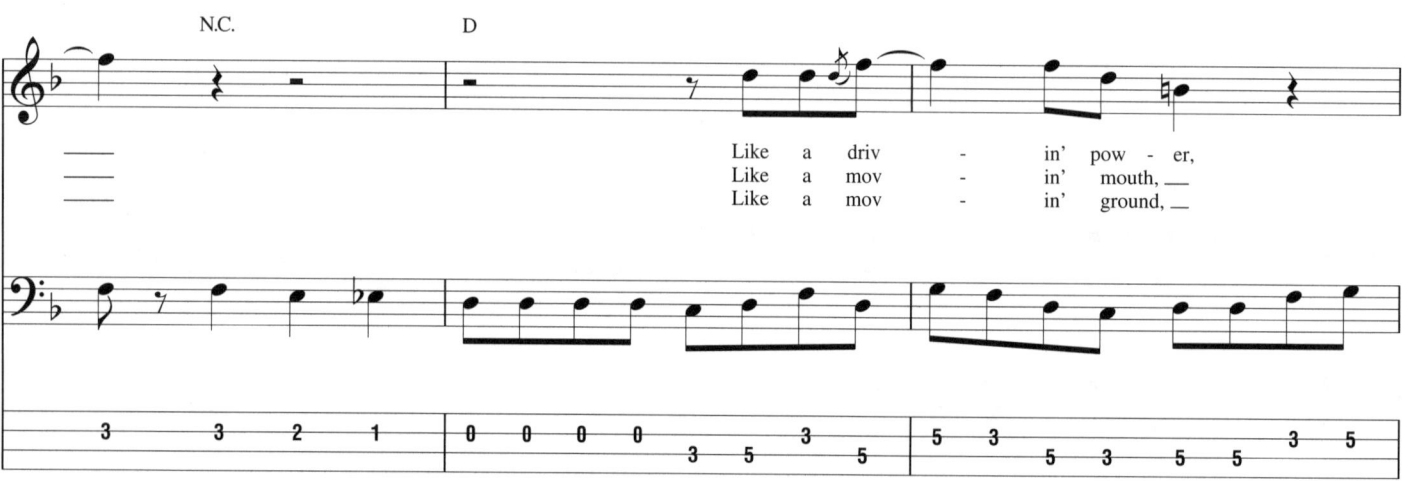

Like a driv - in' pow - er,
Like a mov - in' mouth, __
Like a mov - in' ground, __

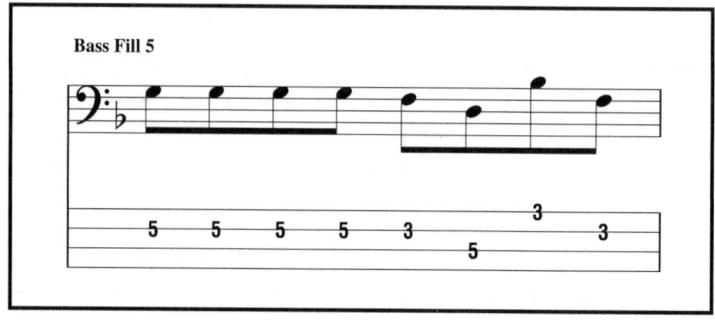

Bass Fill 5

64

2nd time, Bass: w/ Bass Fill 2
3rd time, Bass: w/ Bass Fill 3
4th time, Bass: w/ Bass Fill 6

big fat   tires ___ and ev - 'ry - thing. ___   I love ___ it!
bod - y   con - trol   and ev - 'ry - thing. ___   I love ___ her!
throt - tle con - trol   and ev - 'ry - thing. ___   I love ___ it!

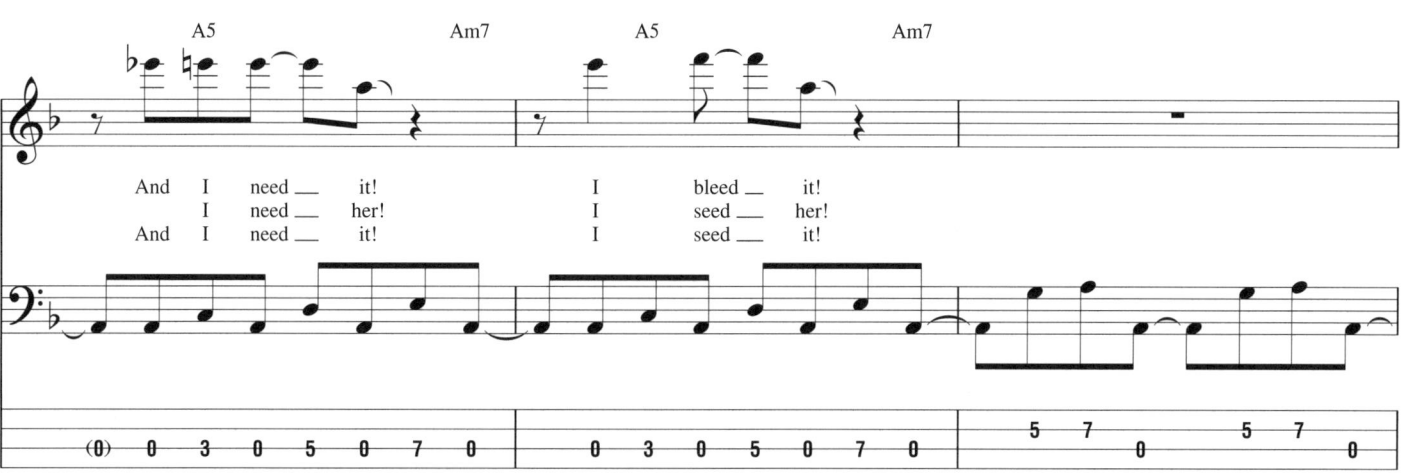

And I   need ___ it!   I   bleed ___ it!
     I   need ___ her!   I   seed ___ her!
And I   need ___ it!   I   seed ___ it!

Bass Fill 2

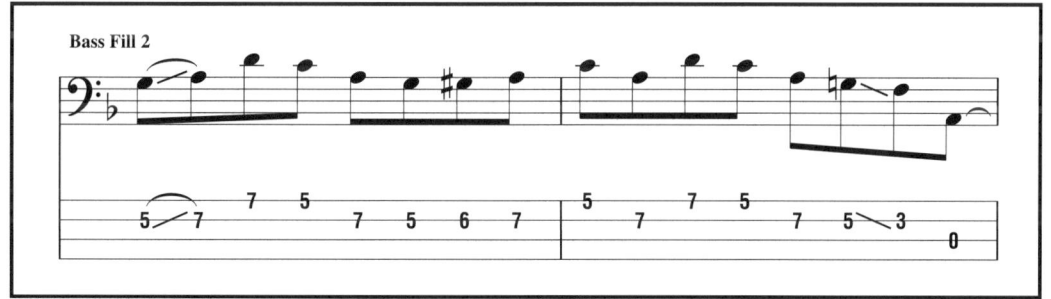

Bass Fill 3

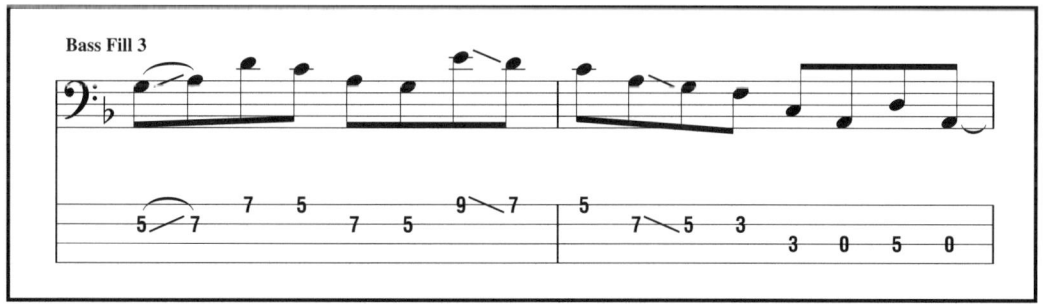

Bass Fill 6

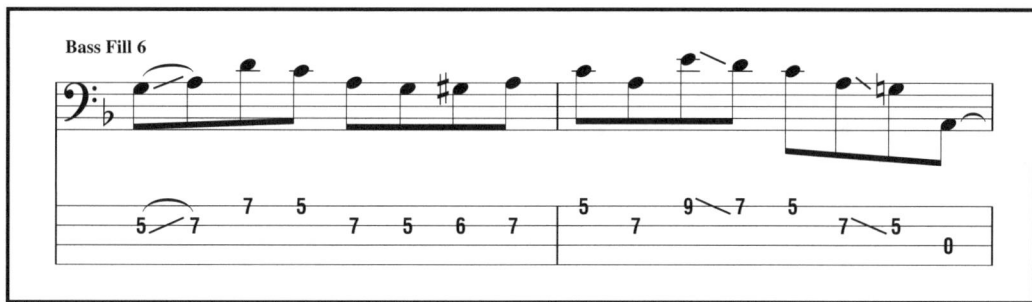

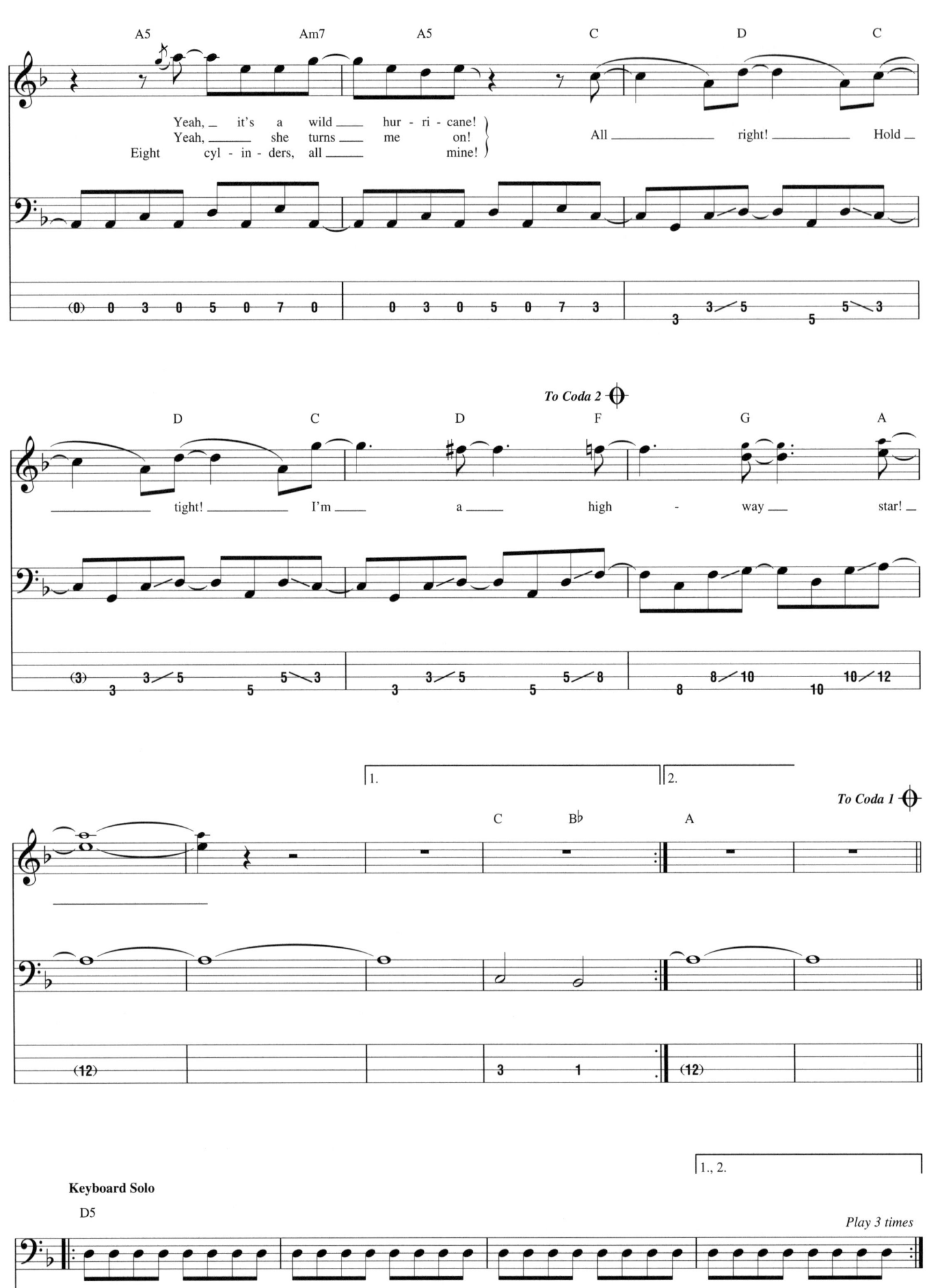

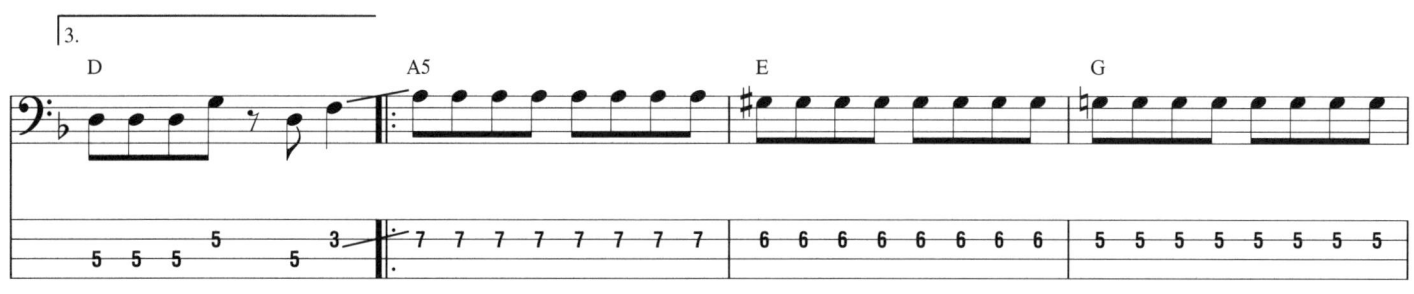

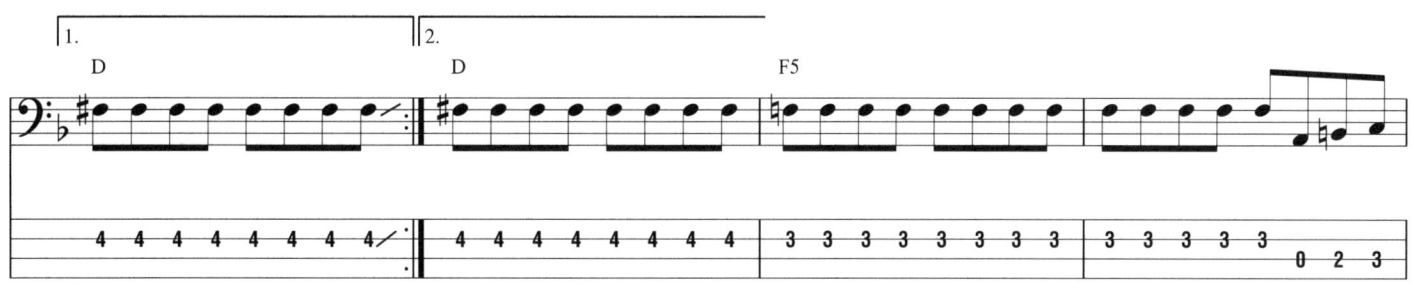

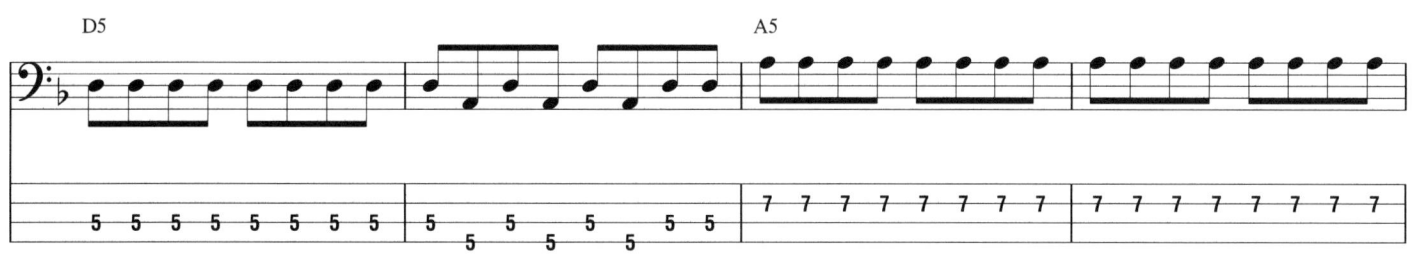

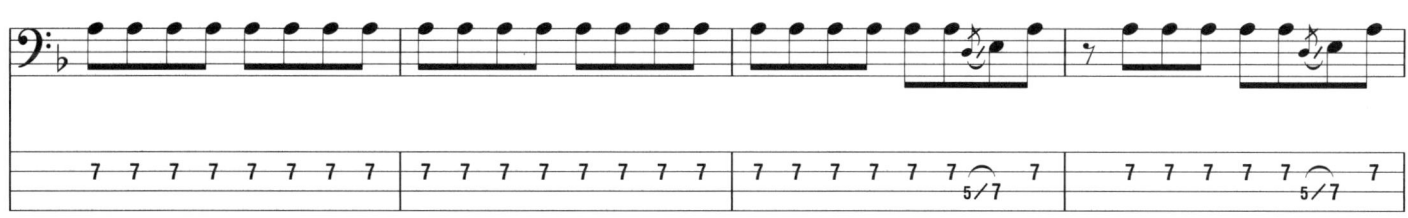

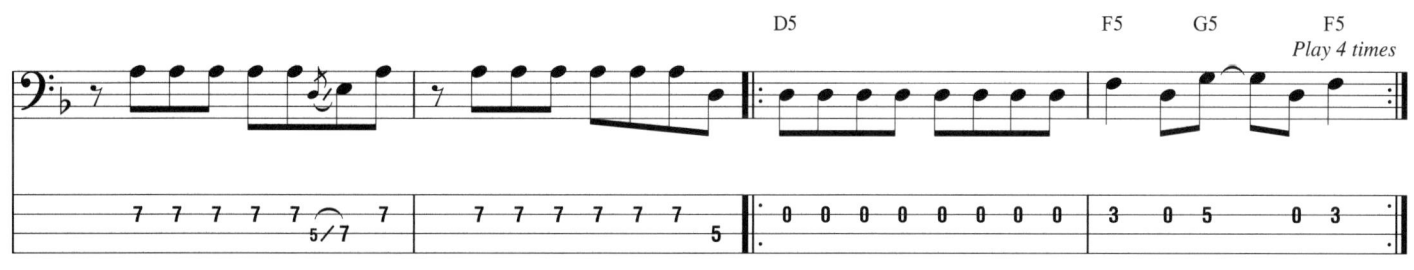

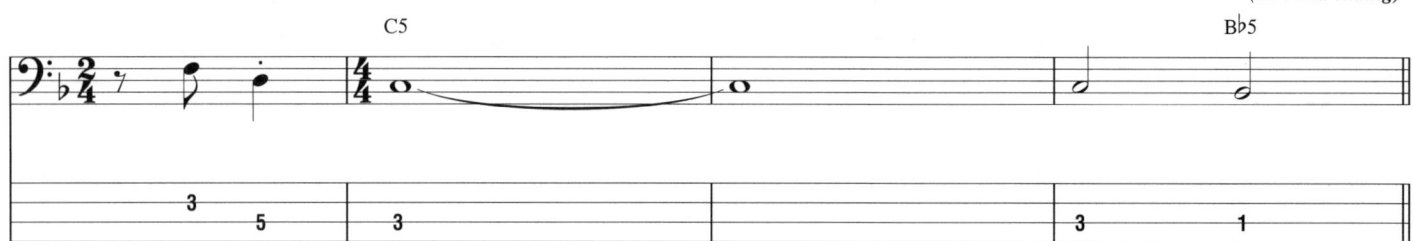

Coda 1

Guitar Solo

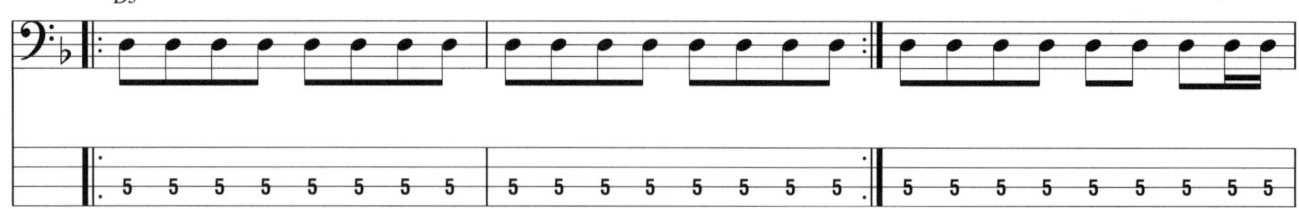

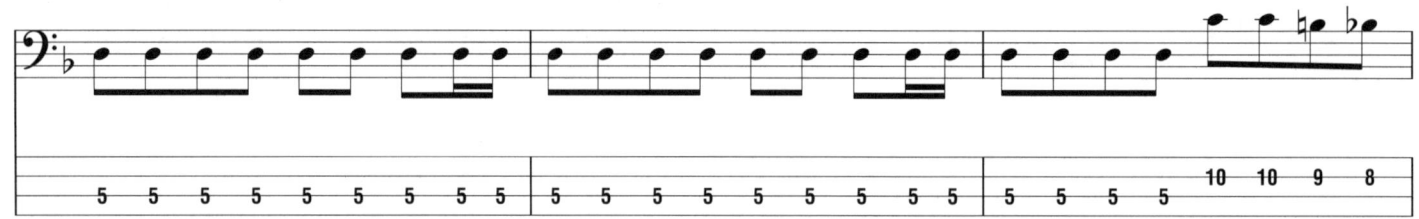

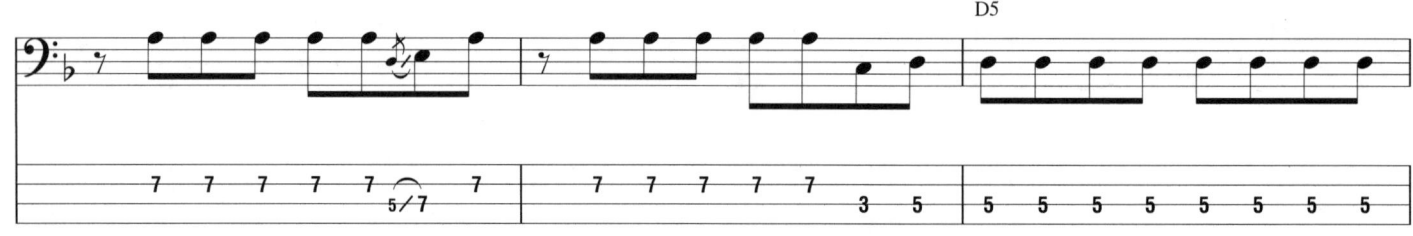

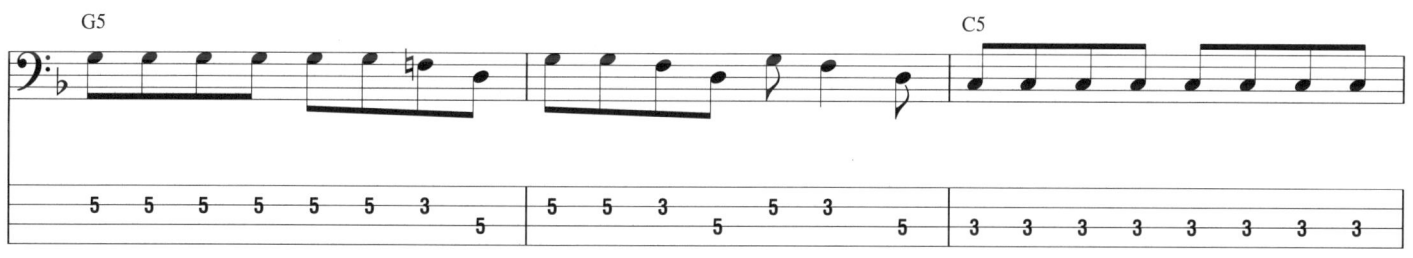

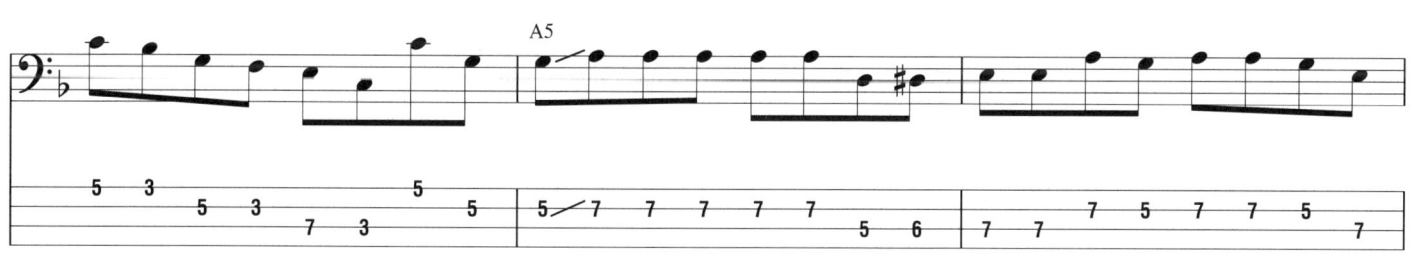

⊕ Coda 2

Free time

I'm So Sick

Words and Music by Sameer Bhattacharya, Jared Hartmann, Kirkpatrick Seals, James Culpepper and Lacey Mosley

Drop D tuning
(low to high) D-A-D-G

*Chord symbols reflect implied harmony.

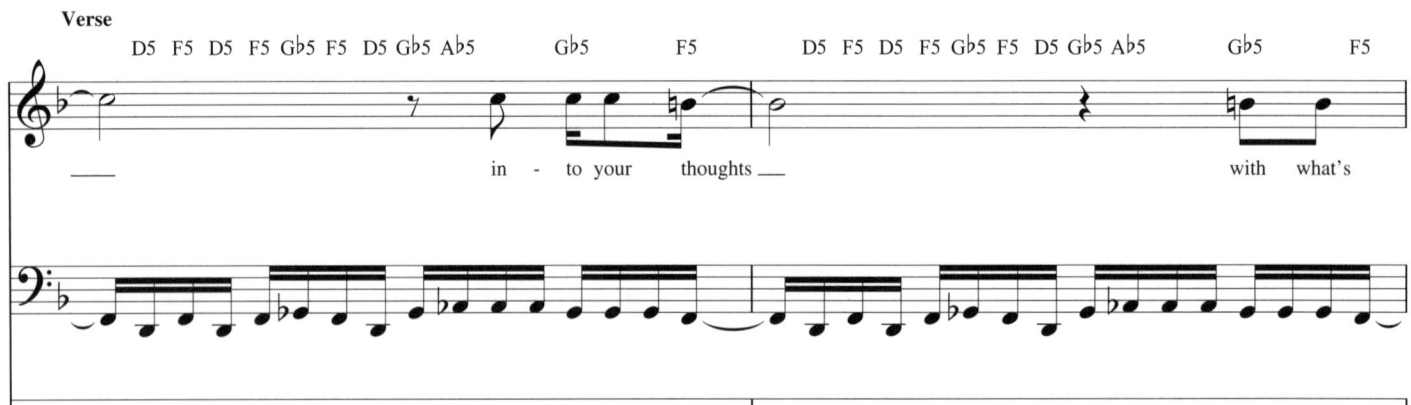

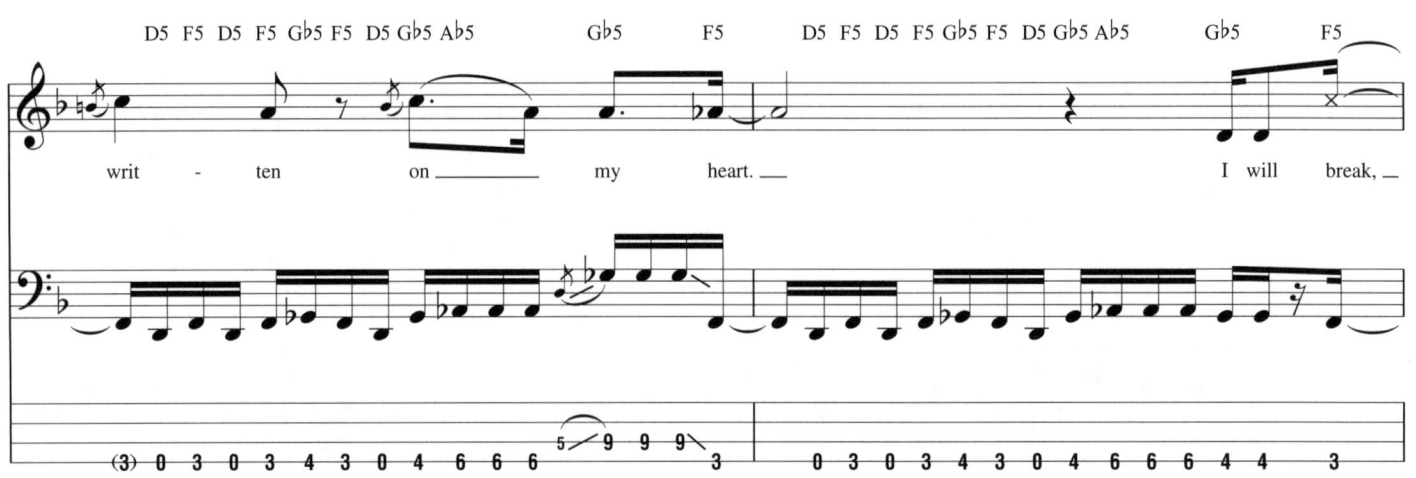

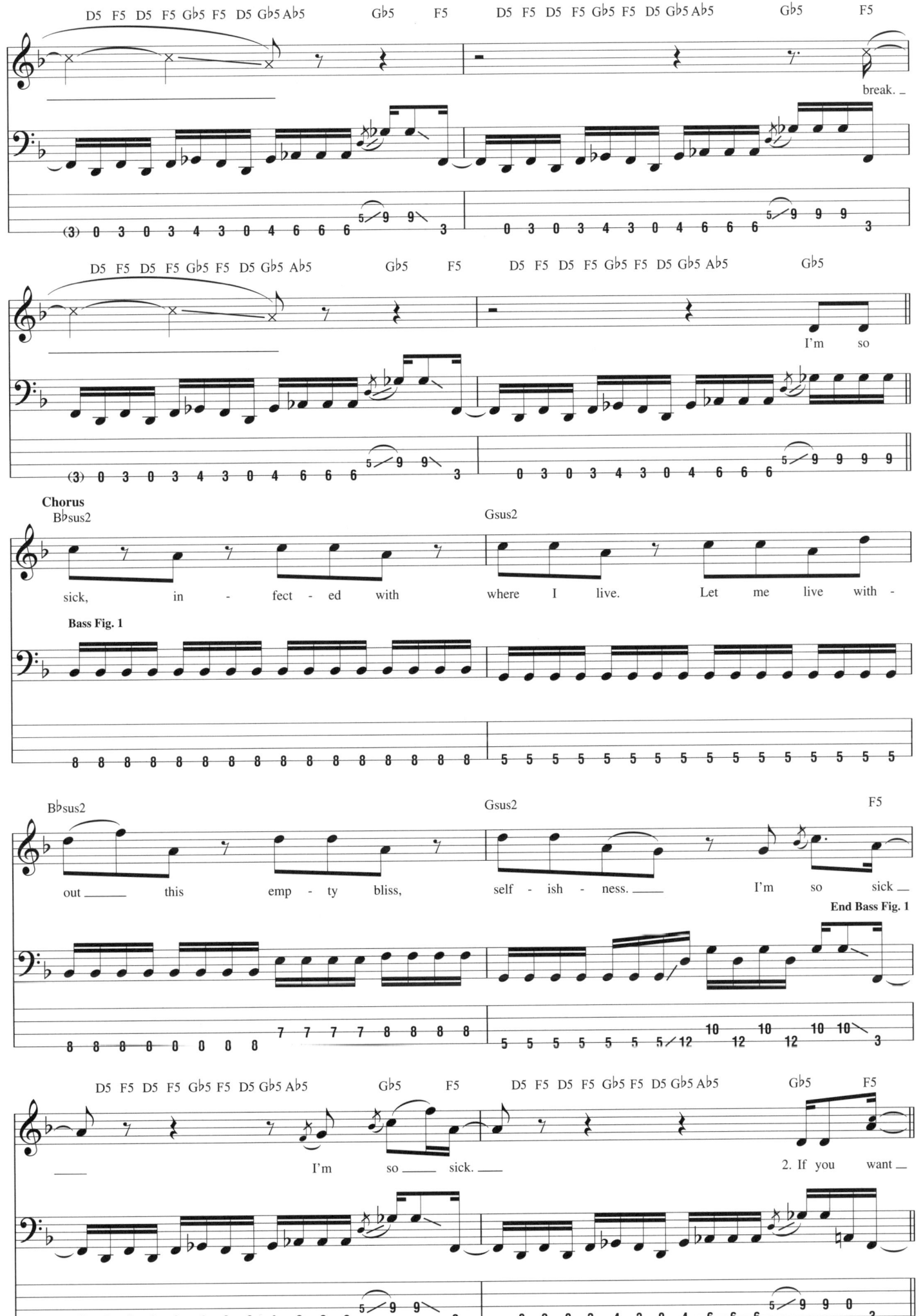

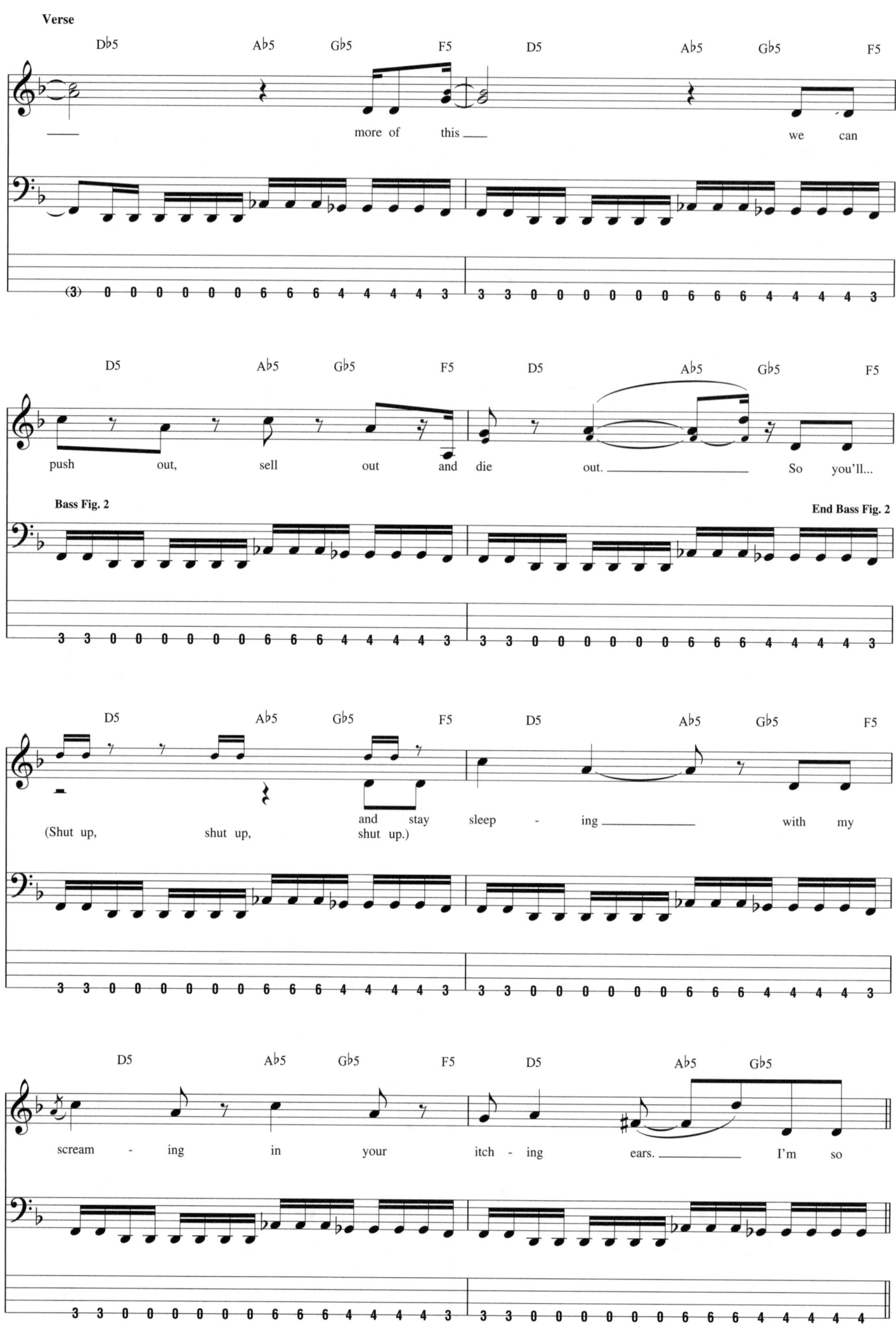

74

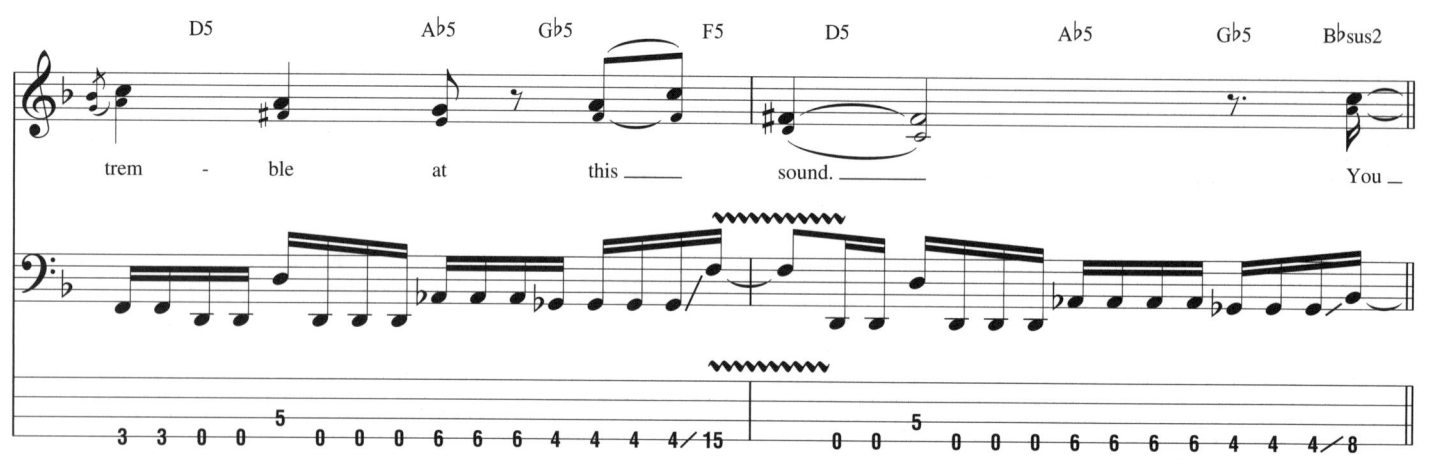

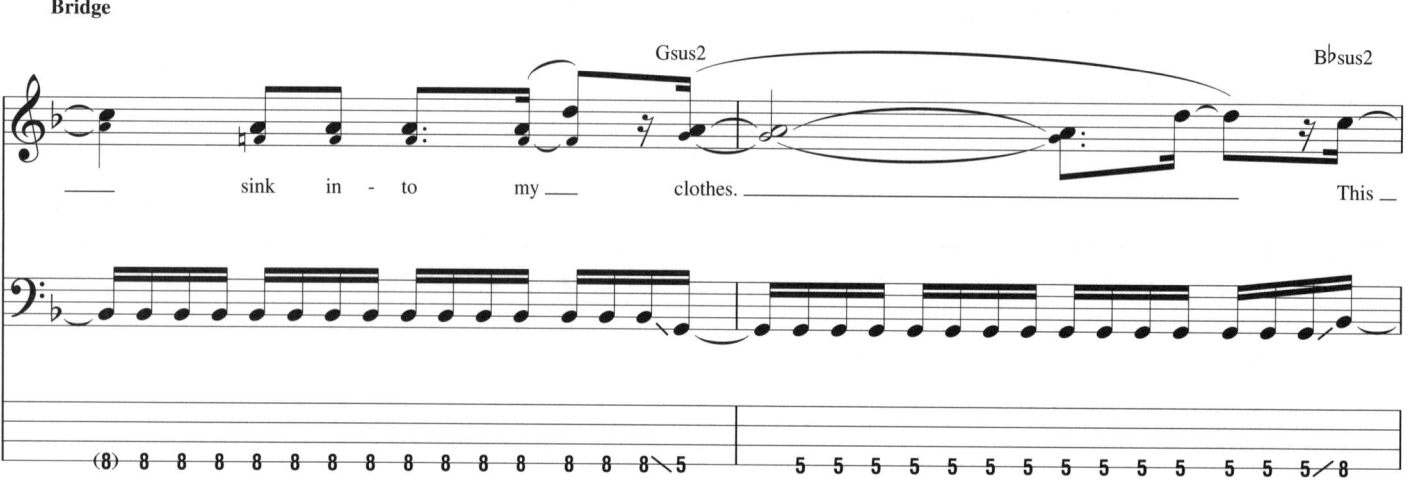

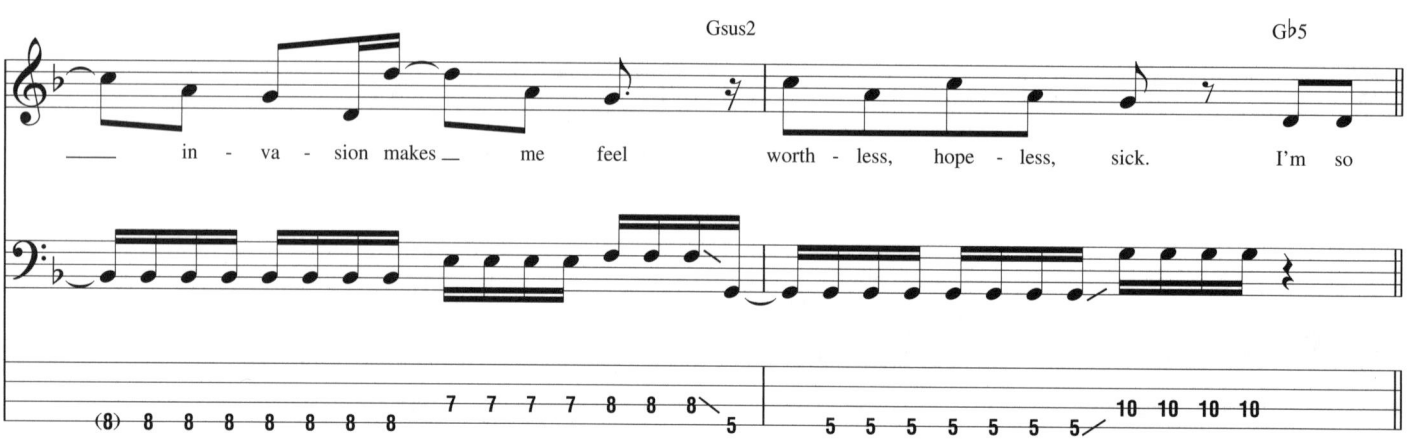

In Bloom

Words and Music by Kurt Cobain

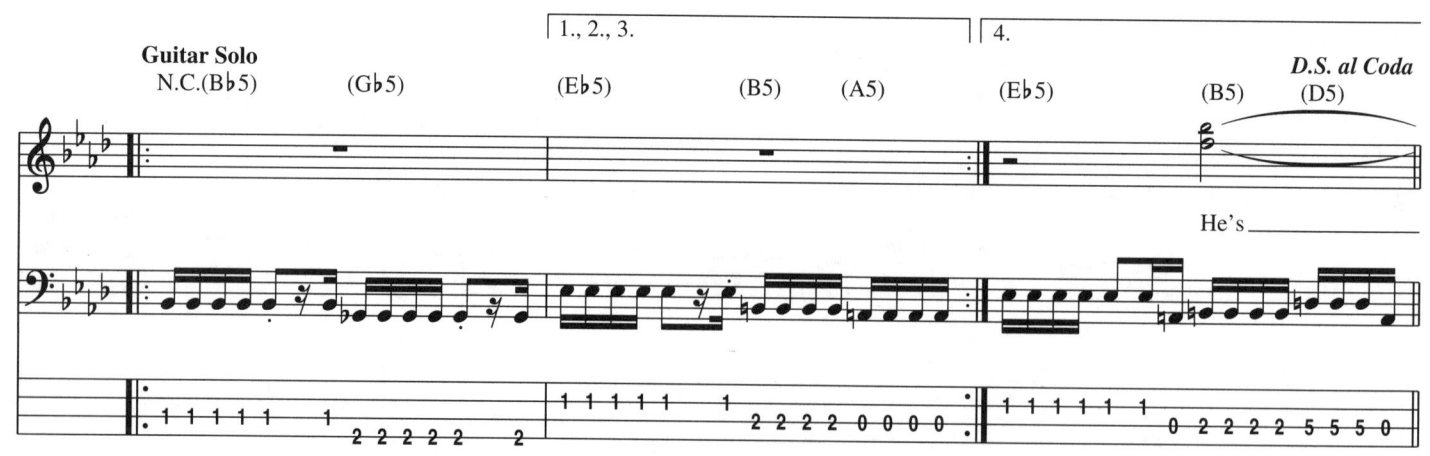

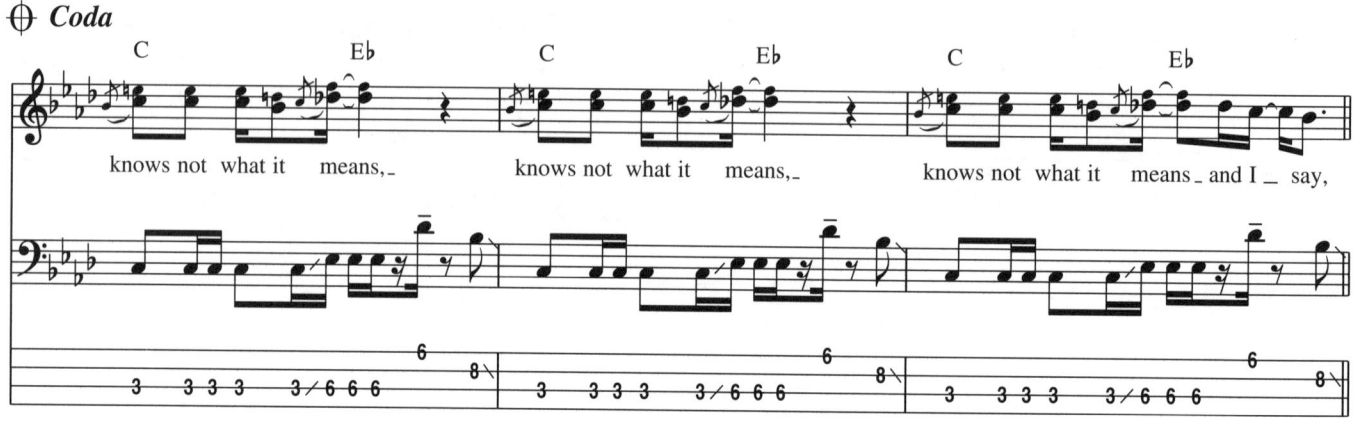

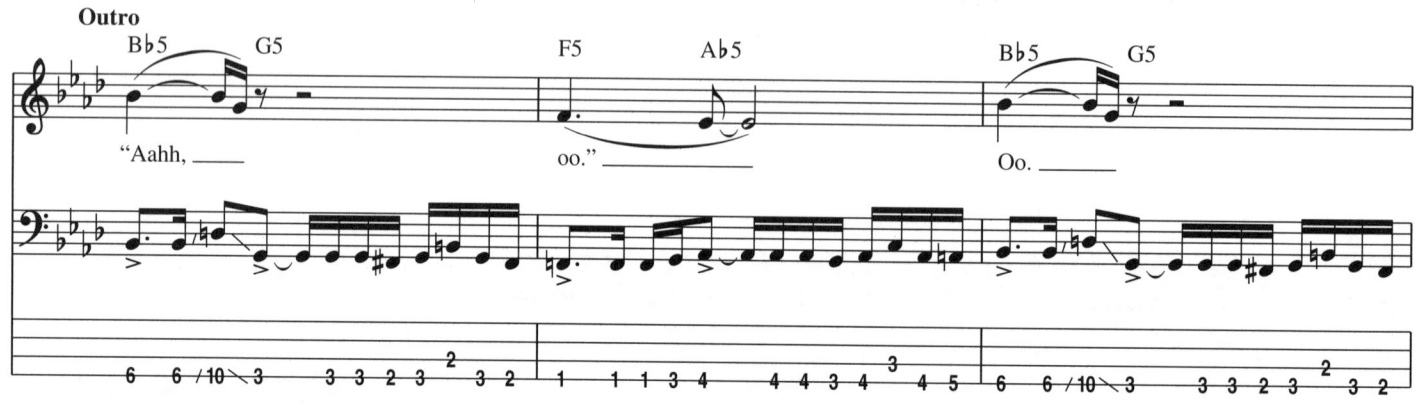

Learn to Fly

Words and Music by Dave Grohl, Nate Mendel and Taylor Hawkins

Intro
Moderately Fast Rock ♩ = 136

Verse

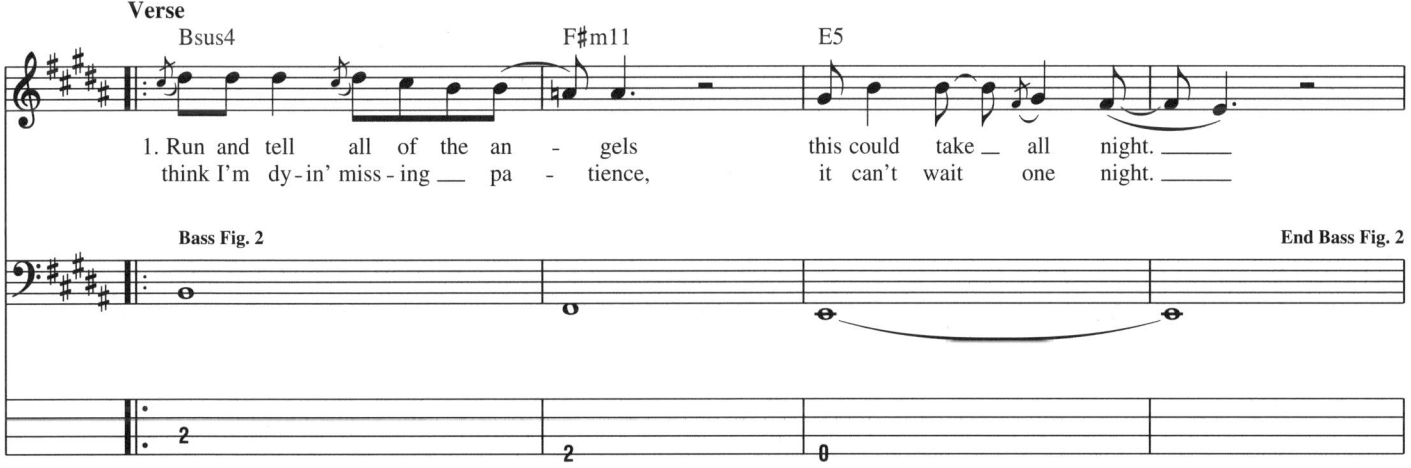

1. Run and tell all of the an – gels this could take __ all night. ____
think I'm dy-in' miss-ing __ pa – tience, it can't wait one night. ____

Bass: w/ Bass Fig. 2, 2 1/2 times

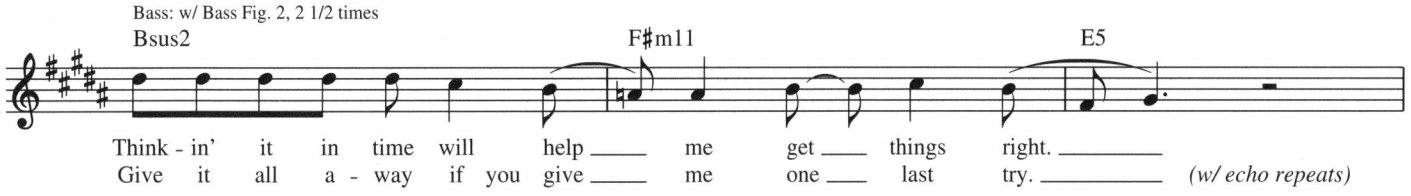

Think – in' it in time will help __ me get __ things right. ____
Give it all a – way if you give __ me one __ last try. ____ *(w/ echo repeats)*

Hook me up a new rev - o - lu - tion, 'cause this one is ___ a lie. ___
We'll live ___ hap - pi - ly ev - ___ er trapped _ if you ___ just save _ my life. _

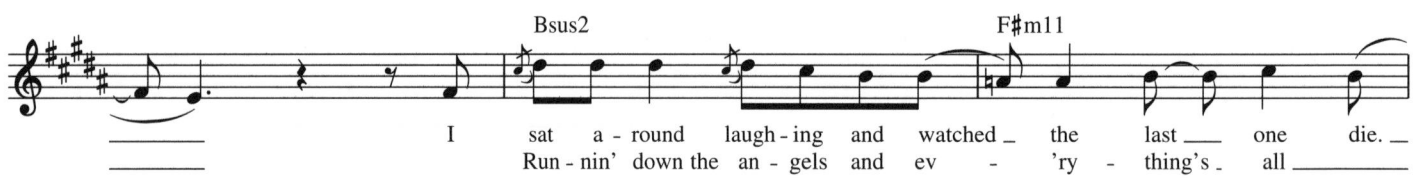

_____ I sat a - round laugh - ing and watched _ the last ___ one die. _
_____ Run - nin' down the an - gels and ev - 'ry - thing's _ all _____

𝄋 Chorus

Bass: w/ Bass Fig. 1, 1st 5 meas.

____ *(w/ echo repeats)*
____ right. _____ I'm look - in' to the sky to save ___ me,

Bass

look - in' for a sign of life. ___ I'm look - in' for some - thin' to help _

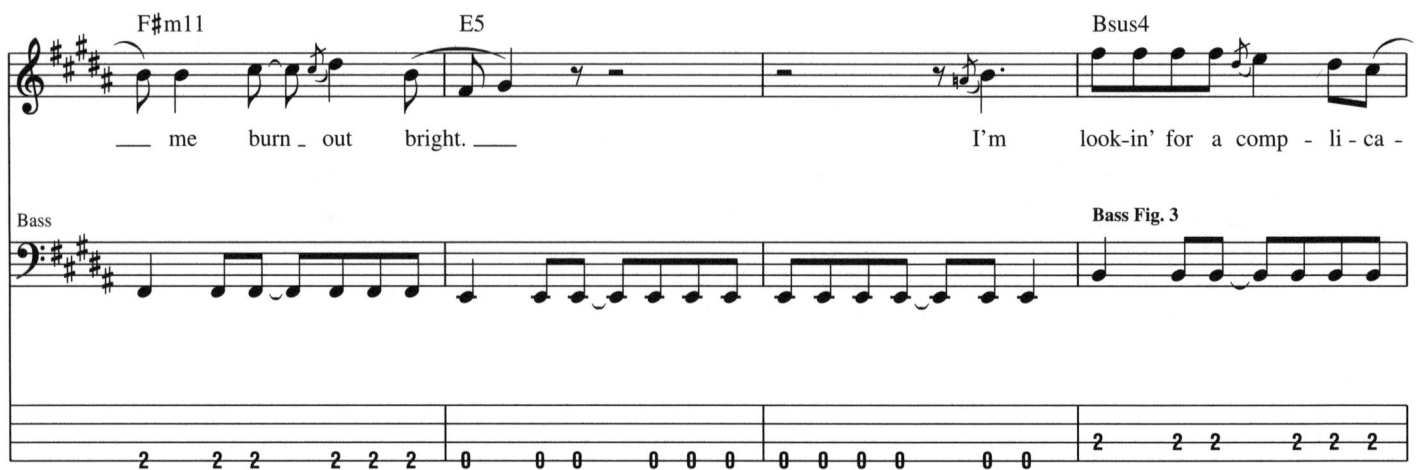

_ me burn _ out bright. ___ I'm look - in' for a comp - li - ca -

Bass

Bass Fig. 3

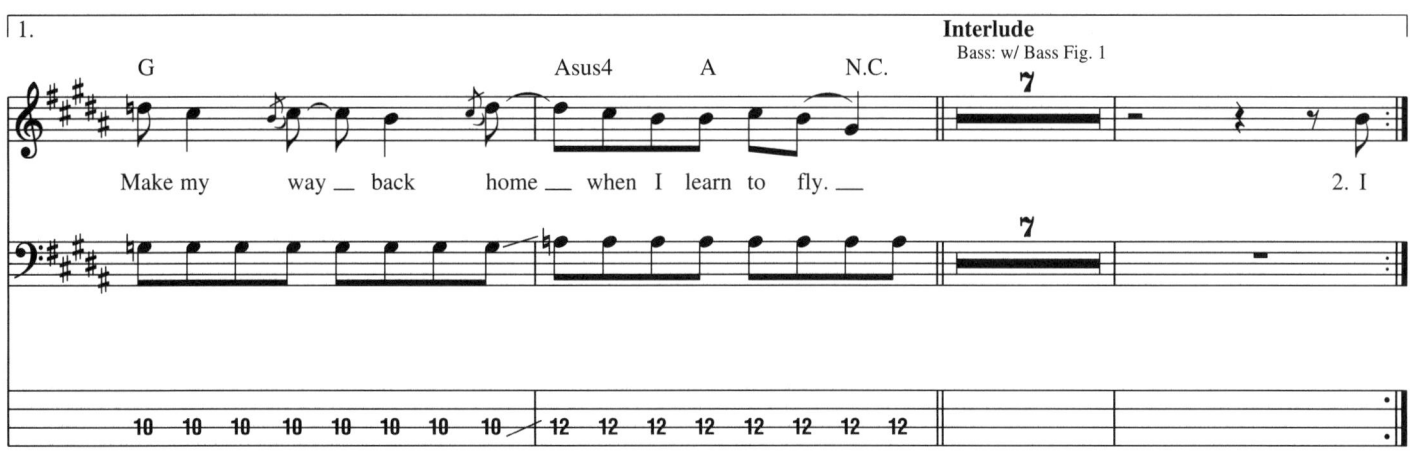

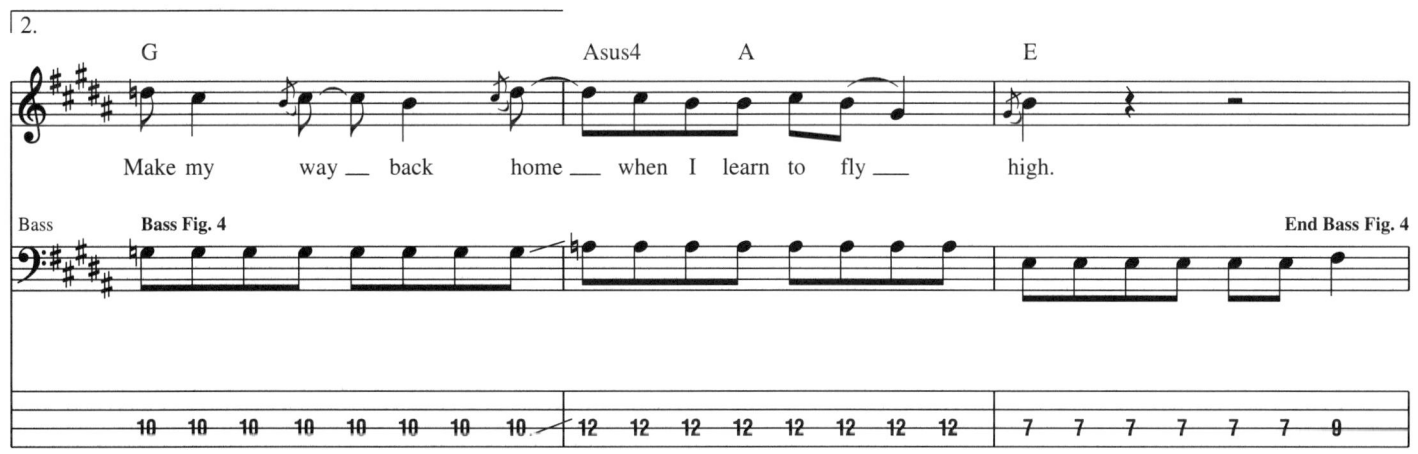

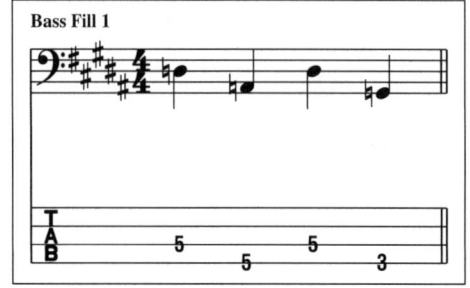

Outro-Chorus

Bass: w/ Bass Fig. 1

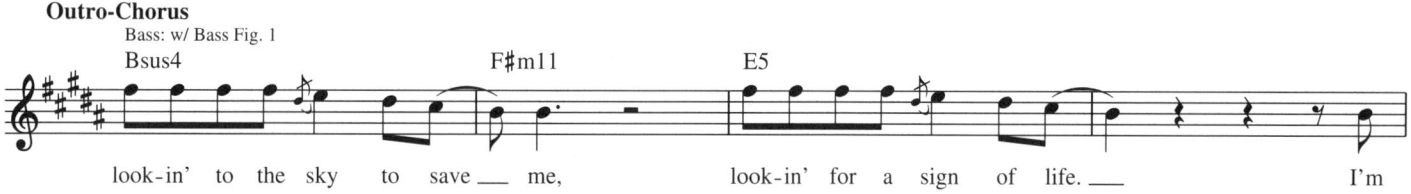

look-in' to the sky to save __ me, look-in' for a sign of life. __ I'm

look-in' for some-thin' to help __ me burn __ out bright. _____ I'm

Bass: w/ Bass Fig. 3

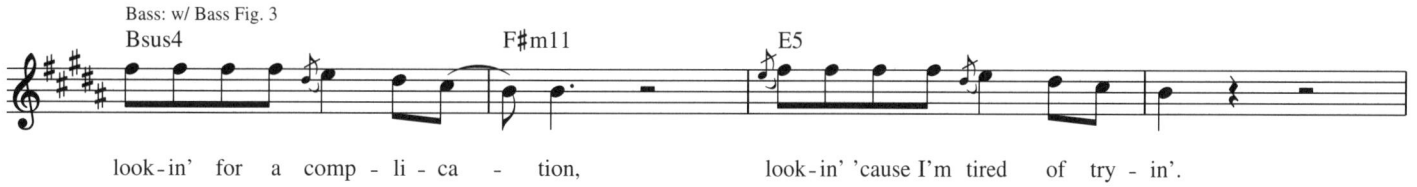

look-in' for a comp-li-ca-tion, look-in' 'cause I'm tired of try-in'.

Bass: w/ Bass Fig. 4, 2 2/3 times

Make my way __ back home __ when I learn to fly __ high. Make my way __ back home __

__ when I learn to fly. Make my way __ back home __ when I learn __ to...(w/ echo repeats)

Outro

Bass

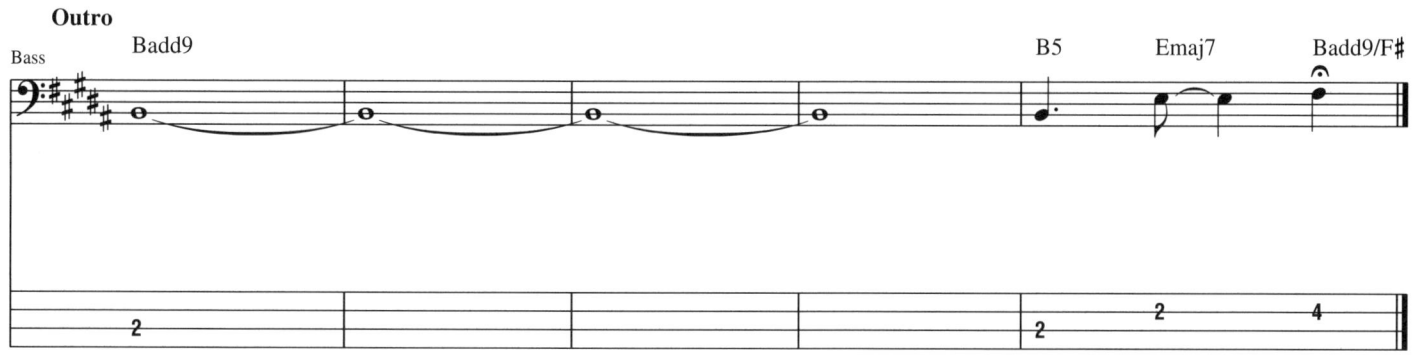

Long Time

Words and Music by Tom Scholz

*2nd time, vocal tacet on beat 1.

I'm just, a, mov - in' on. _____

(Well, I'm tak - in' my time, _____

You'll for - get a - bout _____ me af - ter I've been gone. _____

And I take what I find. _____ I don't _____

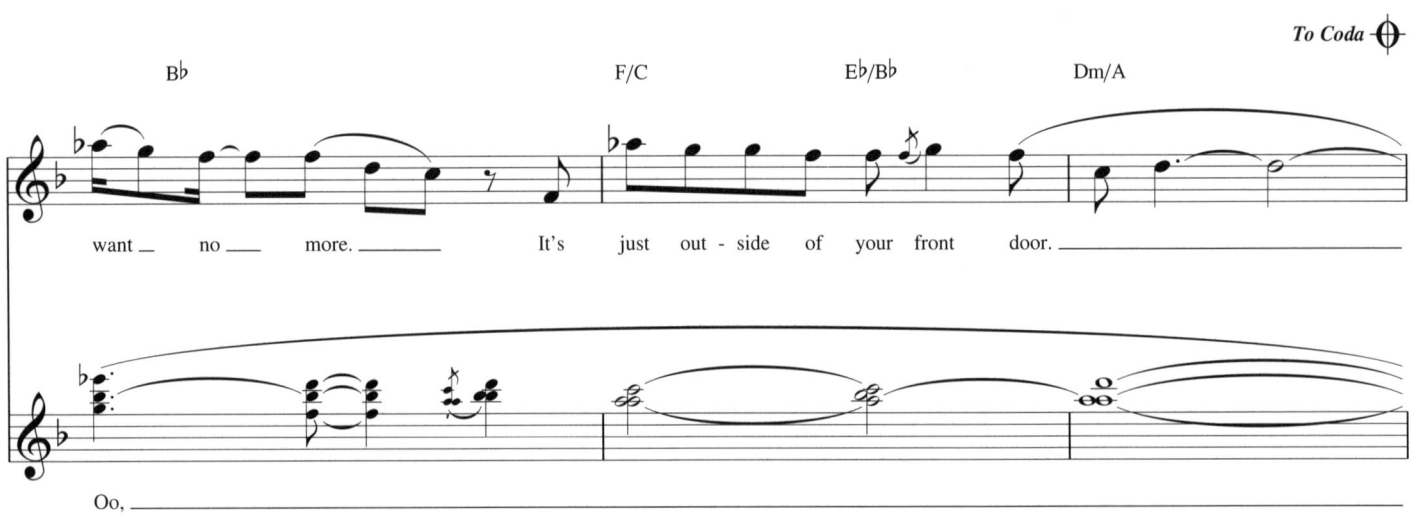

want _____ no _____ more. _____ It's just out - side of your front door. _____

Oo, _____

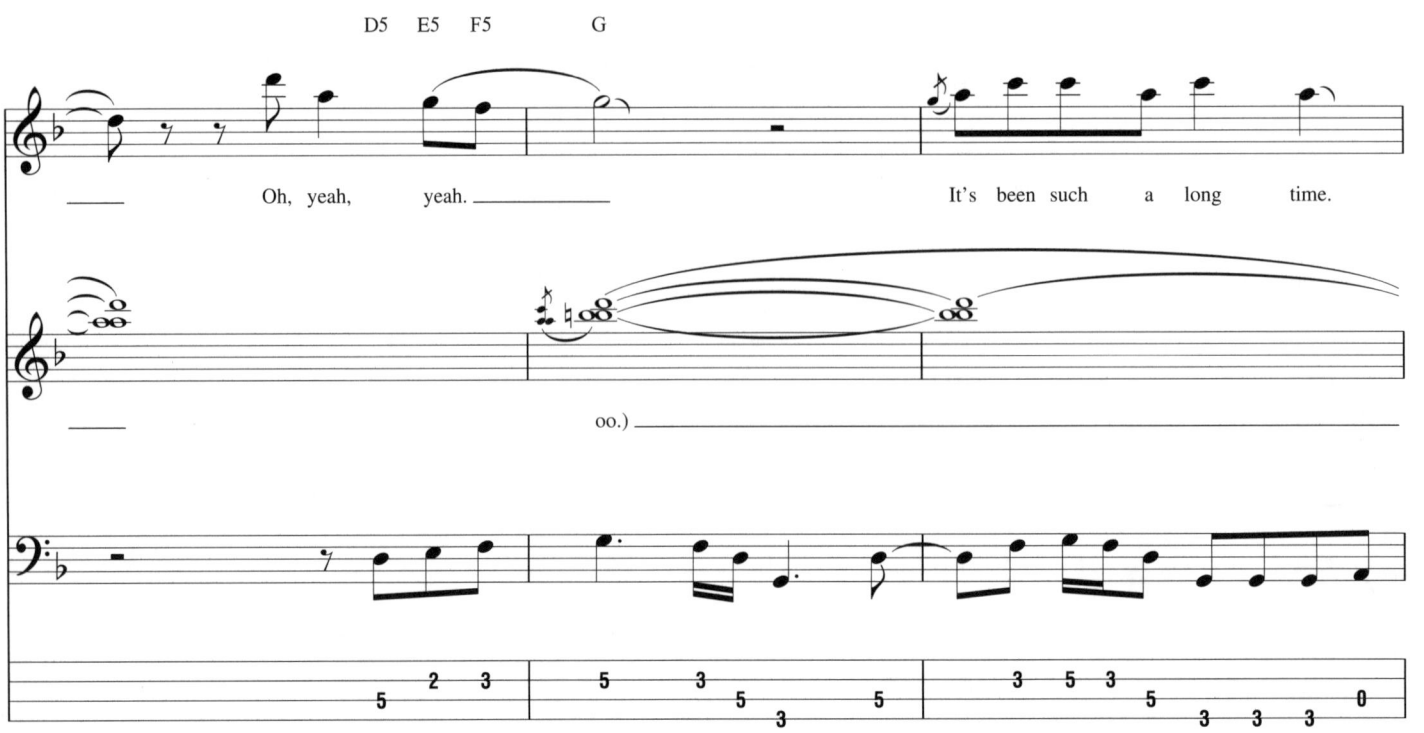

_____ Oh, yeah, yeah. _____ It's been such a long time.

_____ oo.) _____

It's been such a long ___ time, ___

Guitar Solo
Bass: w/ Bass Fig. 1 (last 2 meas., 4 times)

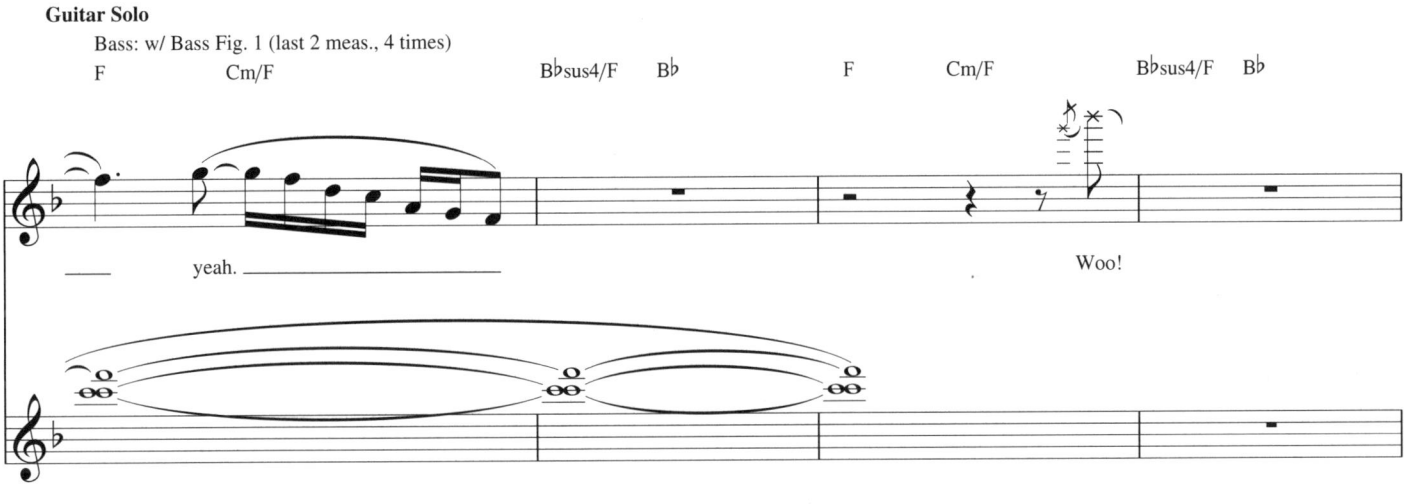

___ yeah. ___   Woo!

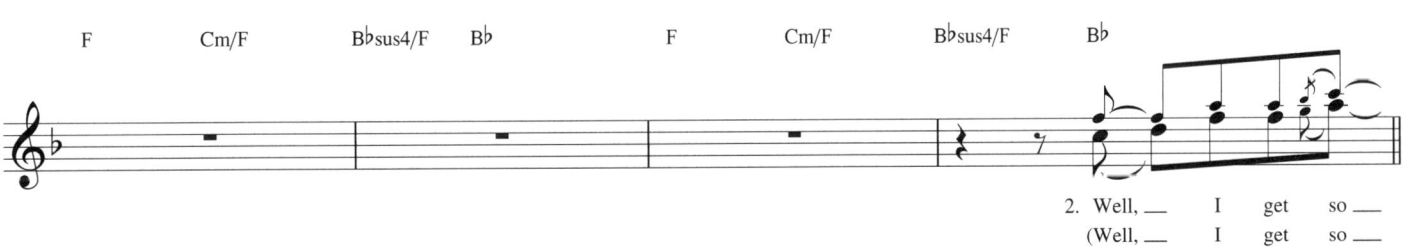

2. Well, ___ I get so ___
(Well, ___ I get so ___

Verse
Bass: w/ Bass Fig. 1

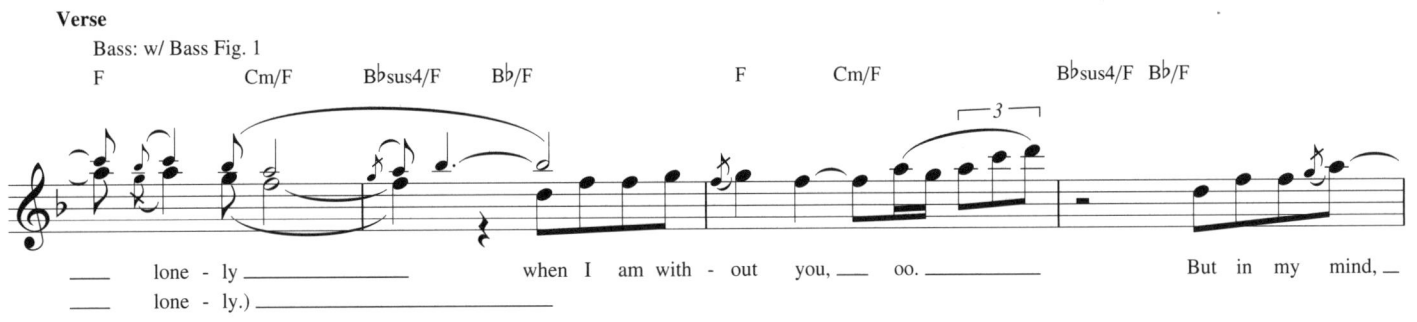

___ lone - ly ___   when I am with - out you, ___ oo. ___   But in my mind, ___
___ lone - ly.) ___

Verse

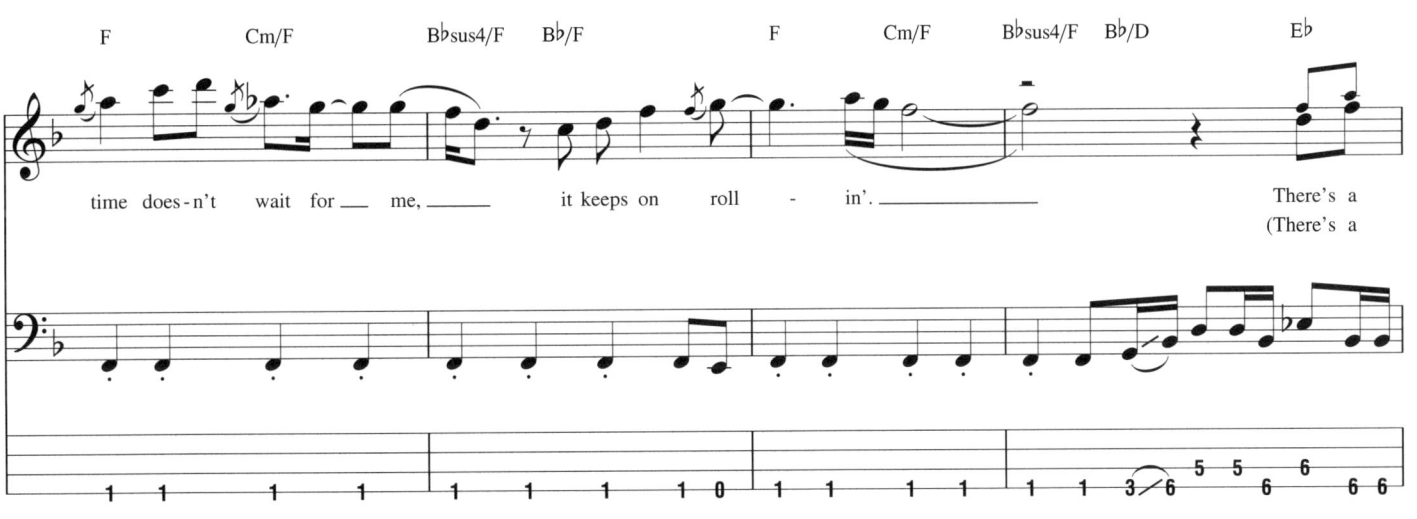

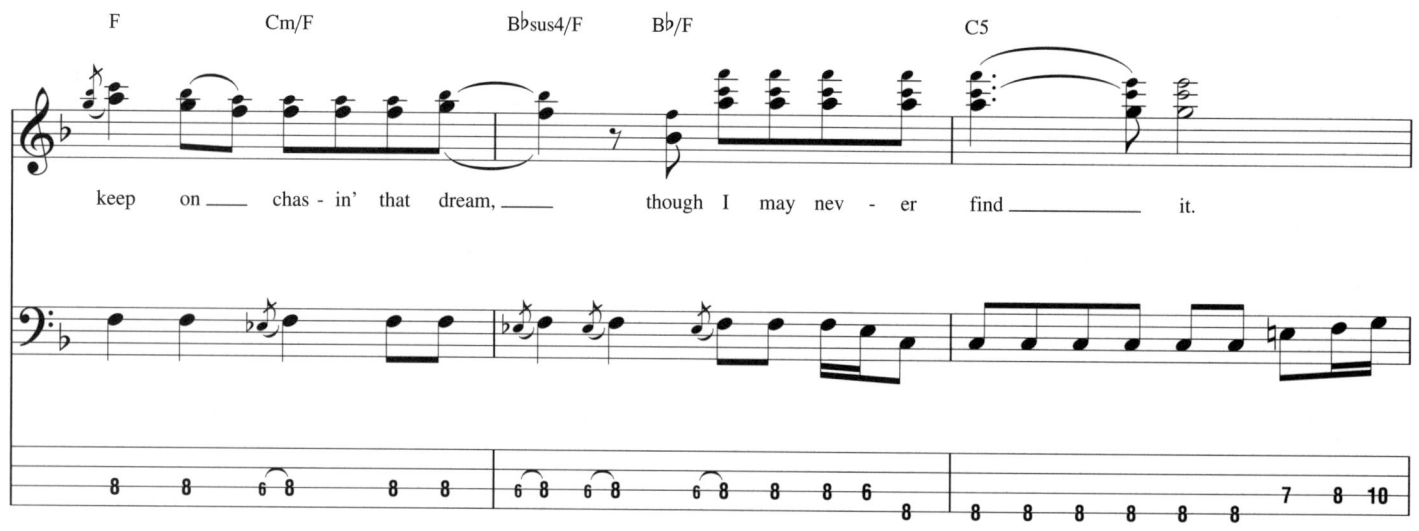

keep on ___ chas - in' that dream, ___ though I may nev - er find _____ it.

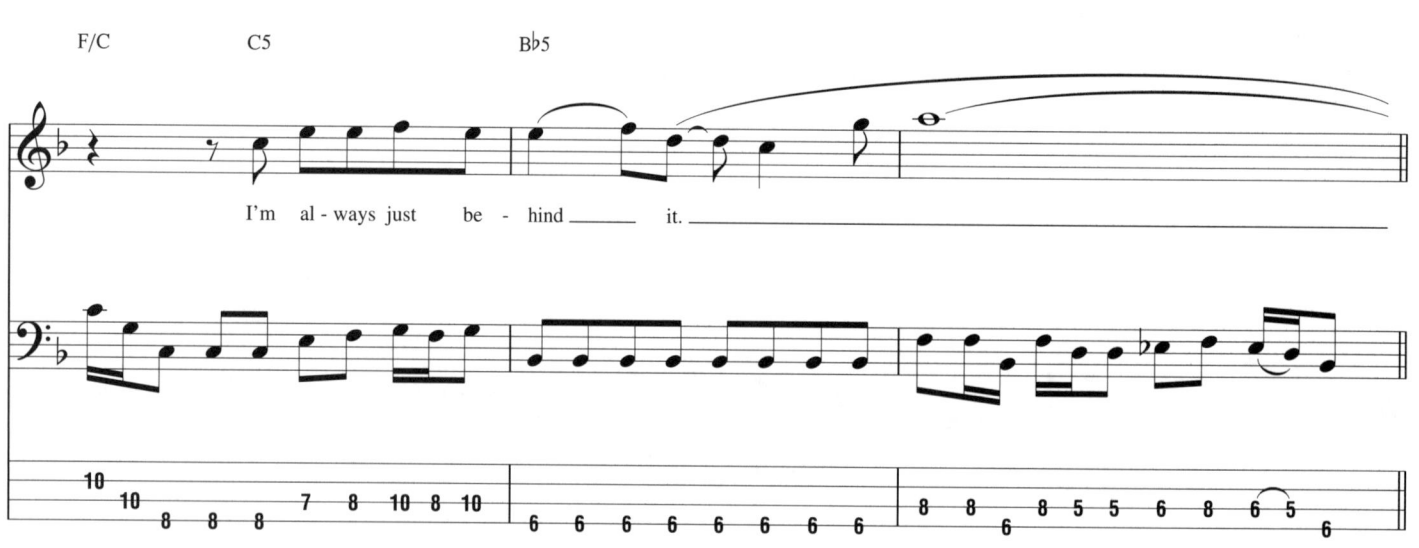

I'm al - ways just be - hind _____ it. ___

Interlude

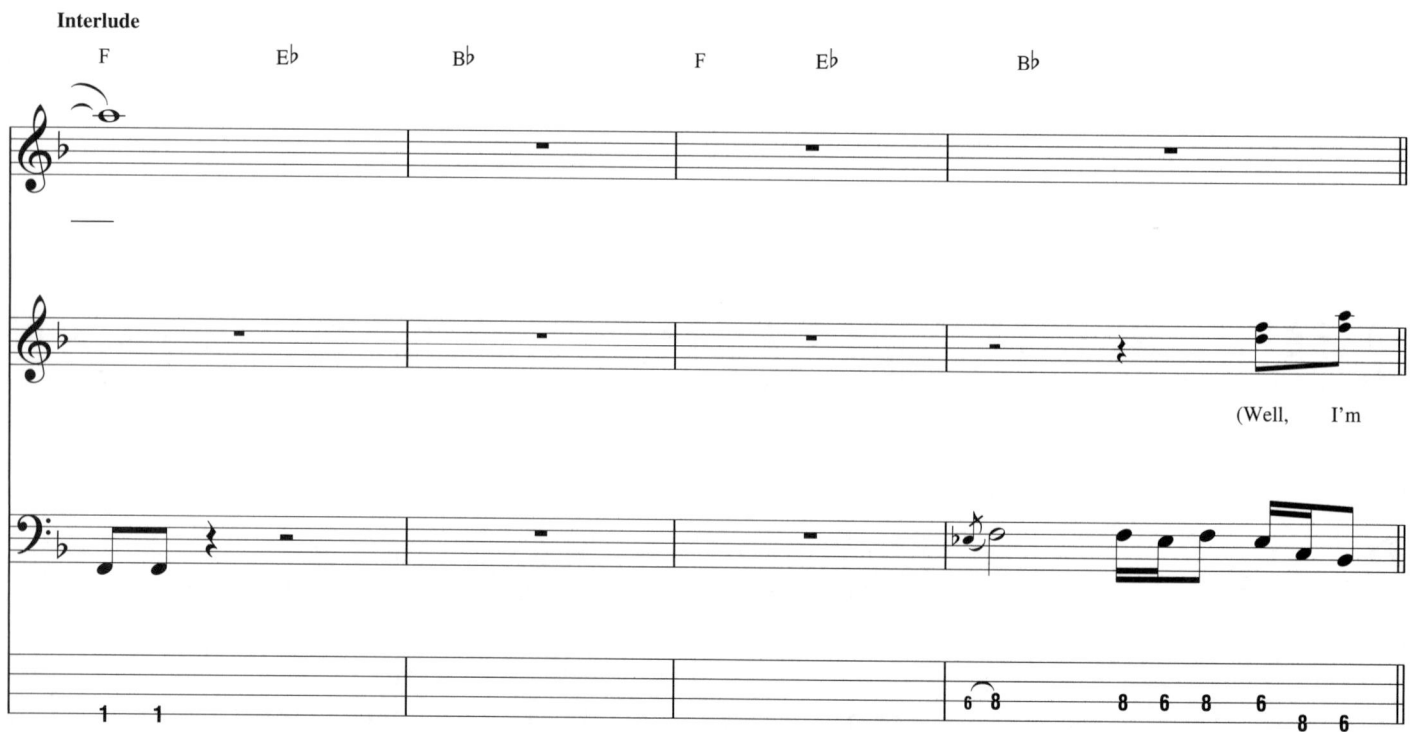

(Well, I'm

Maps

Words and Music by Karen Orzolek, Nick Zinner and Brian Chase

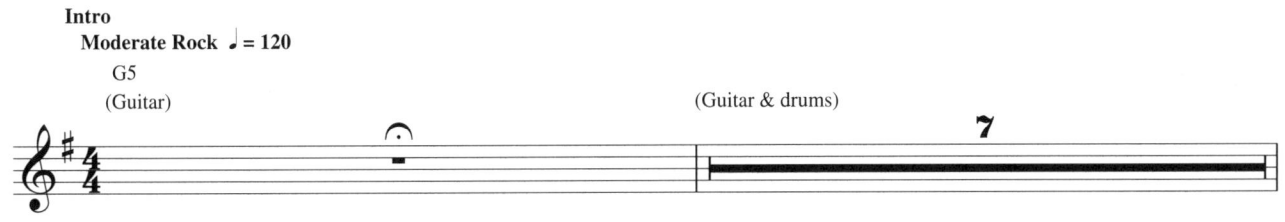

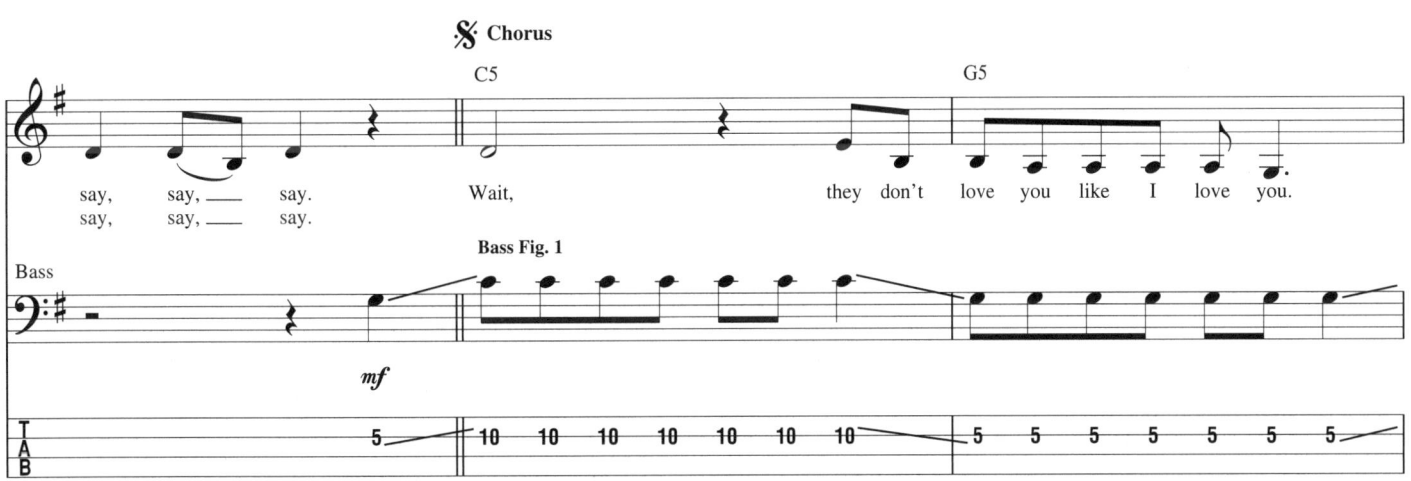

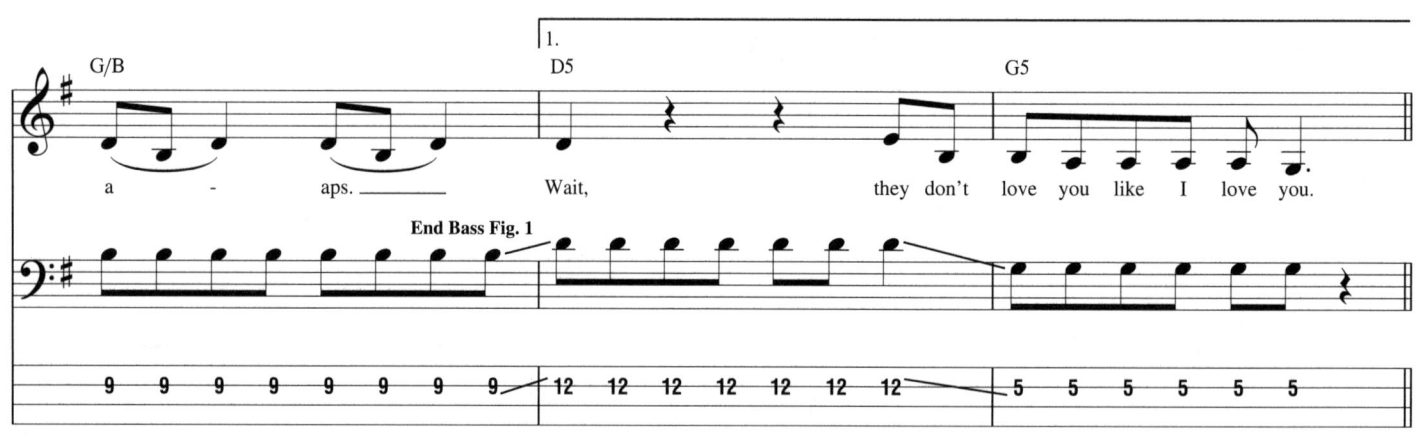

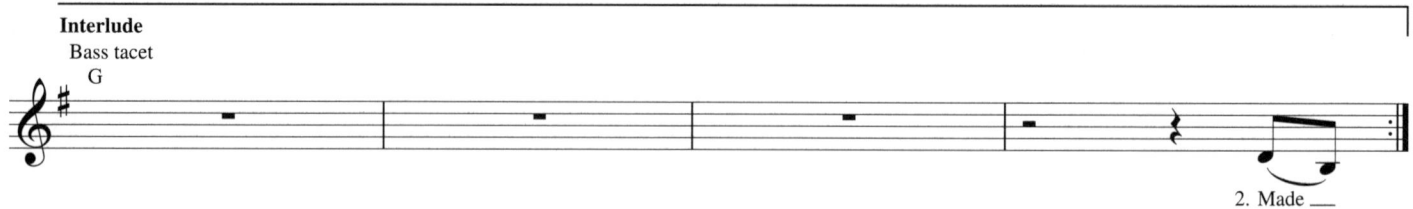

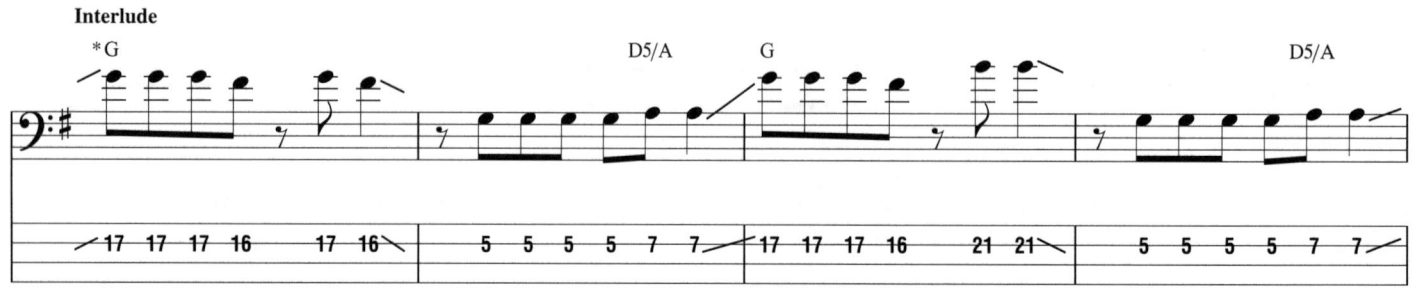

*Chord symbols reflect implied harmony.

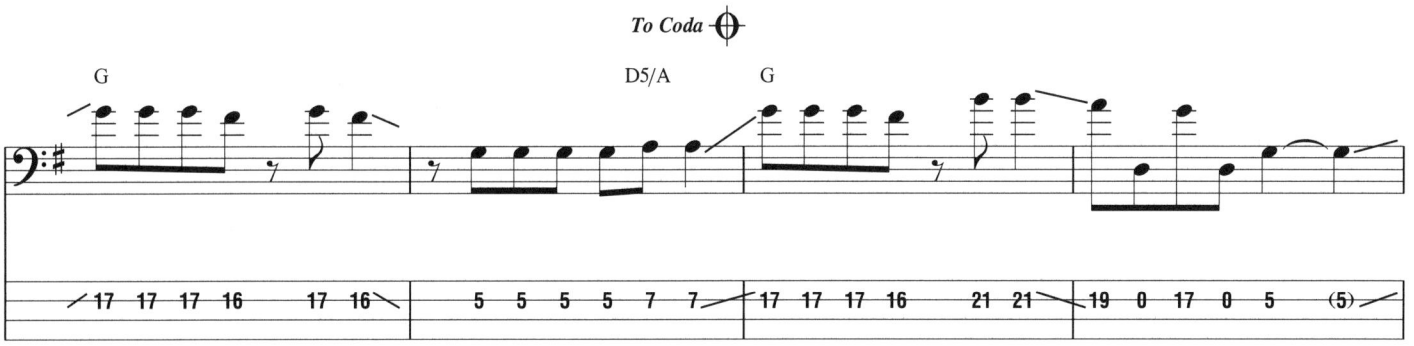

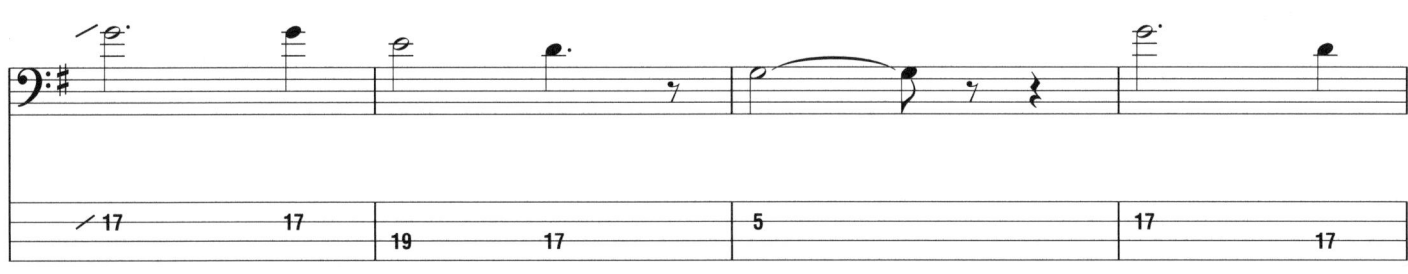

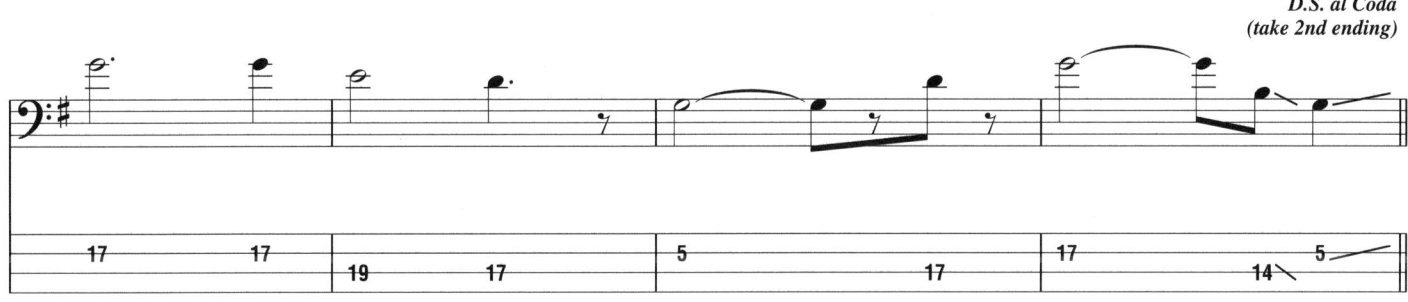

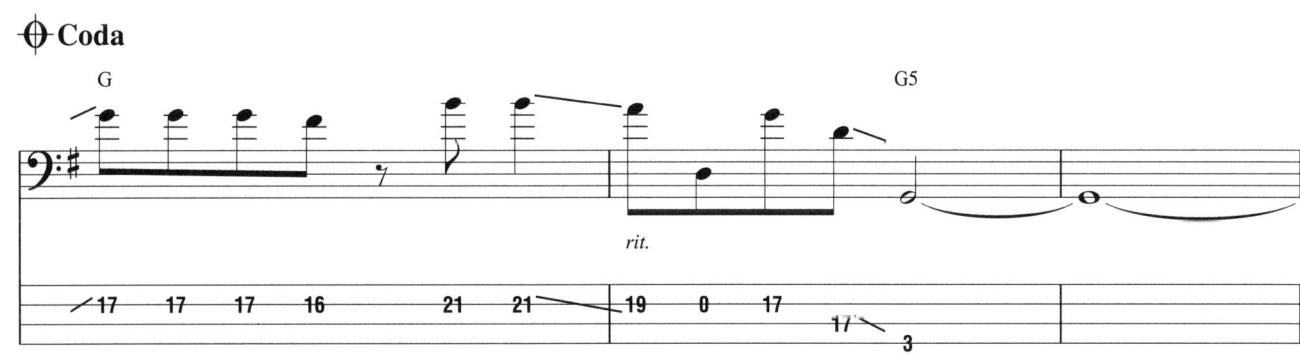

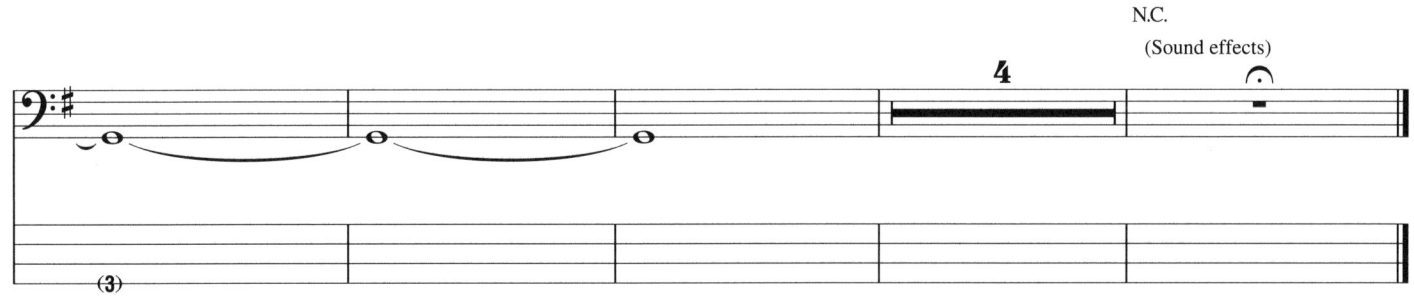

Mississippi Queen

Words and Music by Leslie West, Felix Pappalardi, Corky Laing and David Rea

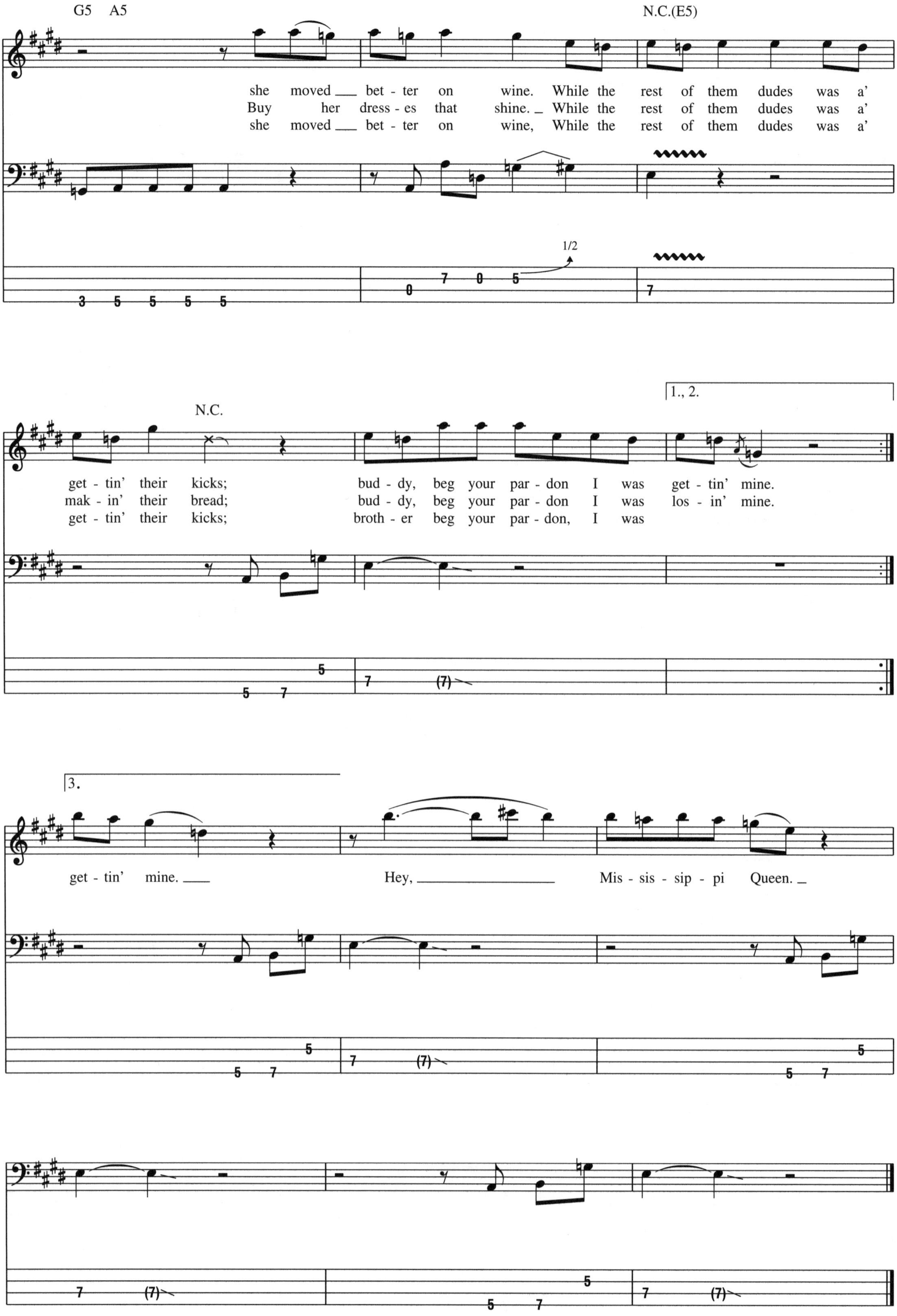
G5 A5
N.C.(E5)
she moved __ bet - ter on wine. While the rest of them dudes was a'
Buy her dress - es that shine. _ While the rest of them dudes was a'
she moved __ bet - ter on wine, While the rest of them dudes was a'
1/2
N.C.
1., 2.
get - tin' their kicks; bud - dy, beg your par - don I was get - tin' mine.
mak - in' their bread; bud - dy, beg your par - don I was los - in' mine.
get - tin' their kicks; broth - er beg your par - don, I was
3.
get - tin' mine. __ Hey, __ Mis - sis - sip - pi Queen. _

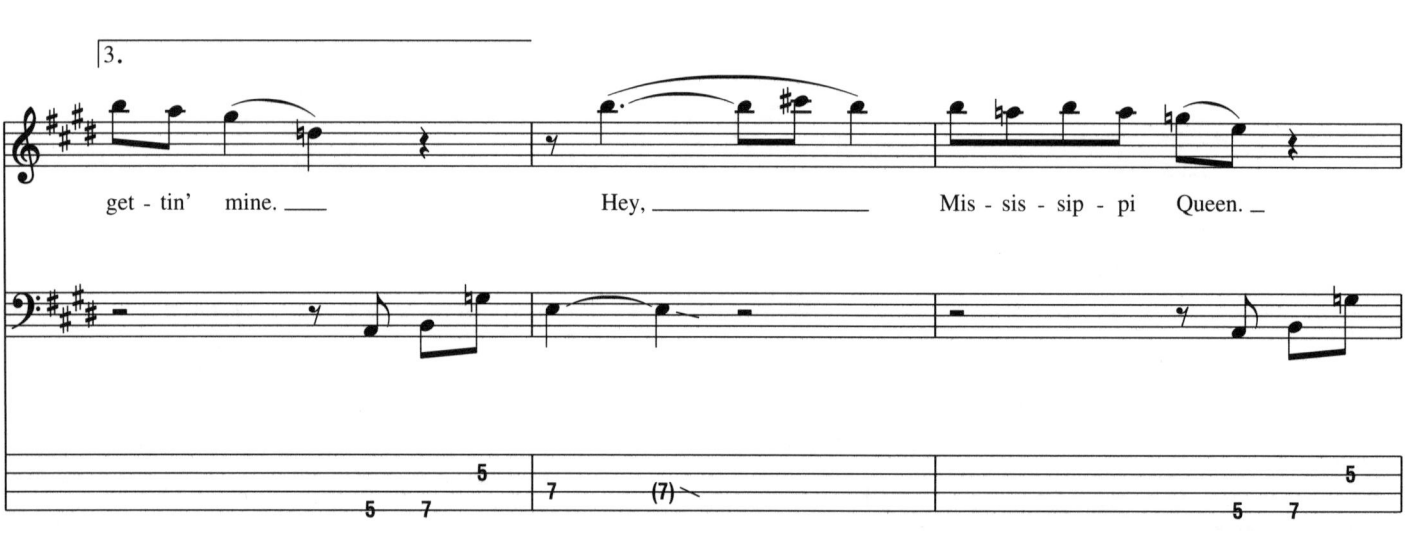

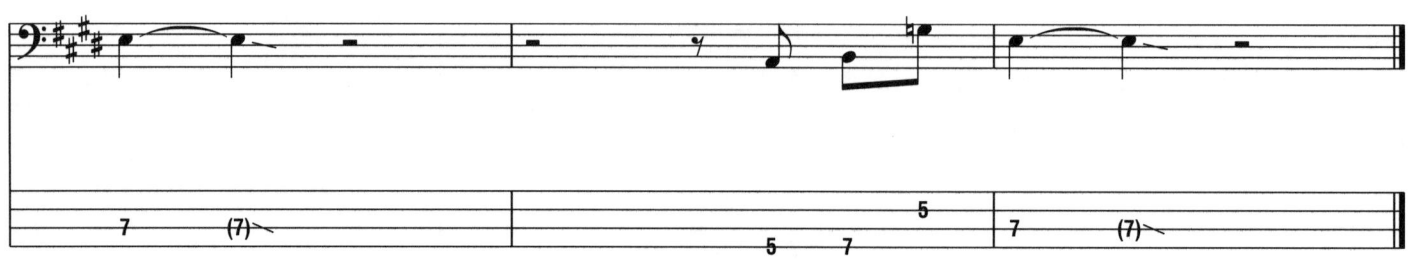

Next to You

Music and Lyrics by Sting

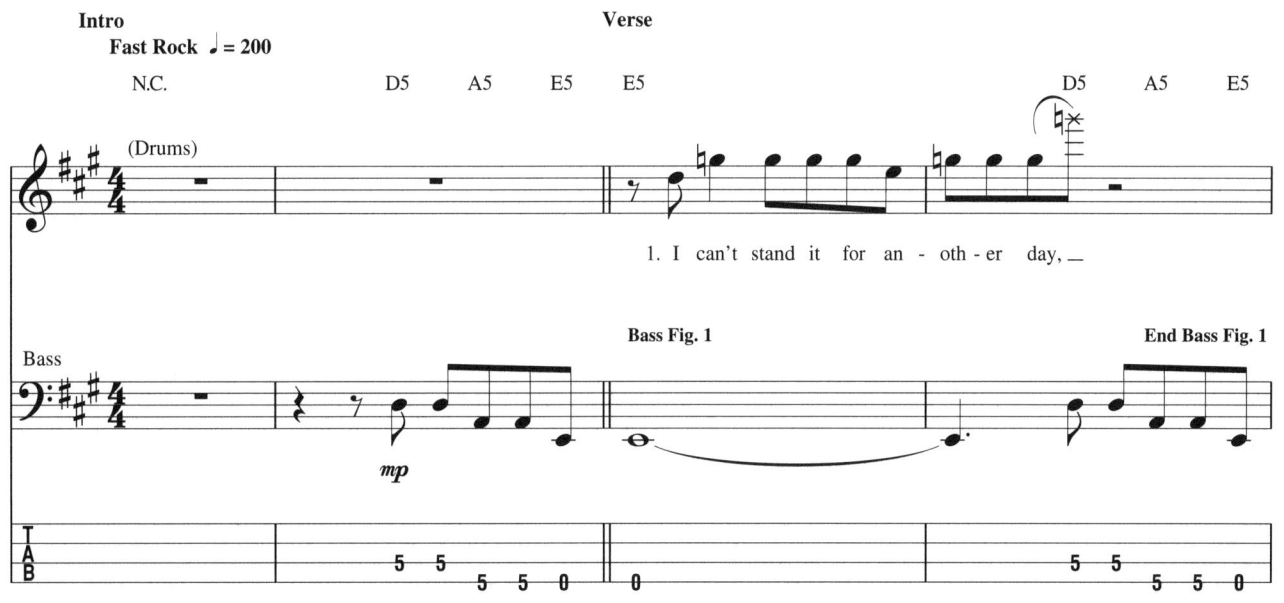

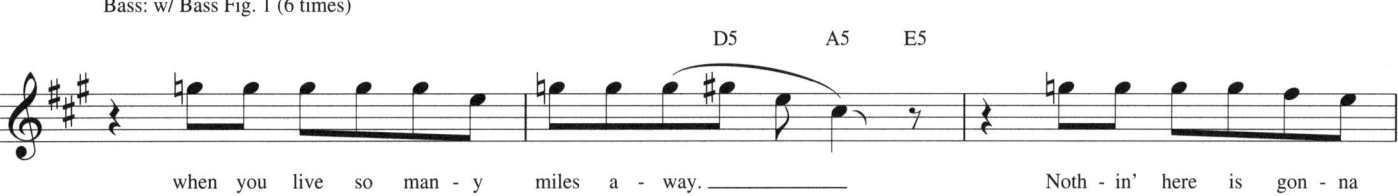

when you live so man-y miles a-way. ____ Noth-in' here is gon-na

make me stay. ____ You took me o-ver, let me find a way. ____

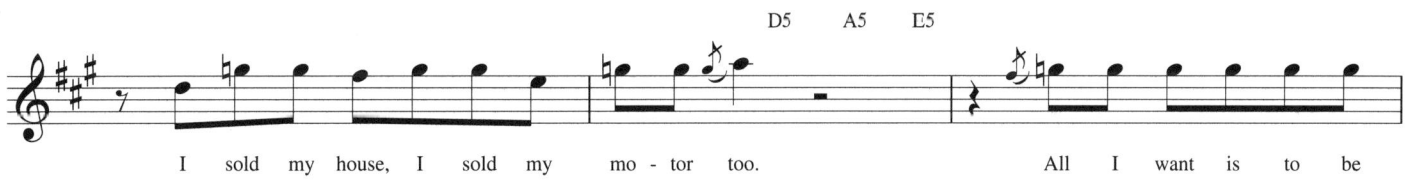

I sold my house, I sold my mo-tor too. All I want is to be

next to you. ____ I'd rob a bank, may-be steal a plane.

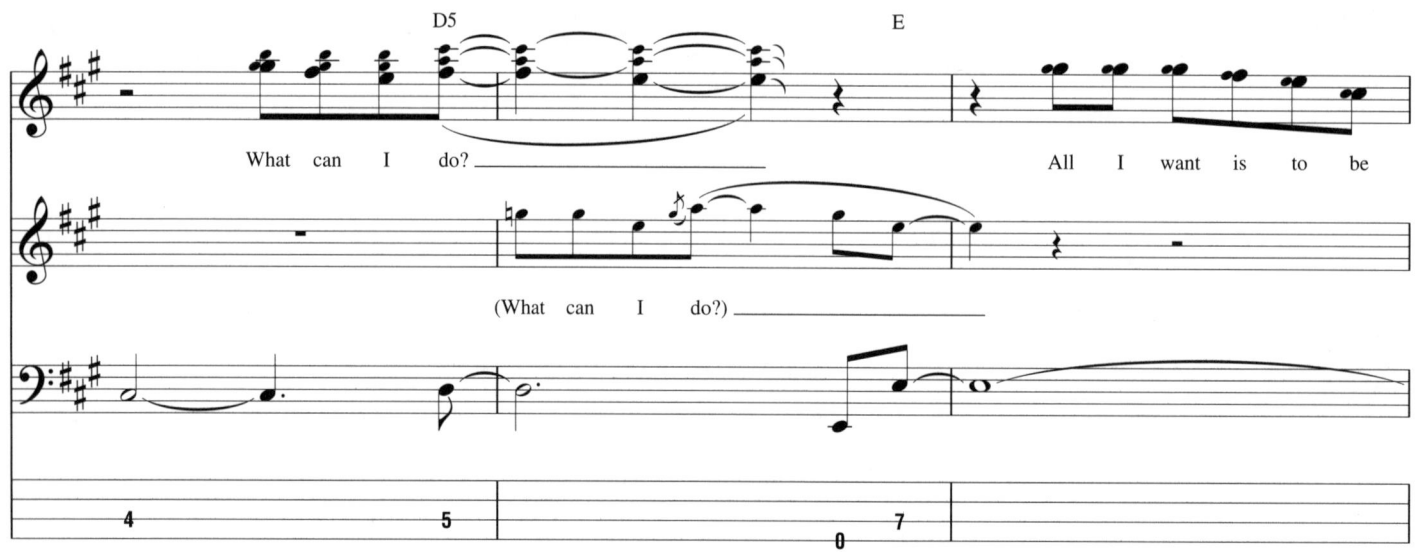

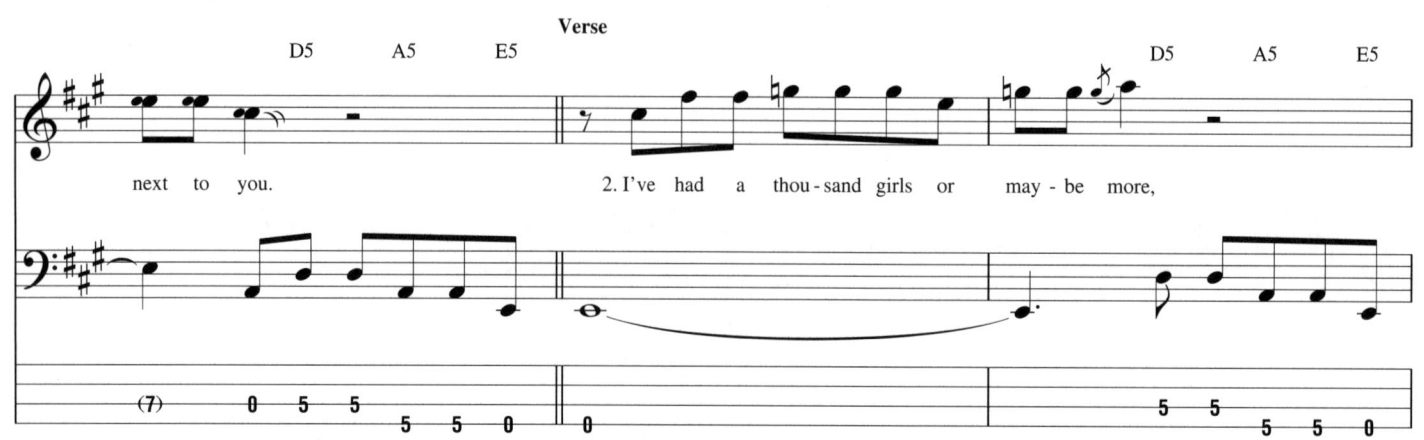

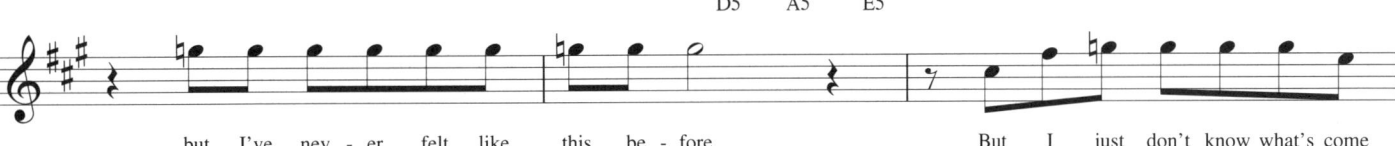

but I've nev - er felt like this be - fore.   But I just don't know what's come

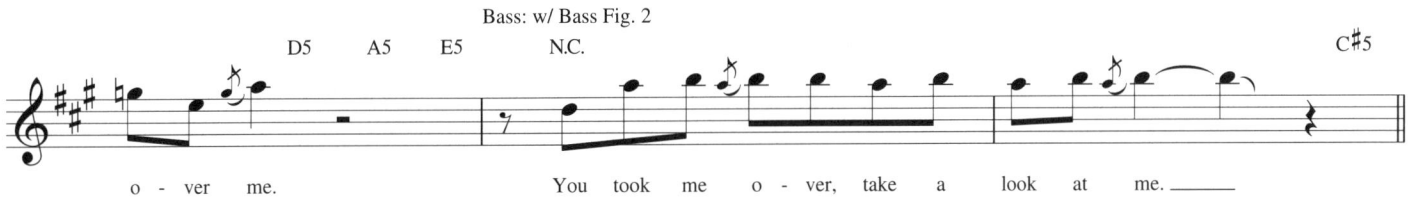

o - ver me.   You took me o - ver, take a look at me. _____

Chorus

What can I do? _____   All I want is to be

next to you. _____   What can I do? _____

All I want is to be next to you. _____   All I want is to be

next to you. _____ All I want is to be next to you. _____

Guitar Solo

All I want is to be next to you. _____

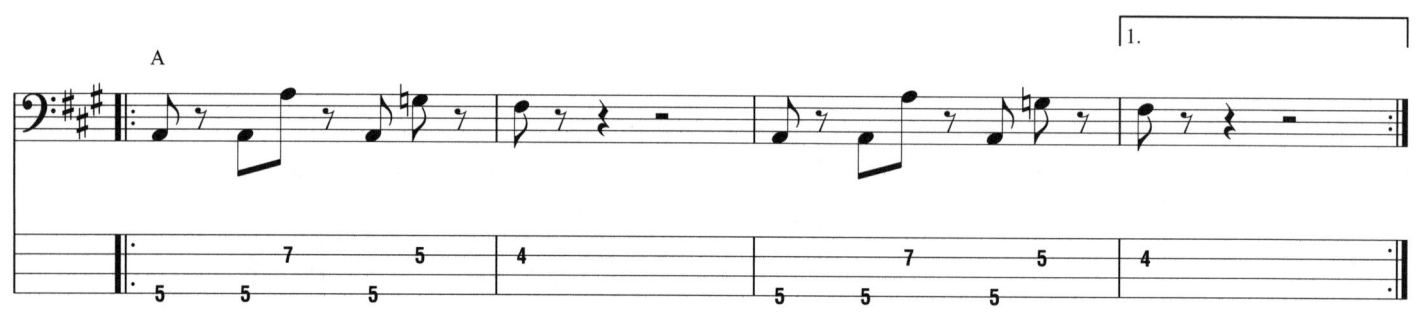

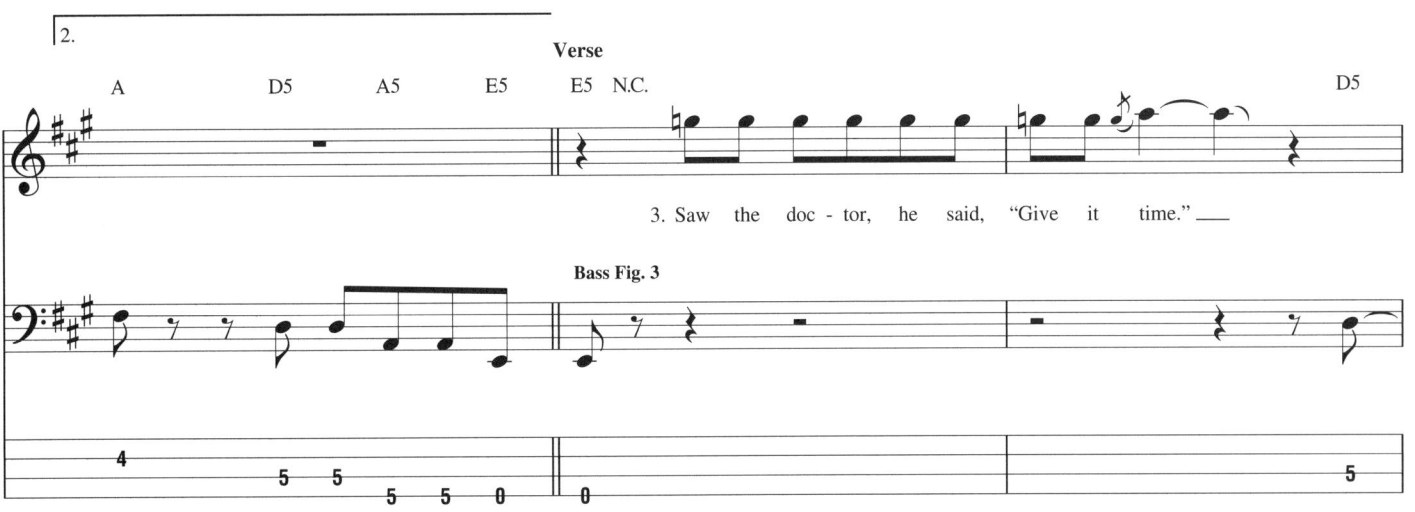

3. Saw the doc - tor, he said, "Give it time." ___

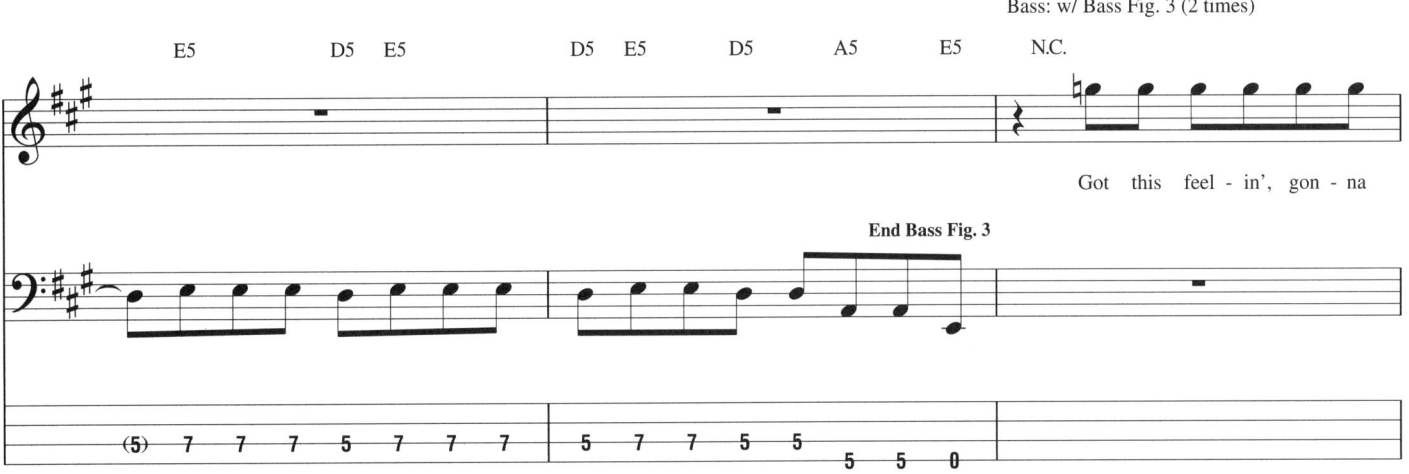

Got this feel - in', gon - na

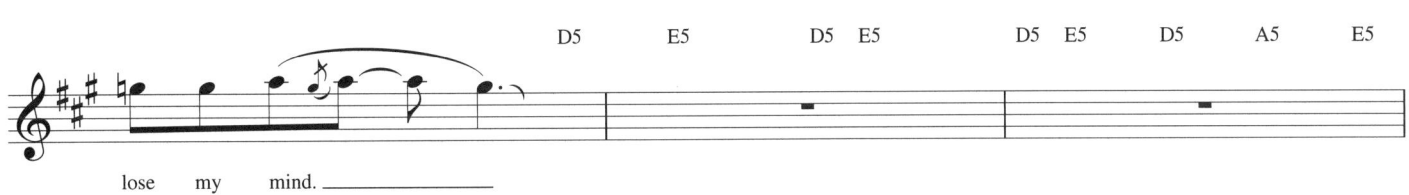

lose my mind. ___

When all it is is just a love af - fair. ___

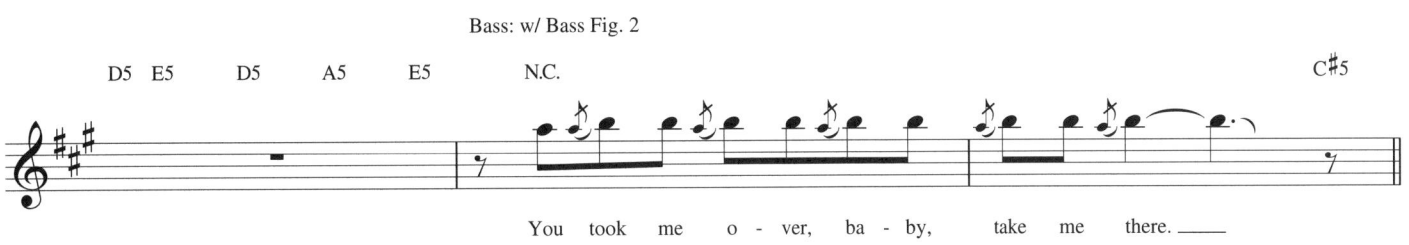

You took me o - ver, ba - by, take me there. ___

Outro-Chorus

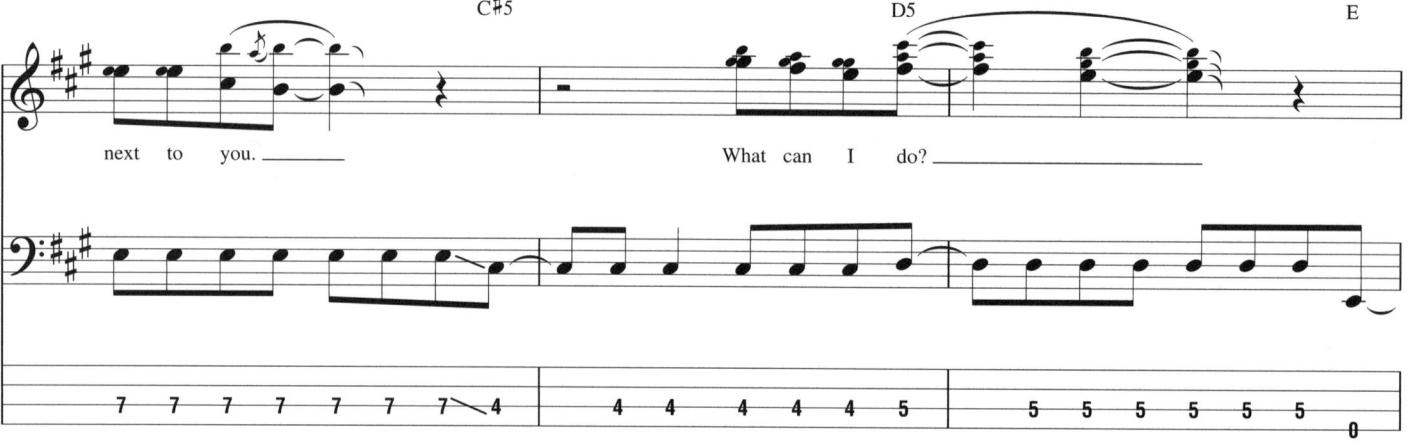

Paranoid

Words and Music by Anthony Iommi, John Osbourne, William Ward and Terence Butler

Intro
Fast Rock ♩ = 160

𝄋 Verse

1. Fin-ished with my wo-man 'cause she could not help me with my mind.
2. All day long I think of things but noth-ing seems to sa-tis-fy.
3. I need some-one to show me that lead-ing light that I can't find.

Peo-ple think I'm in-sane be-cause I
Think I'll lose my mind if I don't find;
I can't see the things that make true hap-

Bass Fill 1

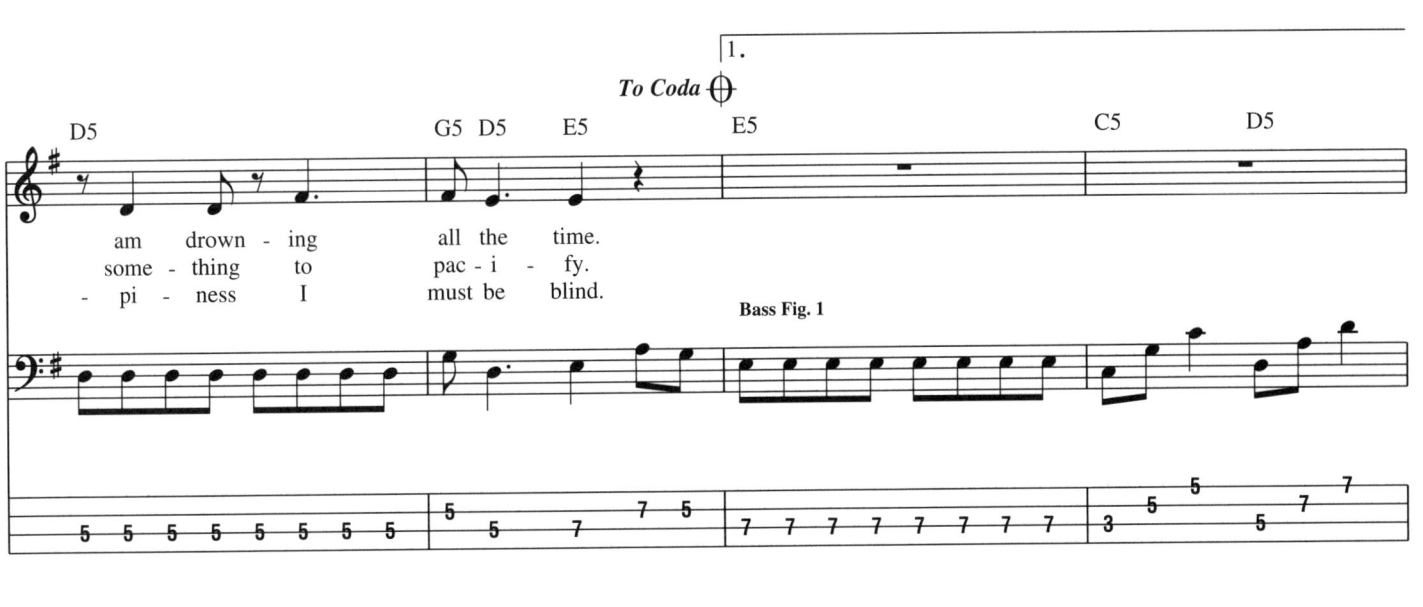

am drown - ing all the time.
some - thing to pac - i - fy.
- pi - ness I must be blind.

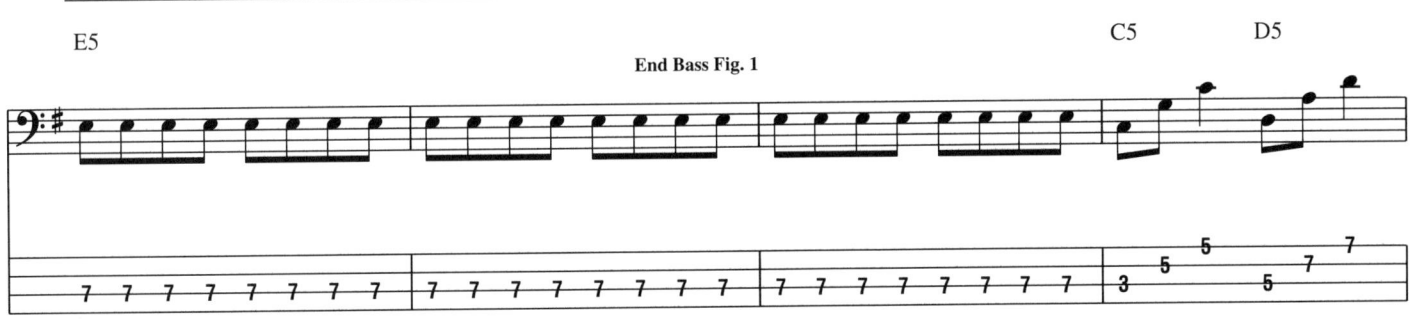

Can you help me

cut you from my brain. _____

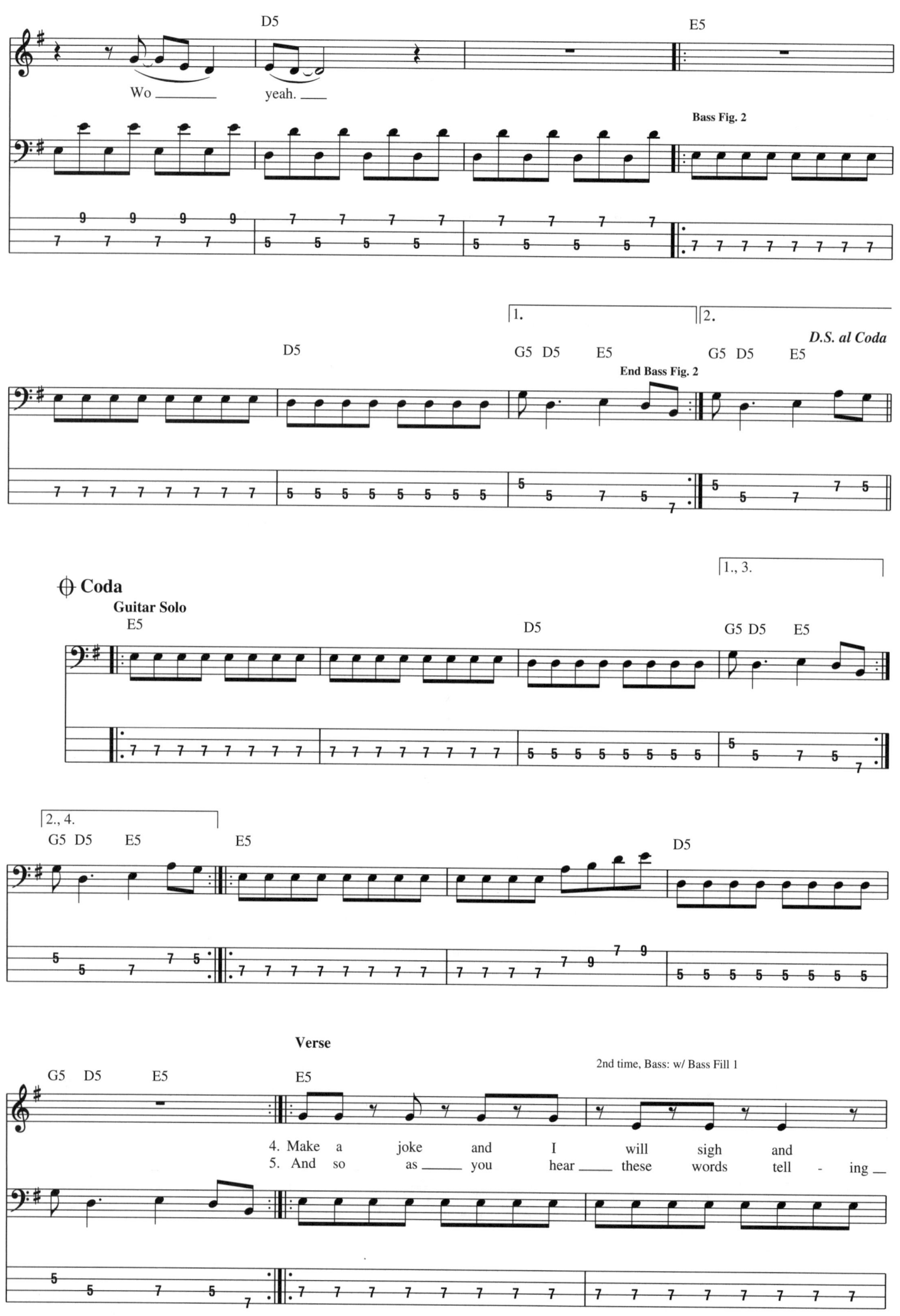

Wo ____ yeah. ____

4. Make a joke and I will sigh and
5. And so as ____ you hear ____ these words tell - ing ____

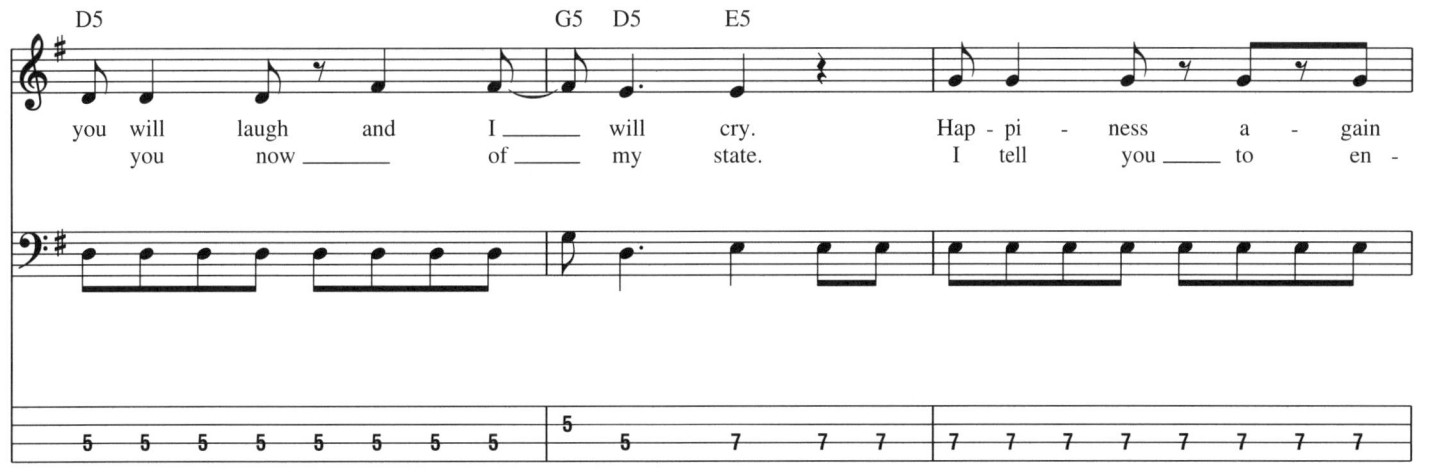

you will laugh and I ___ will cry. Hap - pi - ness a - gain
you now ___ of ___ my state. I tell you ___ to en -

2nd time, Bass: w/ Bass Fill 1

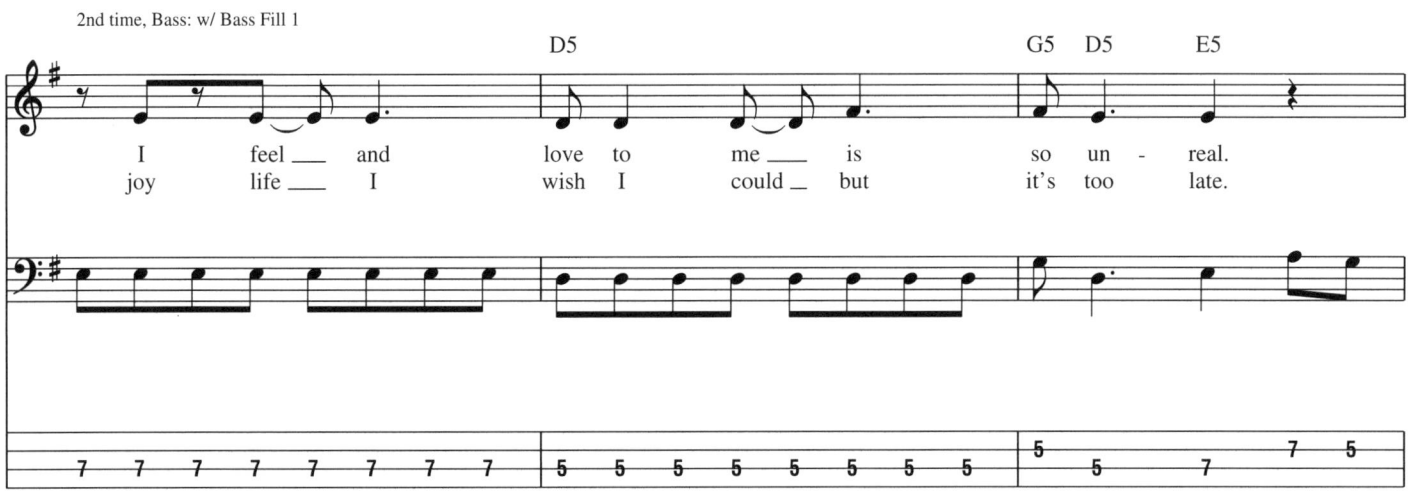

I feel ___ and love to me ___ is so un - real.
joy life ___ I wish I could ___ but it's too late.

1.

Bass: w/ Bass Fig. 1 (2 times)

2.

Bass: w/ Bass Fig. 2

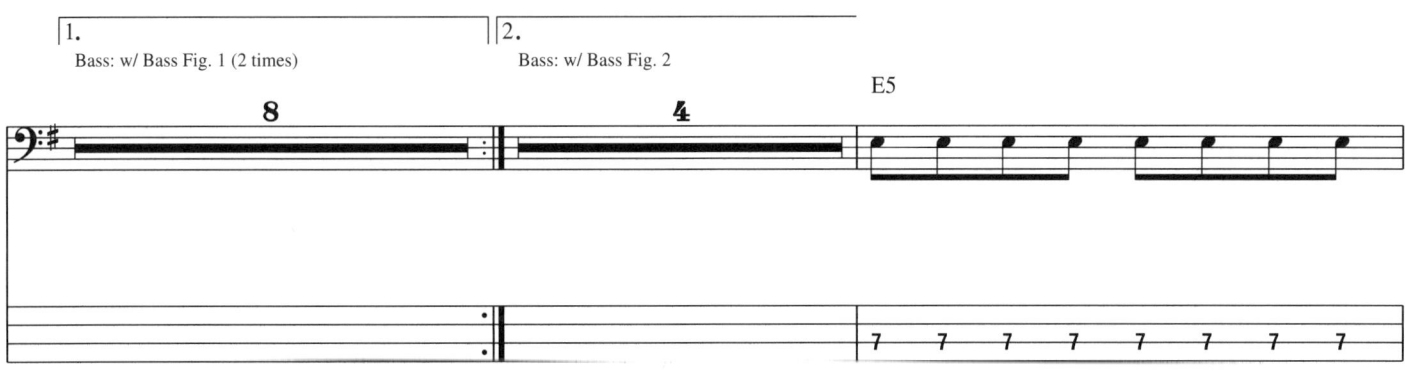

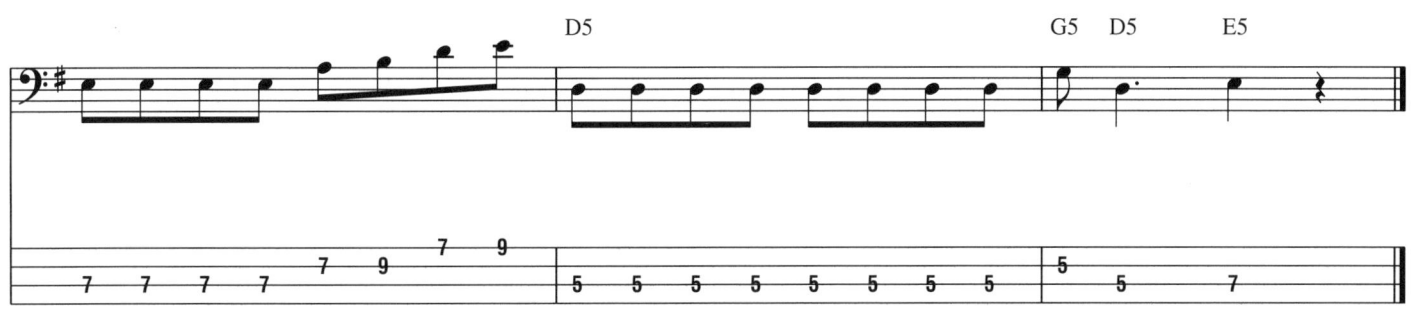

Run to the Hills

Words and Music by Steven Harris

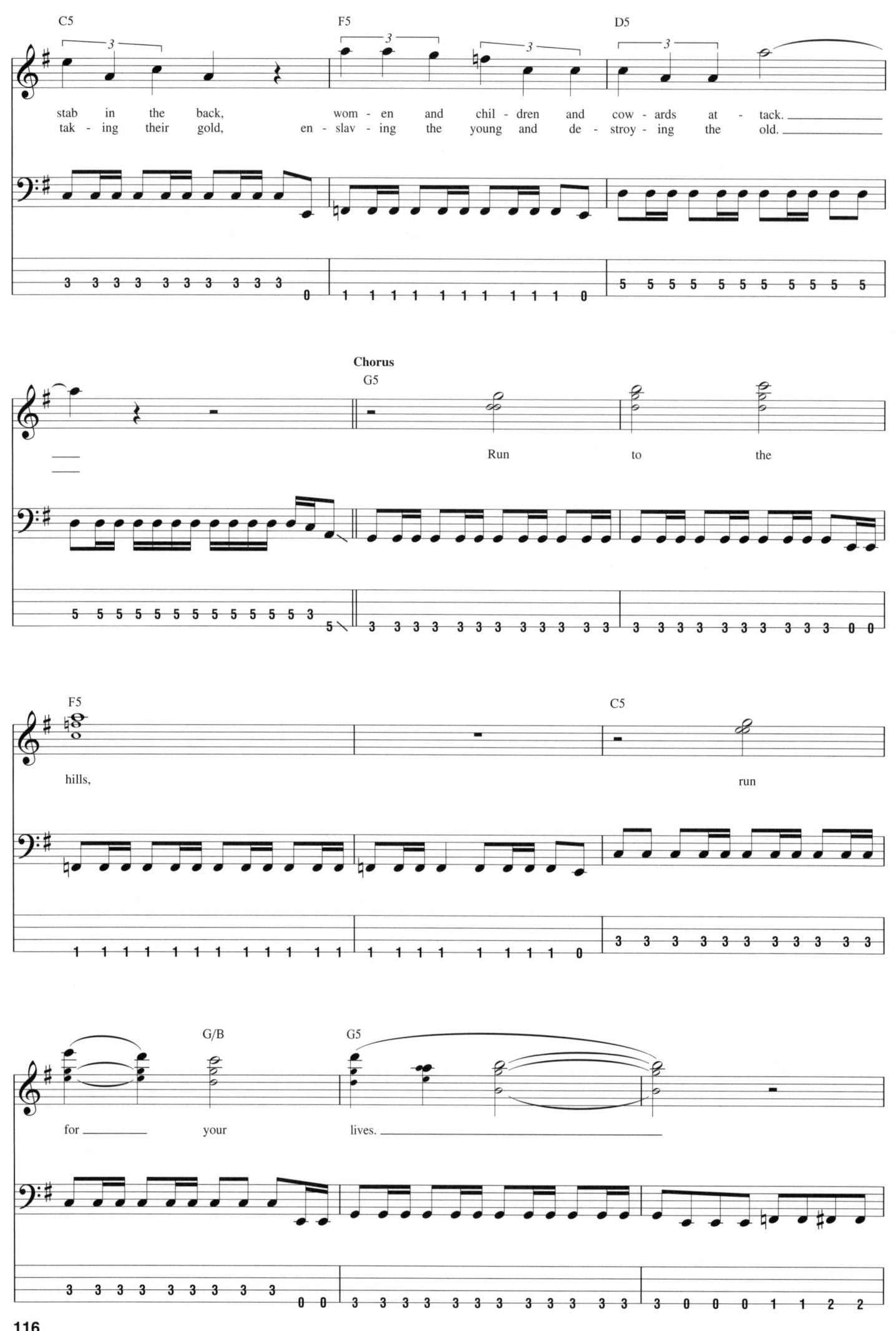

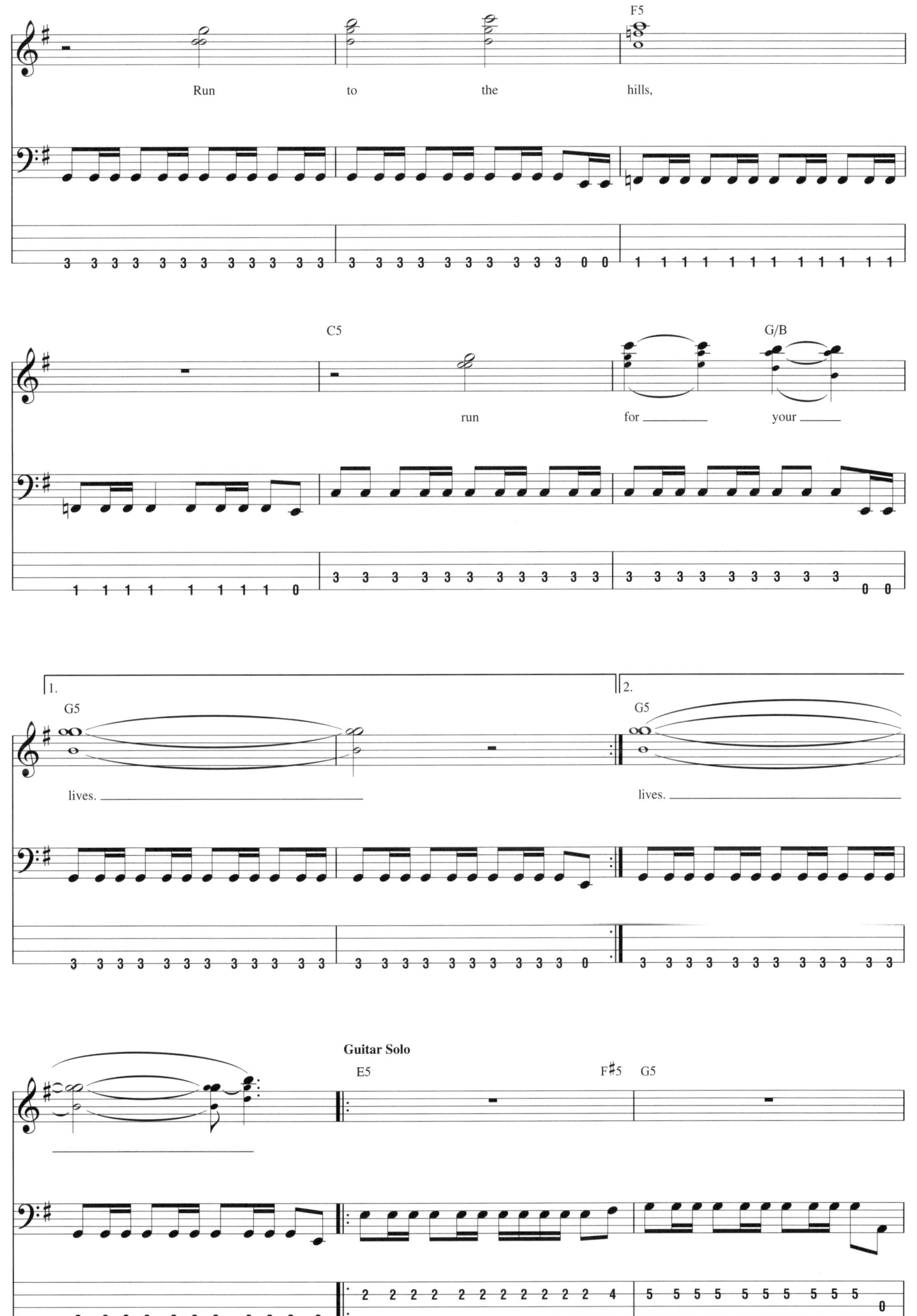

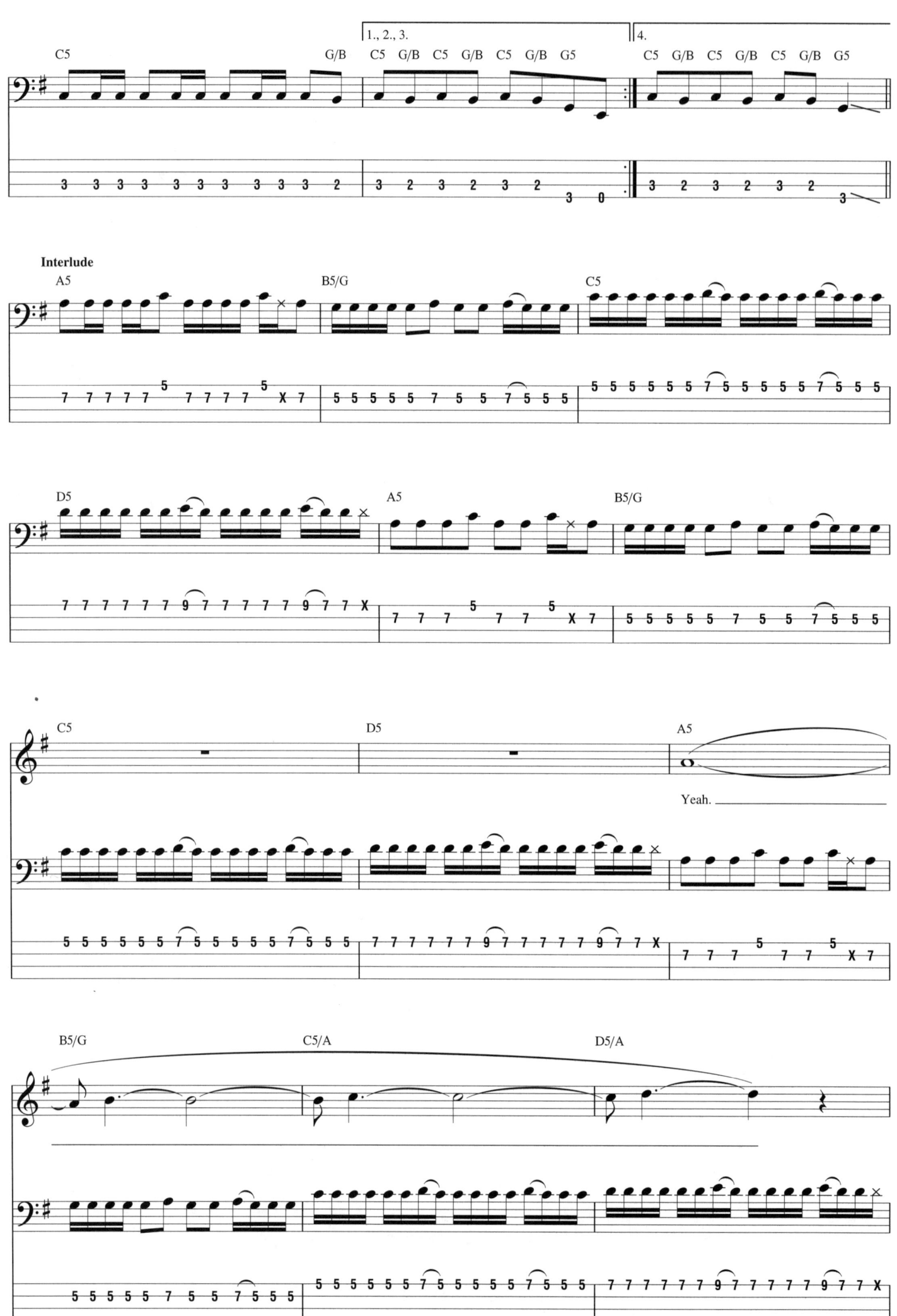

119

Bass: w/ Bass Fig. 2 (2 1/2 times)

F5   C5

Run   to   the   hills,   run

G/B   G5

for _____ your _____ lives. _________________________________ Run   to   the

F5   C5   G/B   G5

hills,   run   for _____ your   lives. ___________

F5

_____   Run   to   the   hills,

Free time

C5   G/B   G5
rit.

run   for   your   life! ____________________________

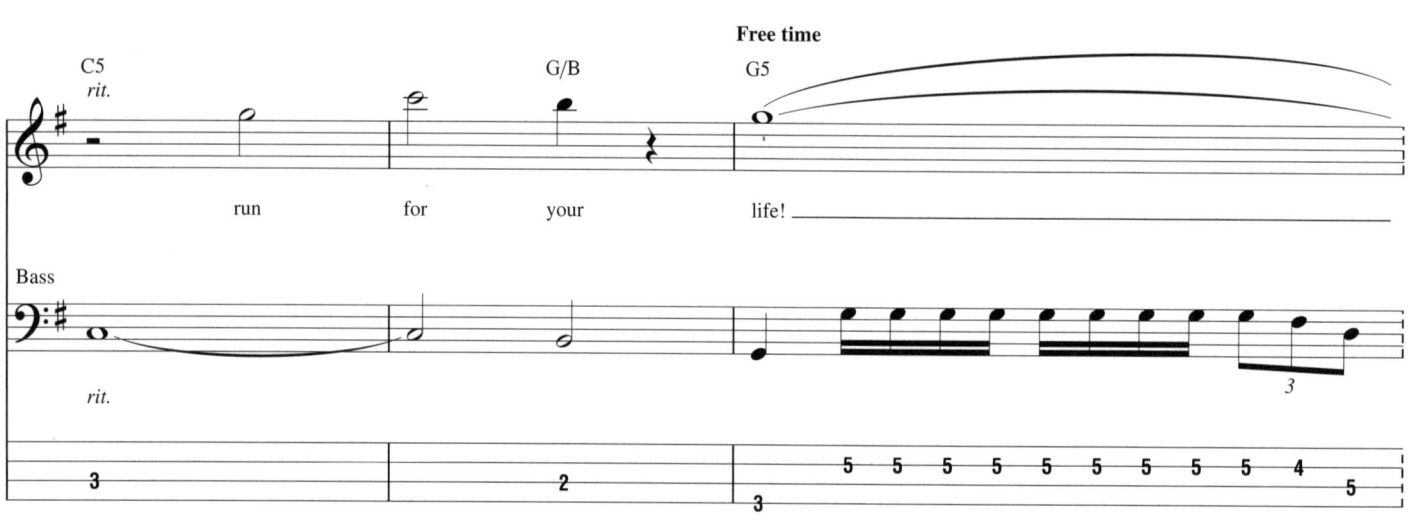

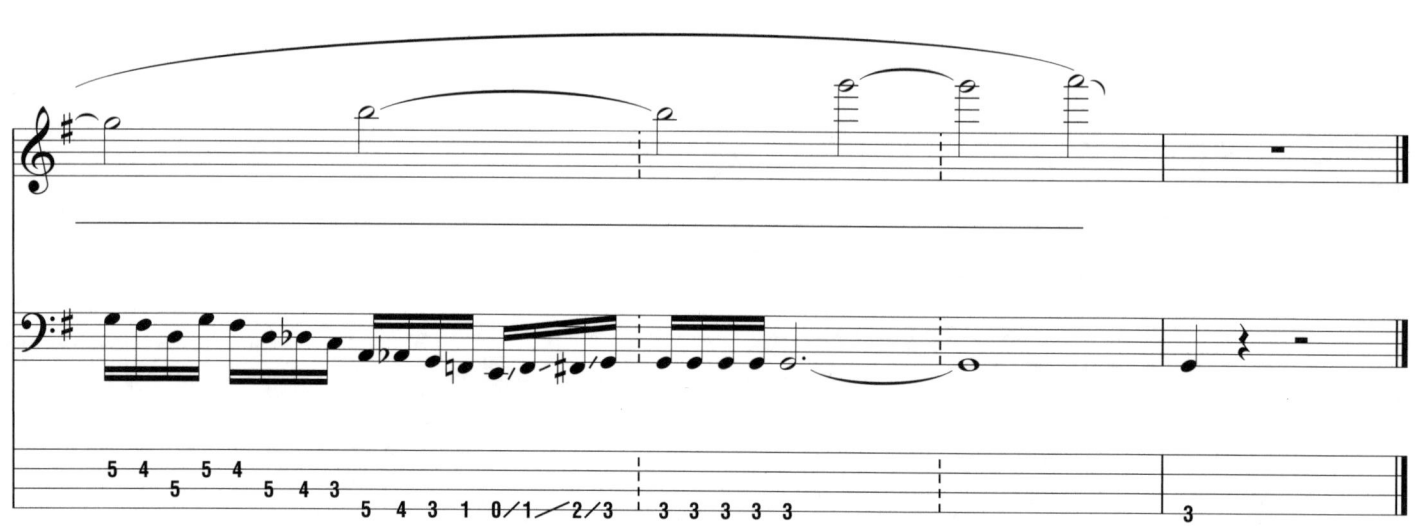

Say It Ain't So

Words and Music by Rivers Cuomo

Tune down 1/2 step:
(low to high) E♭-A♭-D♭-G♭

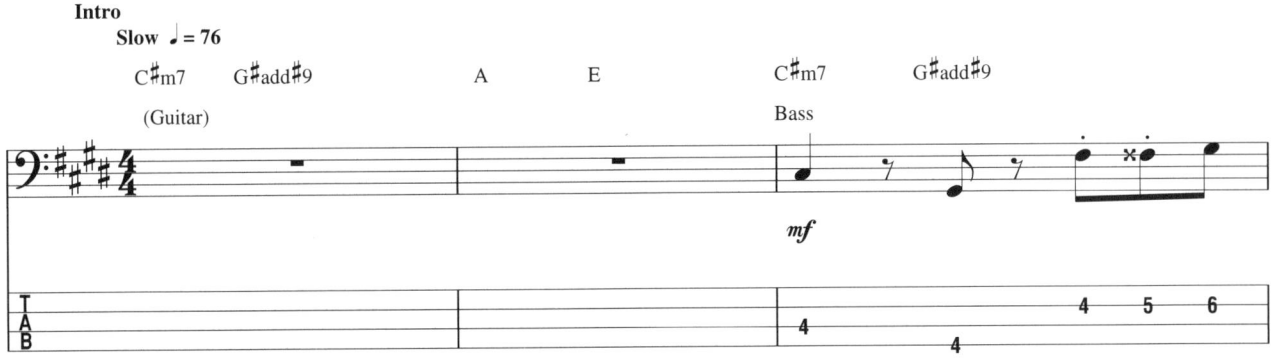

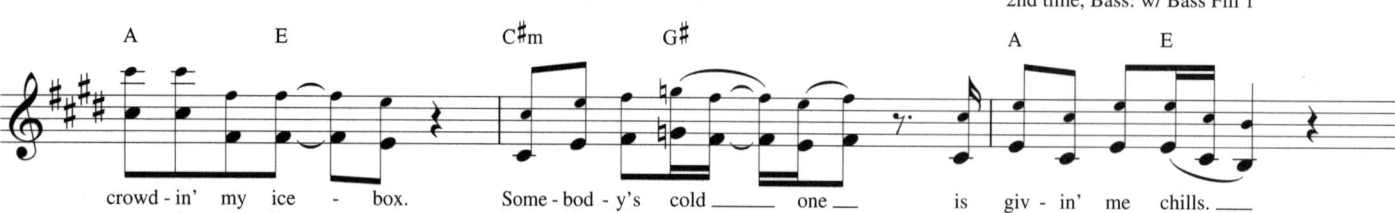

2nd time, Bass: w/ Bass Fill 1

A   E   C#m   G#   A   E

crowd - in' my ice - box. Some - bod - y's cold _____ one _____ is giv - in' me chills. _____
wres - tle with Jim - my. Some - thing is a bub - bling _____ be - hind _____ my back. _____ The

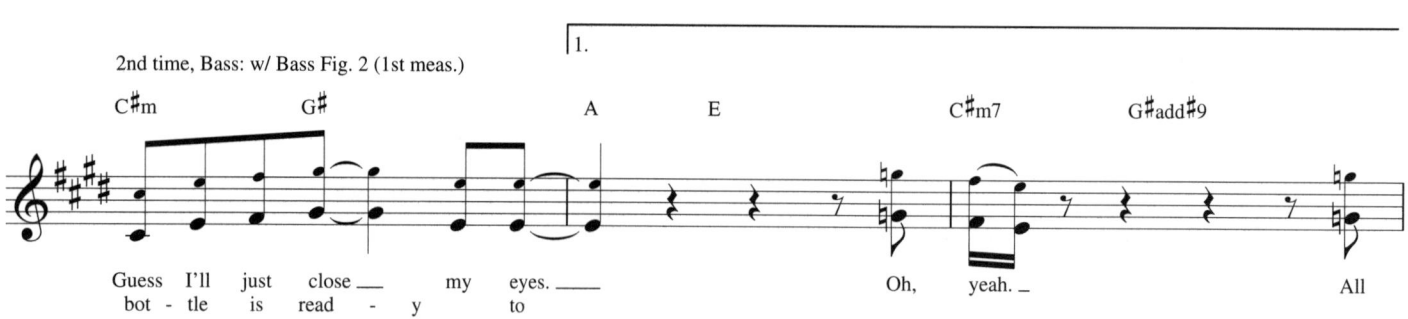

2nd time, Bass: w/ Bass Fig. 2 (1st meas.)

1.

C#m   G#   A   E   C#m7   G#add#9

Guess I'll just close _____ my eyes. _____ Oh, yeah. _____ All
bot - tle is read - y to

Bass: w/ Bass Fig. 2

A   E   C#m   G#   A   E

right. _____ Feels good _____ in - side. _____

2.

𝄋 Chorus

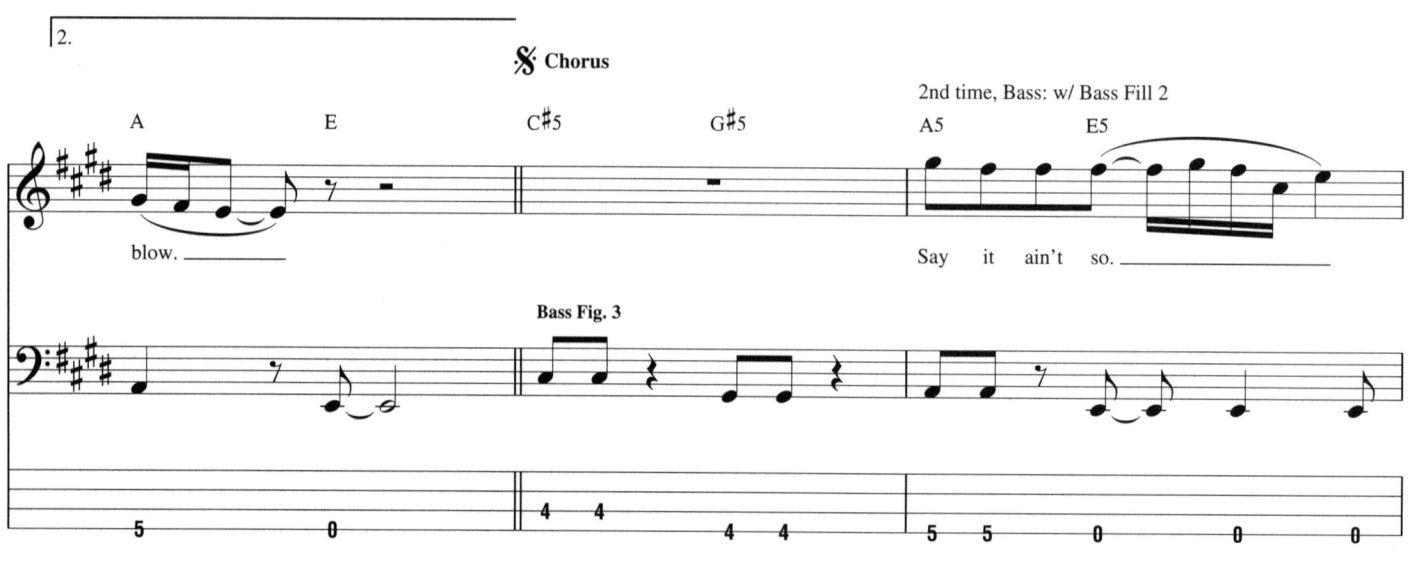

2nd time, Bass: w/ Bass Fill 2

A   E   C#5   G#5   A5   E5

blow. _____ Say it ain't so. _____

Bass Fig. 3

5   0   4   4   4   4   5   5   0   0   0

Bass Fill 1

5   0   6   7

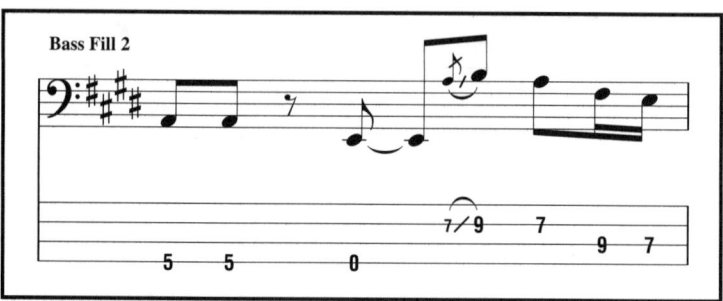

Bass Fill 2

5   5   0   7/9   7   9   7

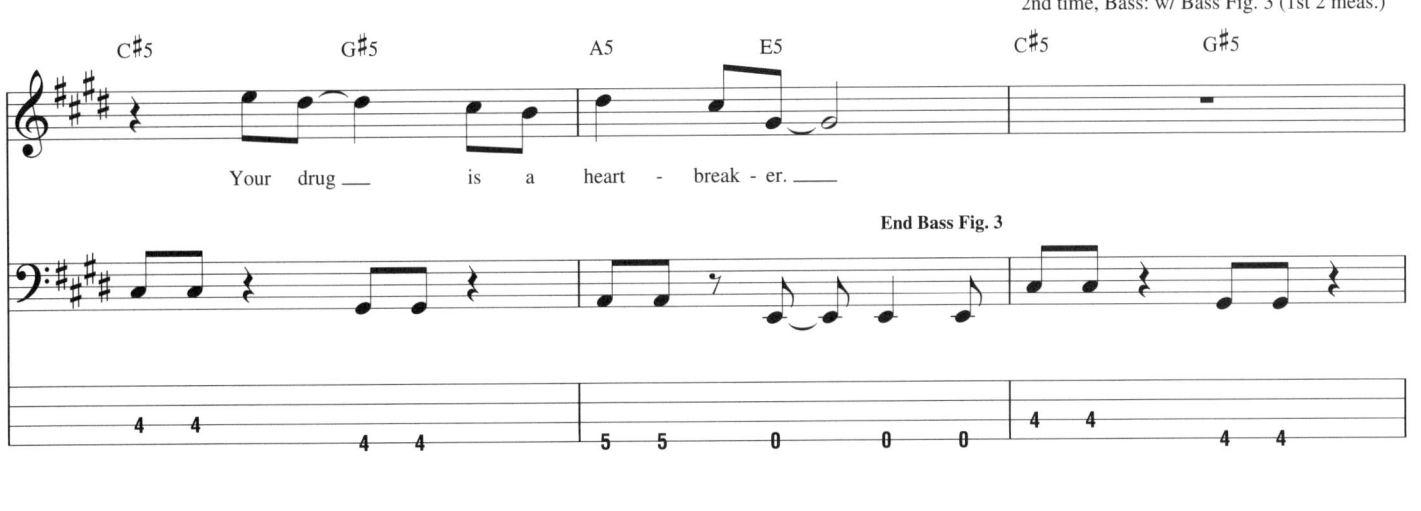

Your drug ___ is a heart - break - er. ___

End Bass Fig. 3

To Coda ⊕

Say it ain't so. ___ My love ___ is a life tak - er. ___

Interlude

Bass: w/ Bass Fig. 1   Bass: w/ Bass Fig. 2

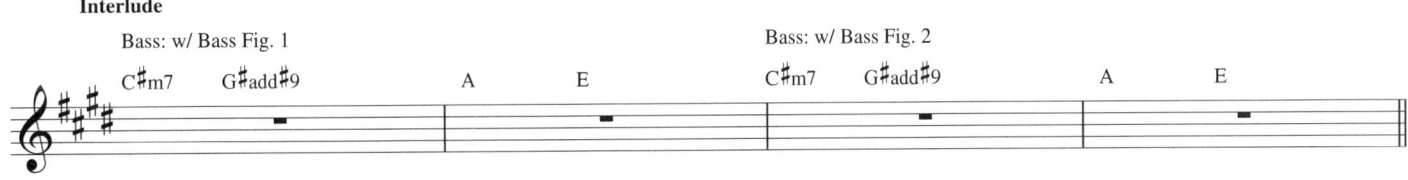

Verse

Bass: w/ Bass Fig. 1 (3 times)

3. I can't con - front ___ you. I nev - er could ___ do that which might hurt ___ you, ___ so

Bass: w/ Bass Fig. 2

try and be cool. ___ When I say this way ___ is a

wa - ter slide a - way from me that takes you fur - ther ev - er - y day, ___ so be

Chorus

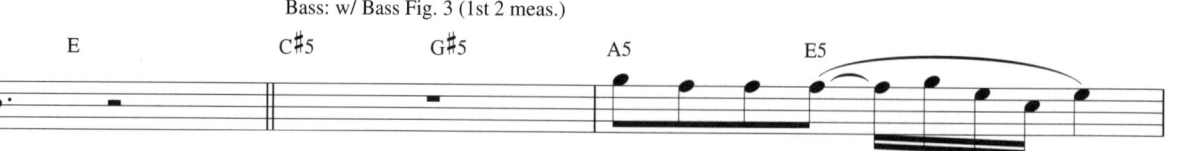

cool. _____

Say it ain't so. _____

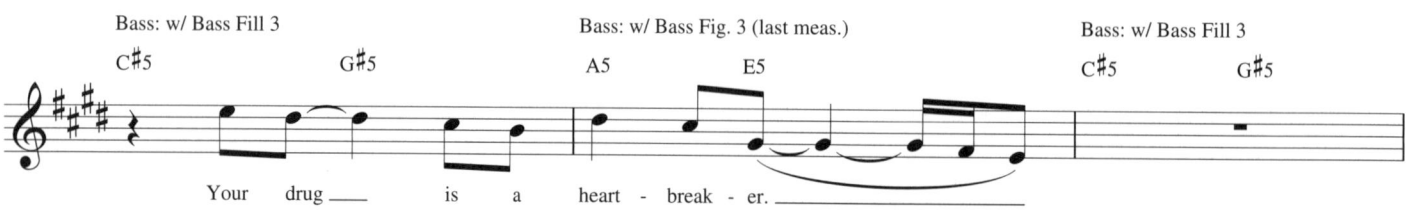

Your drug _____ is a heart - break - er. _____

Say it ain't so. _____

My love _____ is a life tak - er. _____

Bridge

Dear dad - dy, I write you in spite of years of si - lence. You've cleaned up, found Je - sus,

Bass Fill 3

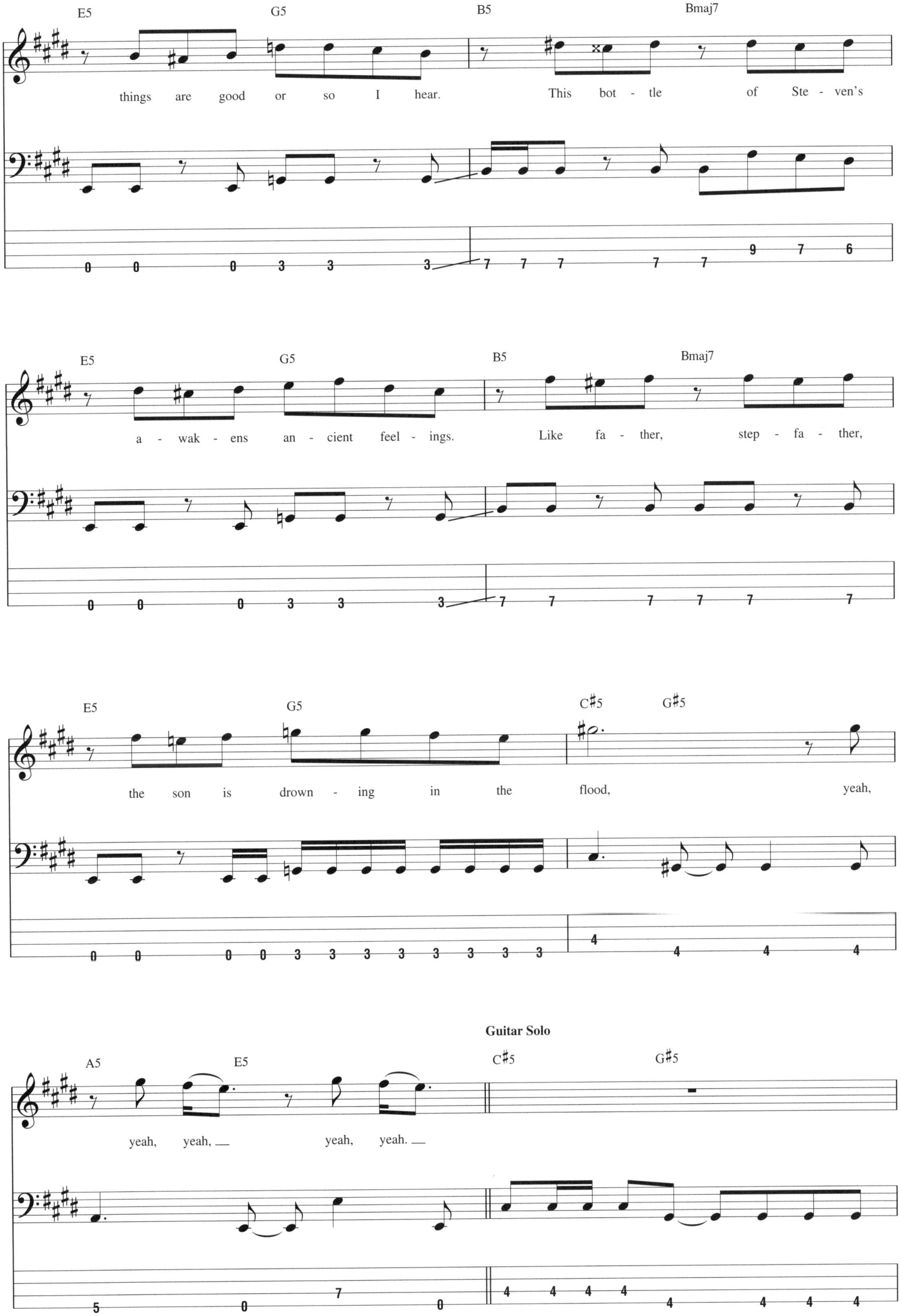

things are good or so I hear. This bot - tle of Ste - ven's

a - wak - ens an - cient feel - ings. Like fa - ther, step - fa - ther,

the son is drown - ing in the flood, yeah,

Guitar Solo

yeah, yeah, ___ yeah, yeah. ___

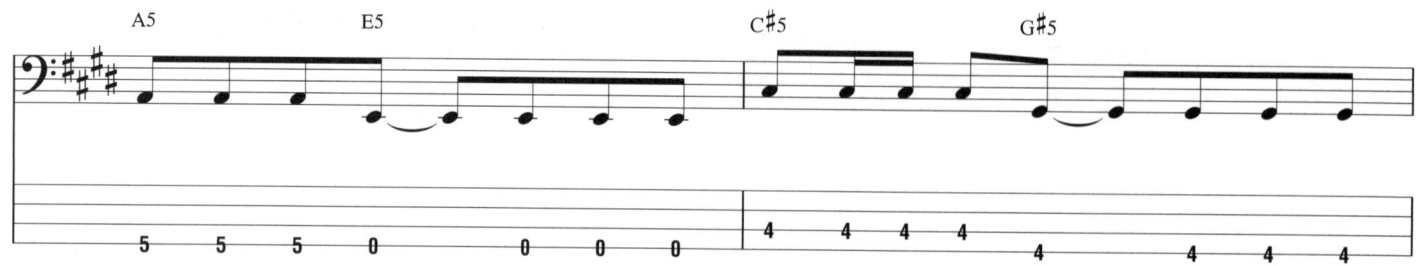

D.S. al Coda

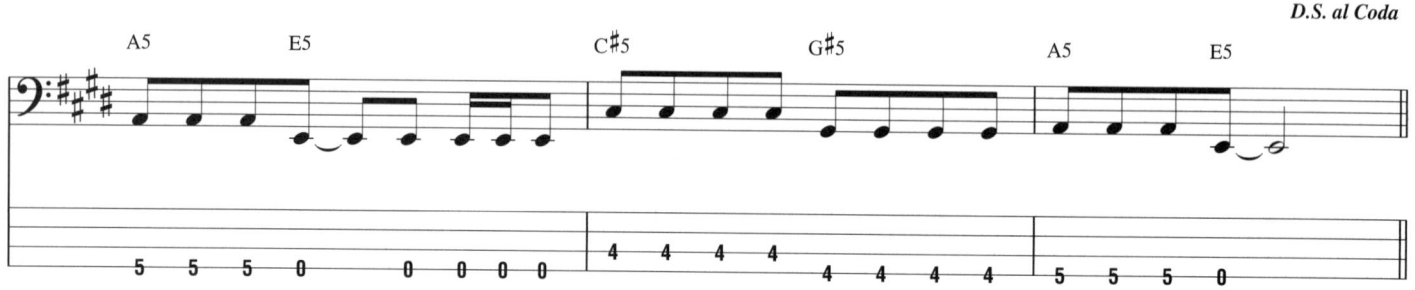

⊕ Coda

My love _____ is a life tak - er. _____

Outro

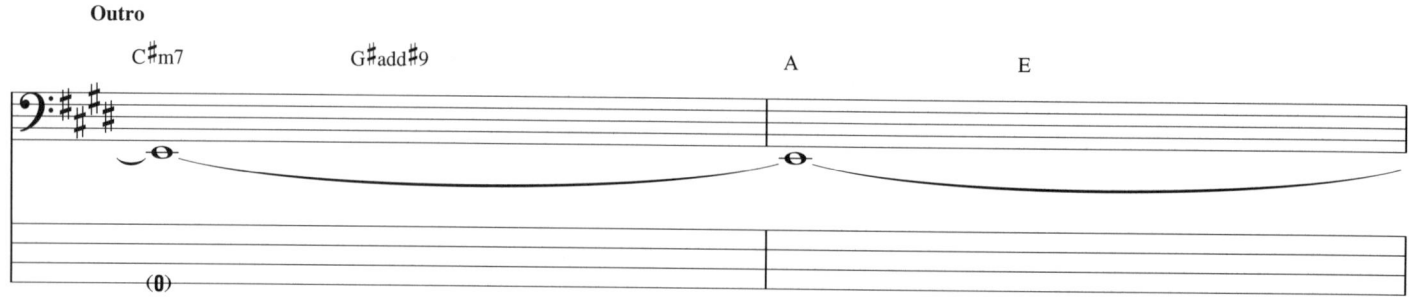

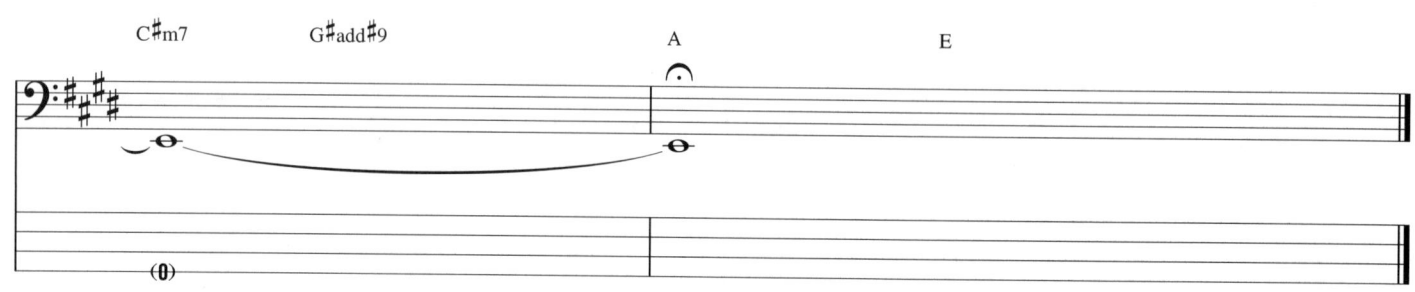

Should I Stay or Should I Go

Words and Music by Mick Jones and Joe Strummer

Whoa!   Ah.   Ah, la!

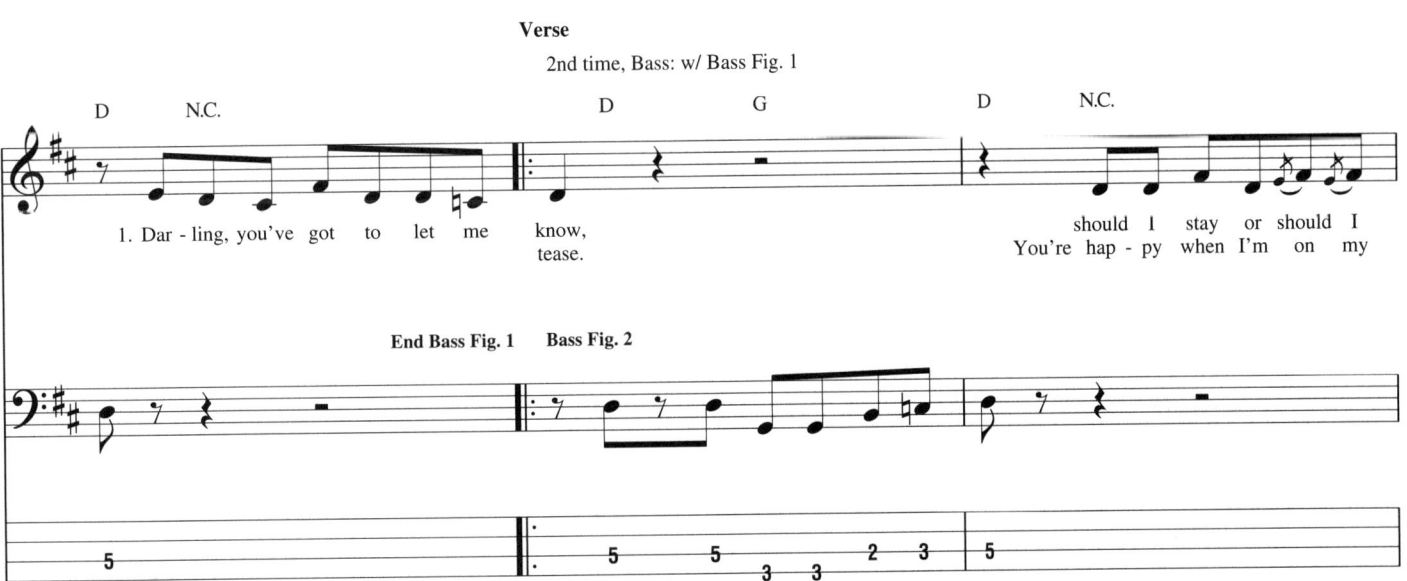

1. Dar - ling, you've got to let me know, tease.

should I stay or should I
You're hap - py when I'm on my

Chorus
Double-time feel
D G D G
go now? Should I stay or should I go now?
Bass Fig. 3
D G F/C
If I go there will be trou - ble,
G D G D
and if I stay it will be dou - ble. So come on and let me
End Bass Fig. 3
A7 D Dsus4 G D N.C.
End double-time feel
know. 3. This in - de - ci - sion's bug - gin'

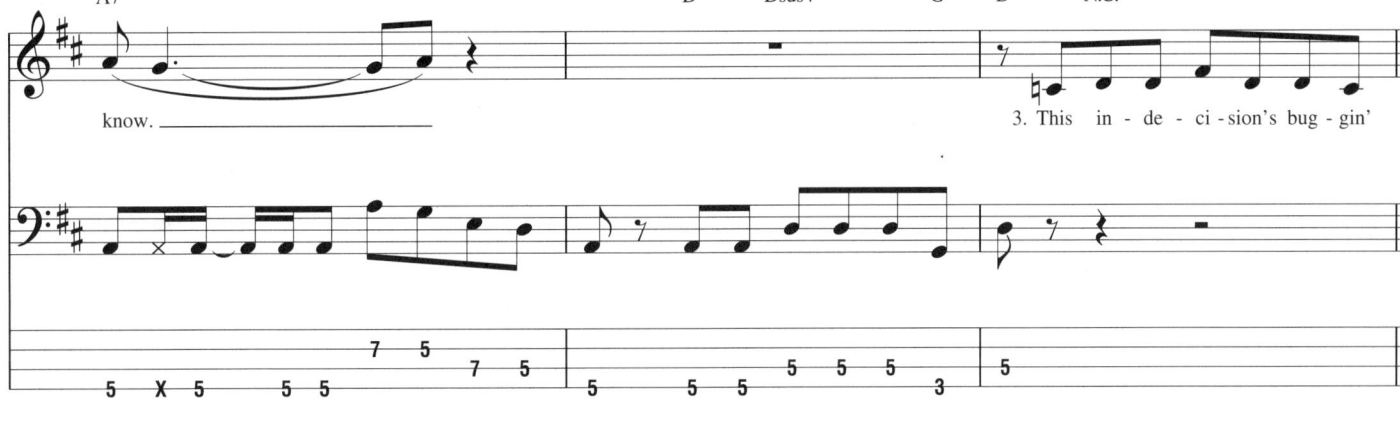

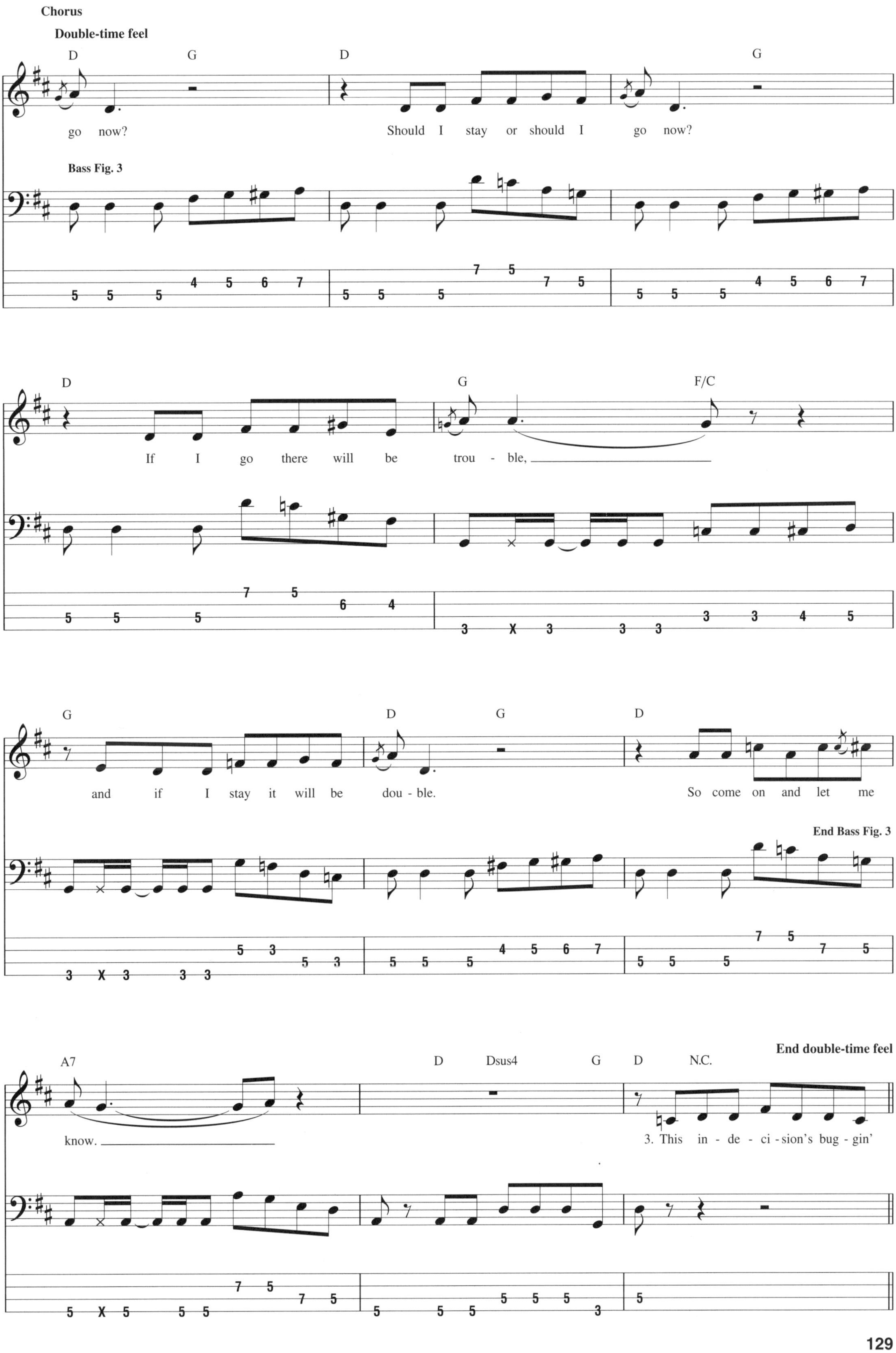

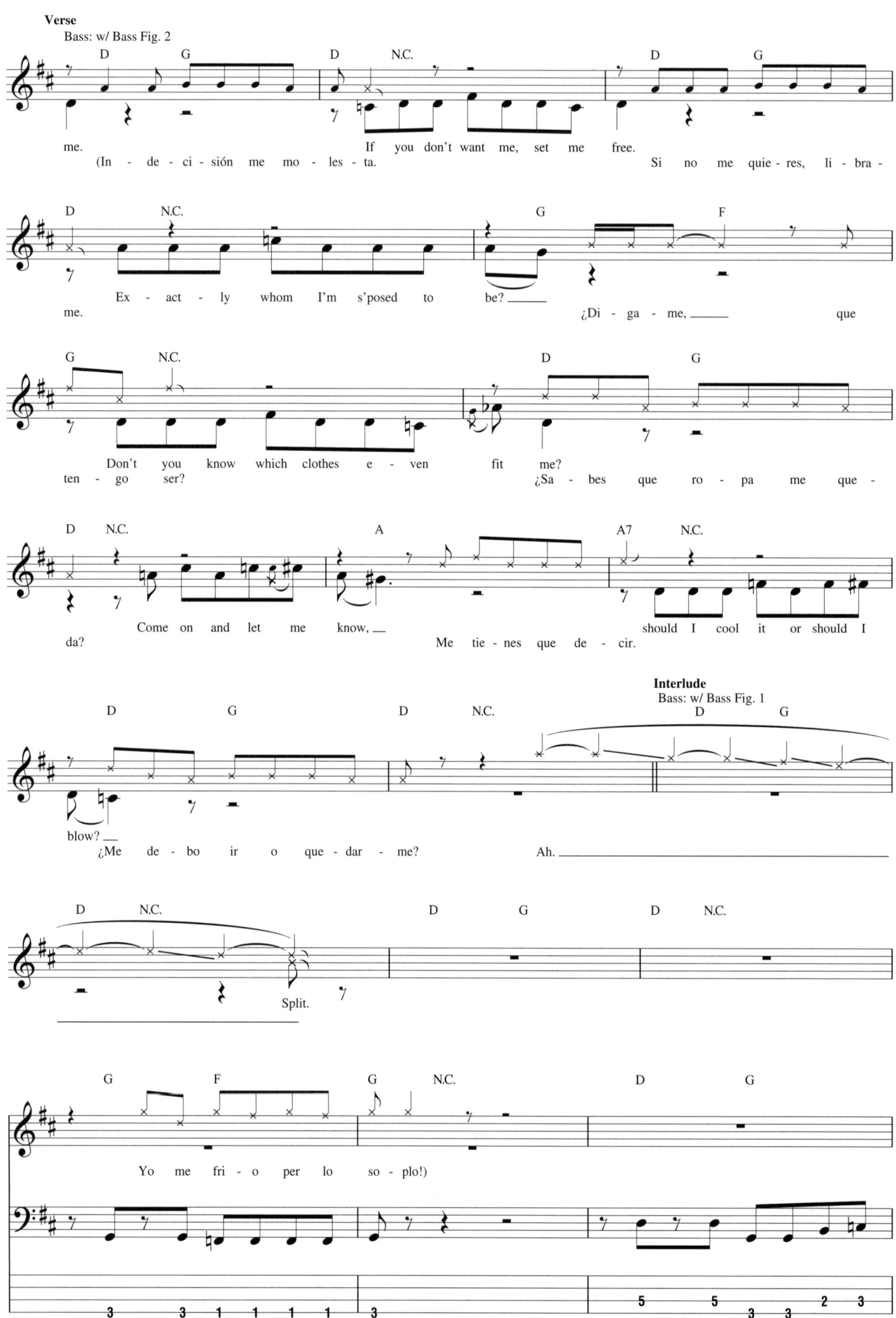

Outro-Chorus
Double-time feel
Bass: w/ Bass Fig. 3

Should I stay or should I go now?
(Yo me fri - o o lo

Should I stay or should I go now?
so - plo.   Yo me fri - o o lo so - plo.

If I go there will be

trou - ble,   Si me voy ___ va ver pe - li - gro,

and if I stay it will be

dou - ble.   si me que - do es do - ble.

So you've got to let me

know, ___   Me tie - nes que de - cir.

should I cool it or should I blow? ___   Yo me fri - o o lo

Should I stay or should I go now? ___ If I go there will be

so - plo. Yo me fri - o o lo so - plo.

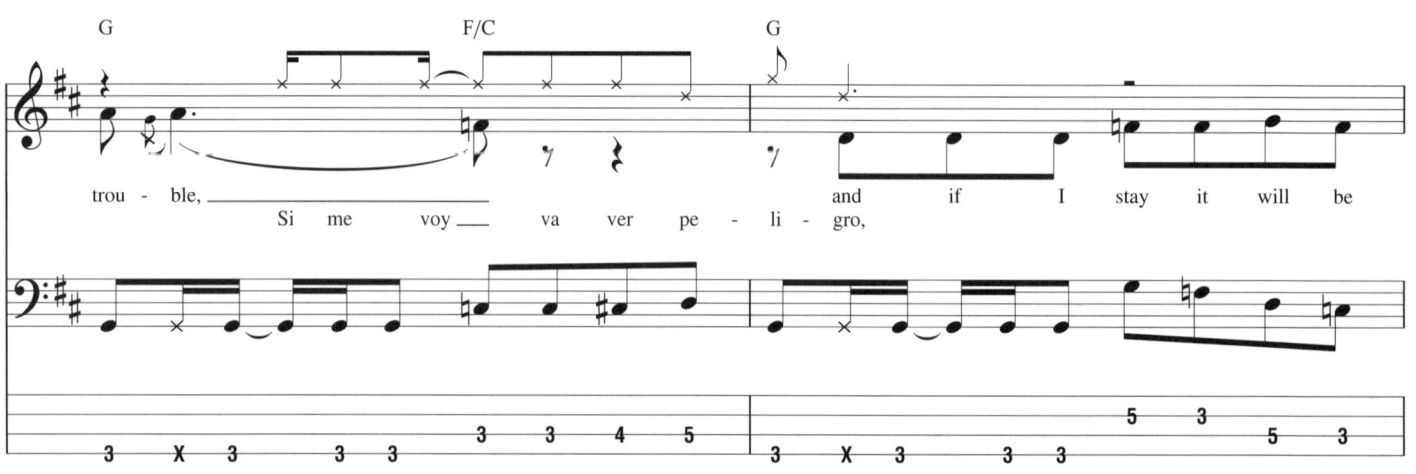

trou - ble, _____ and if I stay it will be

Si me voy ___ va ver pe - li - gro,

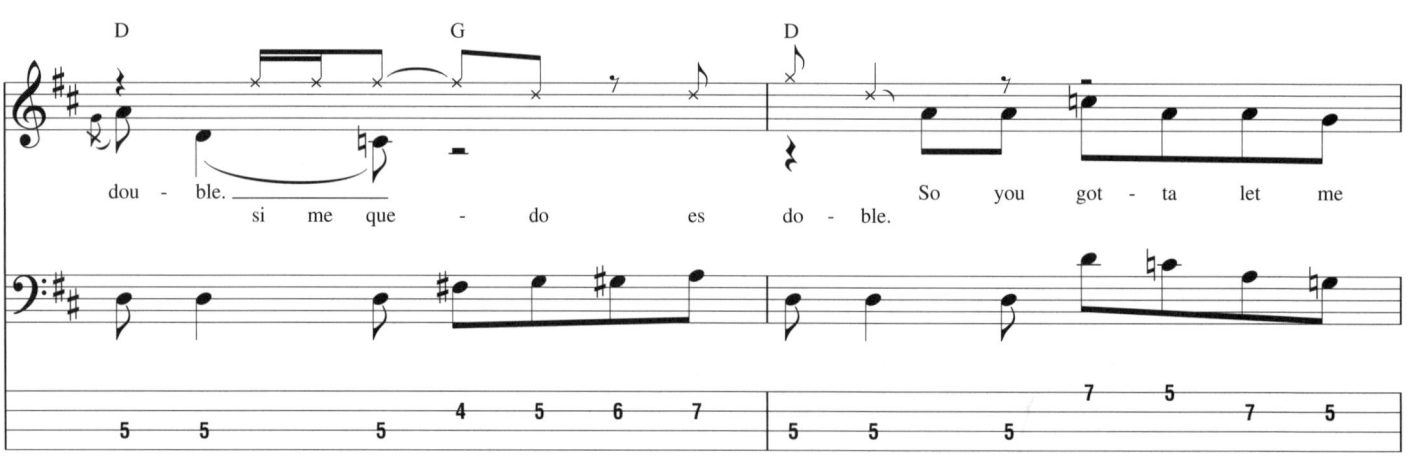

dou - ble. _____ So you got - ta let me

si me que - do es do - ble.

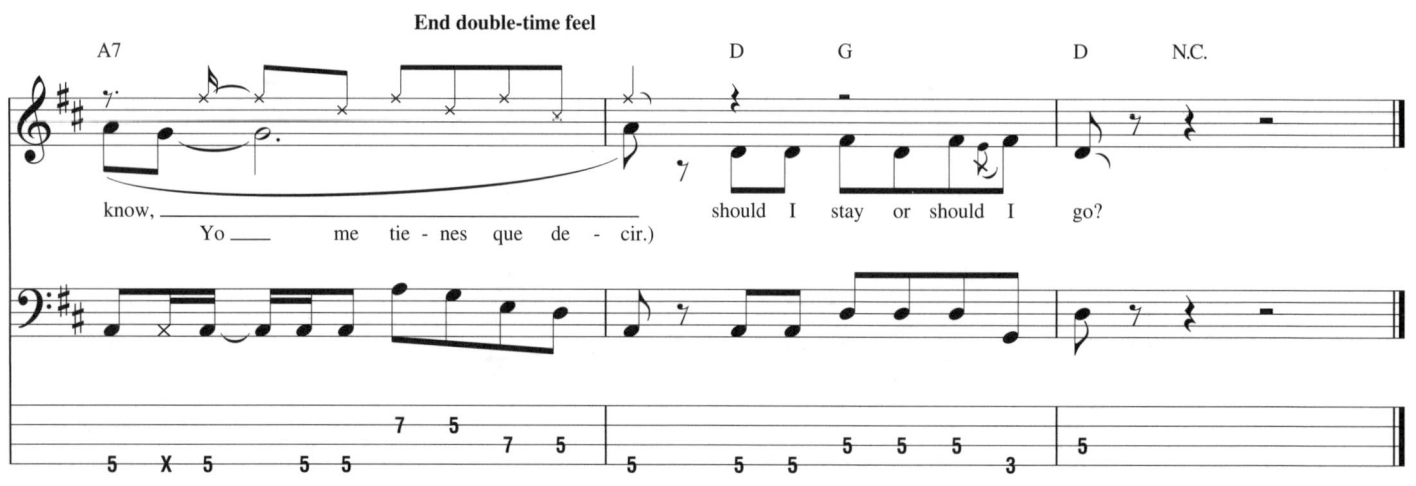

End double-time feel

know, _____ should I stay or should I go?

Yo ___ me tie - nes que de - cir.)

Suffragette City

Words and Music by David Bowie

Intro
Moderate Rock ♩ = 138

Verse

1. (Hey man!) Ah, _____ leave me a - lone, _ you know.

Bass Fig. 1

(Hey, man!) Oh, Hen-ry, get off the phone, _ I got... (Hey, man!) I got to

straight-en my face, __ this mel - low thighed chick __ just put my spine out of place. __

End Bass Fig. 1

w/ Bass Fig. 1

(Hey, man!) My school day's in - sane. __ (Hey, man!) My

work's down the drain. __ (Hey, man!) Uh, she's a tot - al blam blam, __ she

said she had to squeeze it but she... an' then she... Ah, __ don't __

𝄋 Chorus

lean on me, man, 'cause you can't af - ford the tick - et back from Suf - fra - gette Cit -

y! Uh, don't _ lean on me, man, 'cause you ain't got time to check it.

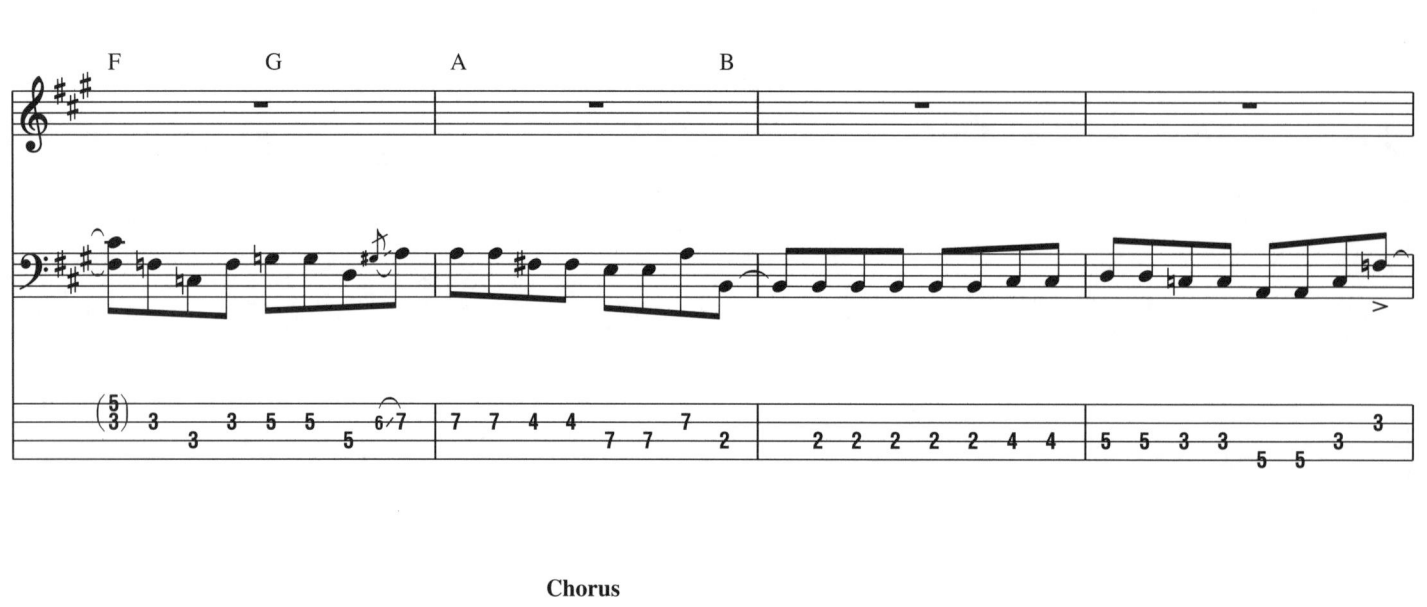

Chorus

Uh, don't _ lean on me, man, 'cause you can't af - ford the tick - et

back from Suf - fra - gette Cit - y! Uh, don't _ lean on me, man, 'cause you

ain't got time to check it. You know my Suf - fra - gette Cit - y! Don't _

Train Kept A-Rollin'

Words and Music by Tiny Bradshaw, Lois Mann and Howie Kay

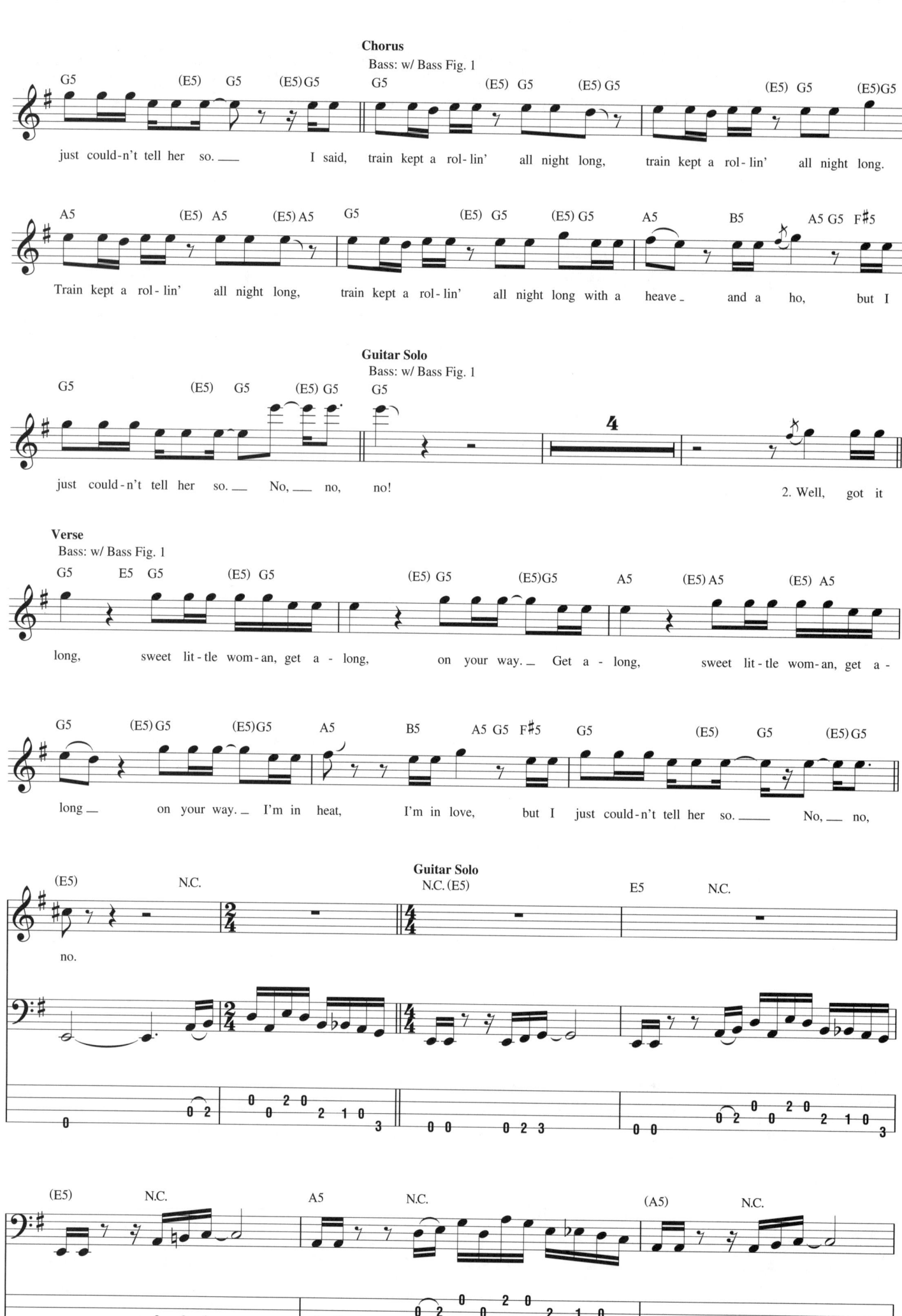

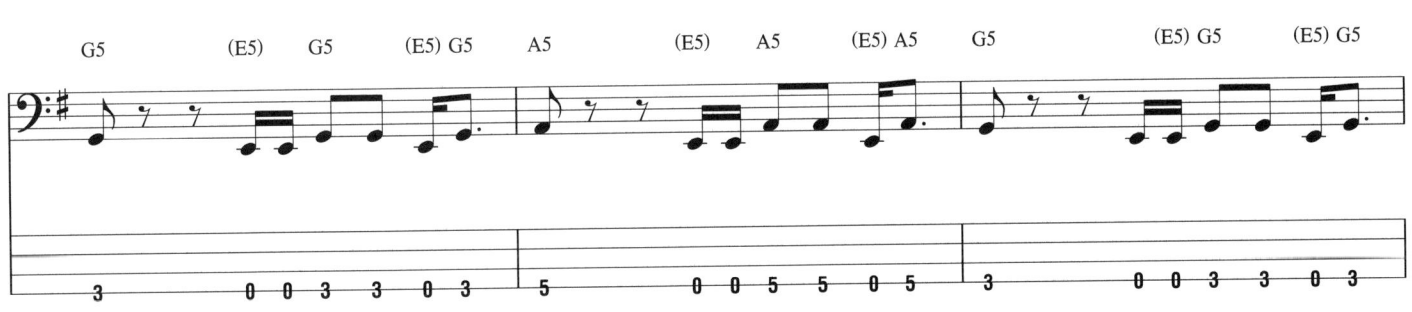

Interlude
Faster ♩ = 198

Bass tacet
(Snare drum & guitar)

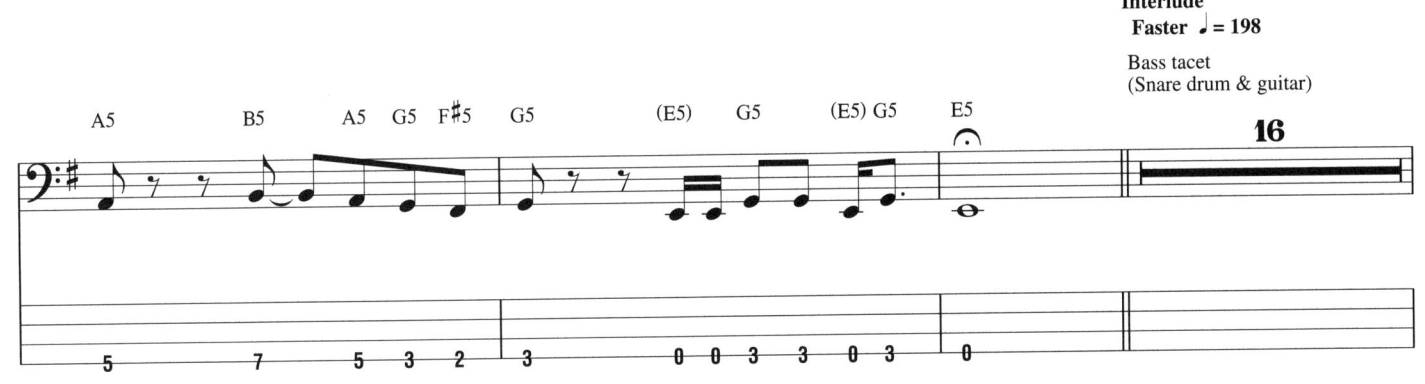

train, I met a dame. She was rath - er hand - some, we kind - a

looked the same. ___ She was pret - ty, from New York ___ Cit - y. I'm

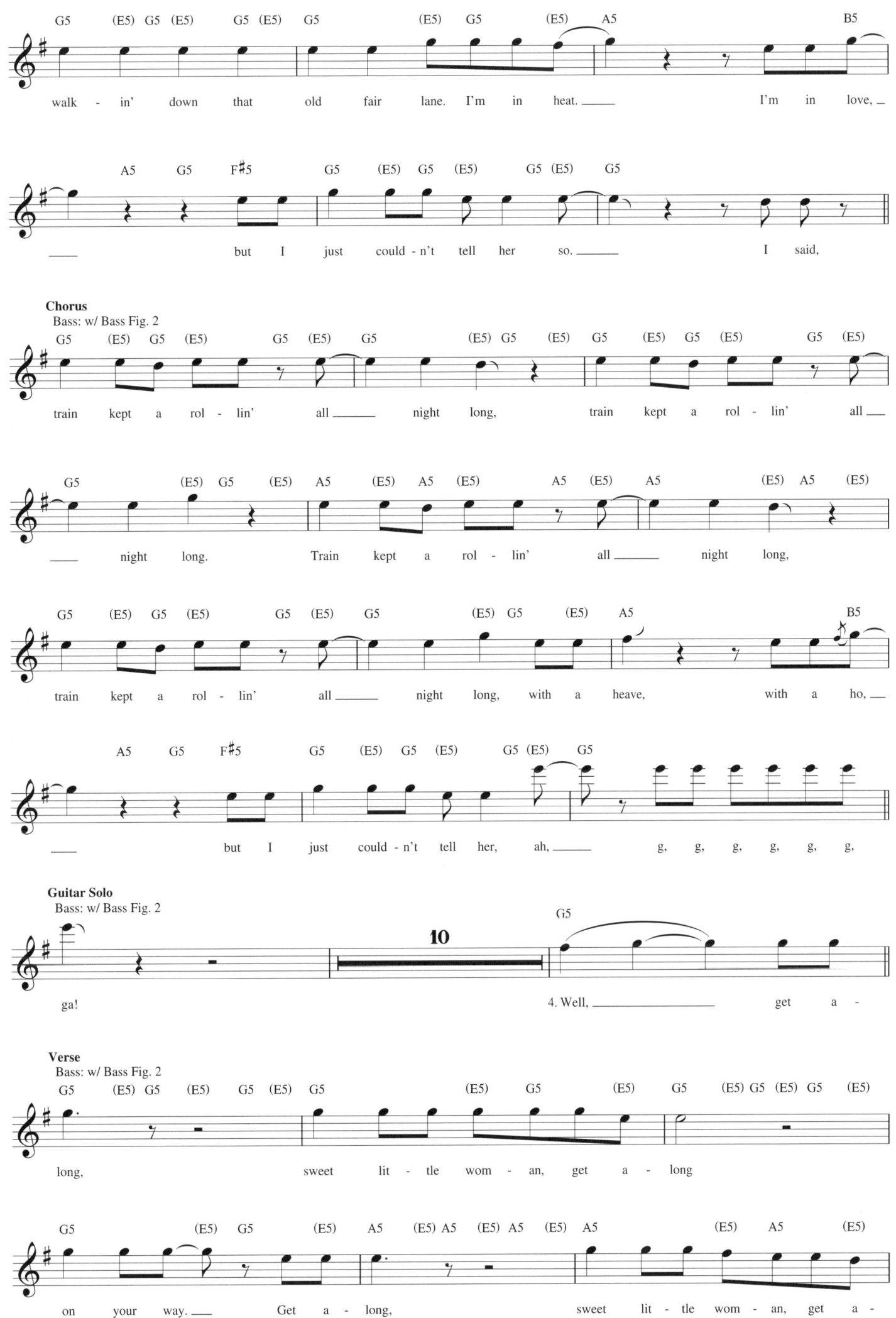

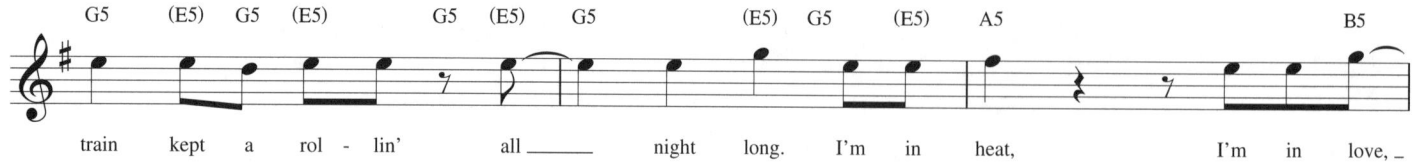

train kept a rol - lin' all _____ night long. I'm in heat, I'm in love,

_____ but I just could - n't tell her, ah, _____ yeh, y - yeah! _____

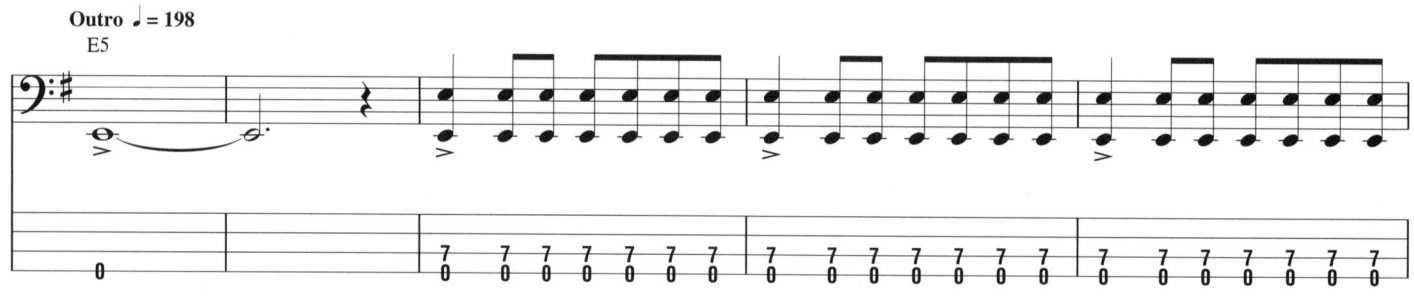

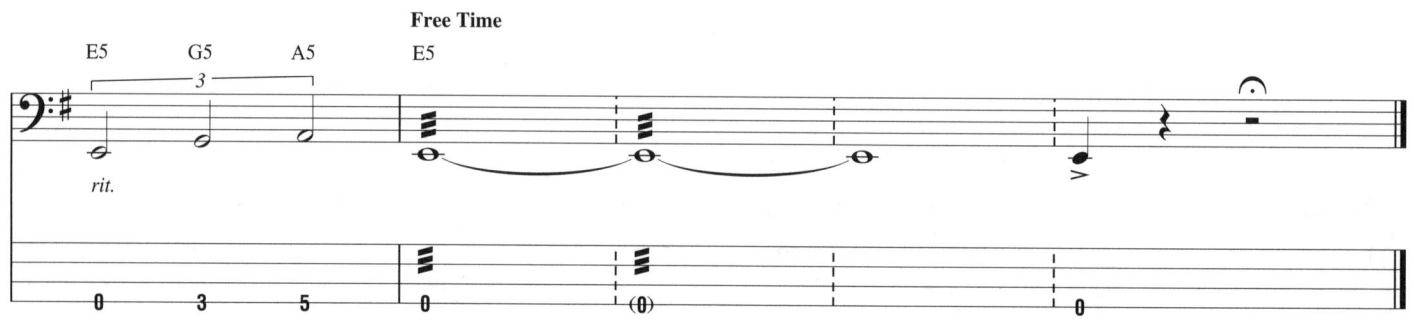

Wanted Dead or Alive

Words and Music by Jon Bon Jovi and Richie Sambora

Welcome Home

Words and Music by Claudio Sanchez, Michael Todd, Joshua Eppard and Travis Stever

Tune down 1/2 step:
(low to high) E♭-A♭-D♭-G♭

Intro

Moderately ♩ = 78

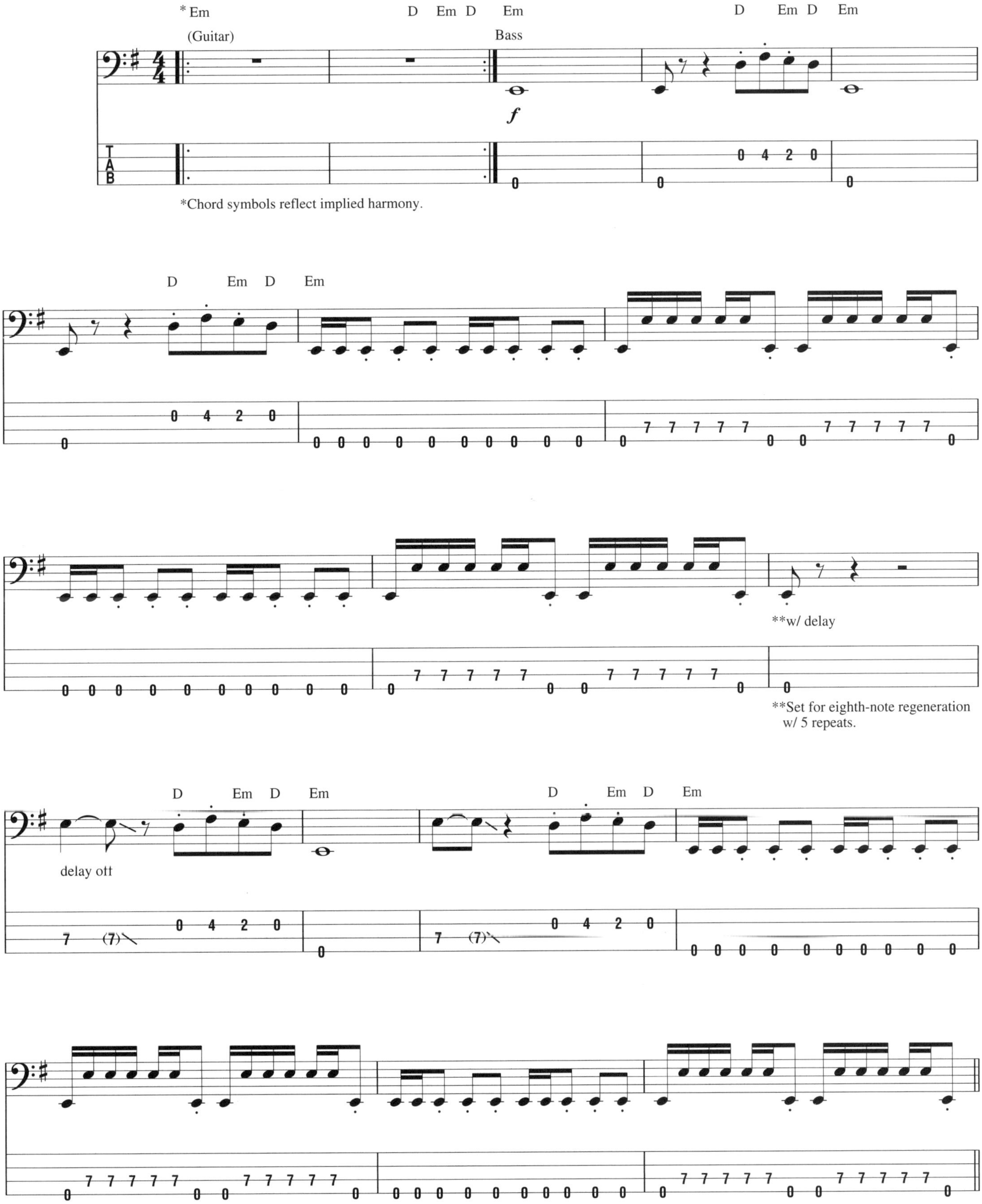

*Em
(Guitar)
D Em D Em
Bass
f
D Em D Em
*Chord symbols reflect implied harmony.
D Em D Em
**w/ delay
**Set for eighth-note regeneration w/ 5 repeats.
D Em D Em
delay off
D Em D Em

Verse

2nd time, Lead Voc.: w/ Voc. Fill 1

E5   C/E

1. You could-'ve been _____ all _____ I want - ed but
2. You stormed _____ off to scar _____ the ar - ma - da, like

Bass Fig. 1

Dsus2/E   E5   D5

you were-n't hon - est, now get in the ground. _____
Je - sus played let - ter, I'll drill through your hands. _____

End Bass Fig. 1

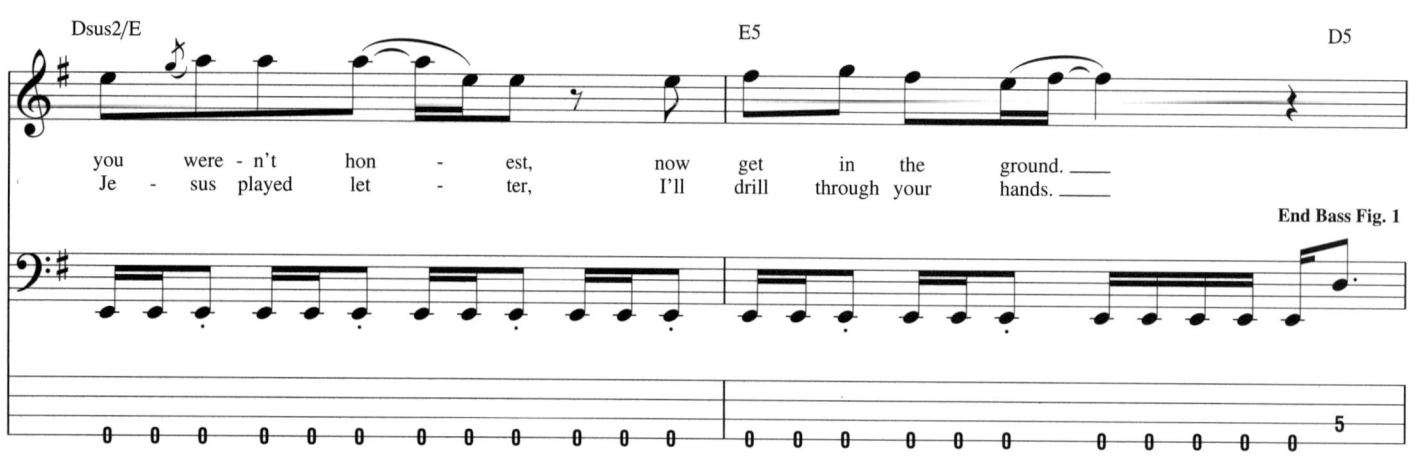

1st time, Bass: w/ Bass Fig. 1 (2 1/2 times)
2nd time, Bass: w/ Bass Fig. 1 (1st meas.)   2nd time, Bass: w/ Bass Fill 1

E5   C/E

You choked _____ off the sur - est of fa - vors, _____ but if
The stone _____ for the curse _____ you have blamed _____ me. With

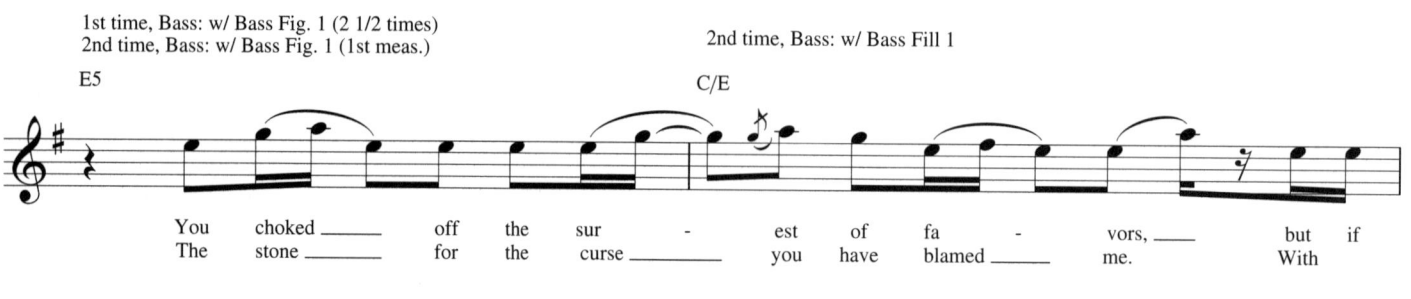

Voc. Fill 1

_3_

songs. _____

Bass Fill 1

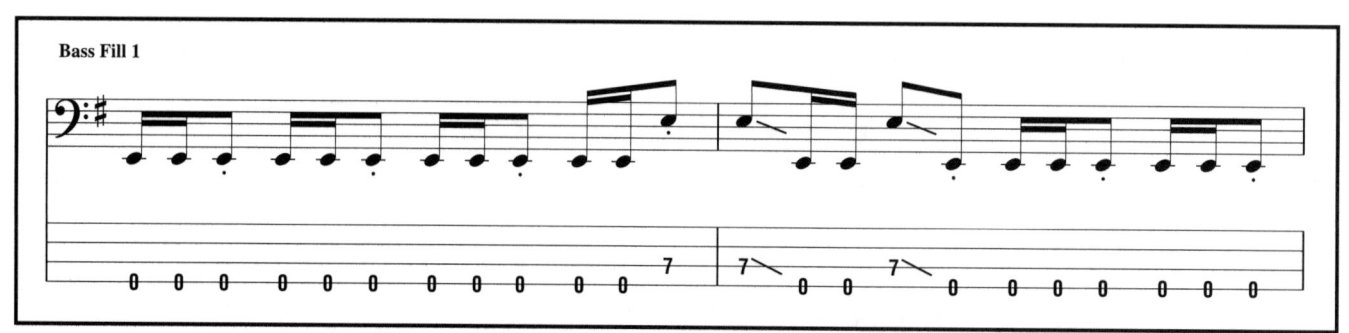

154

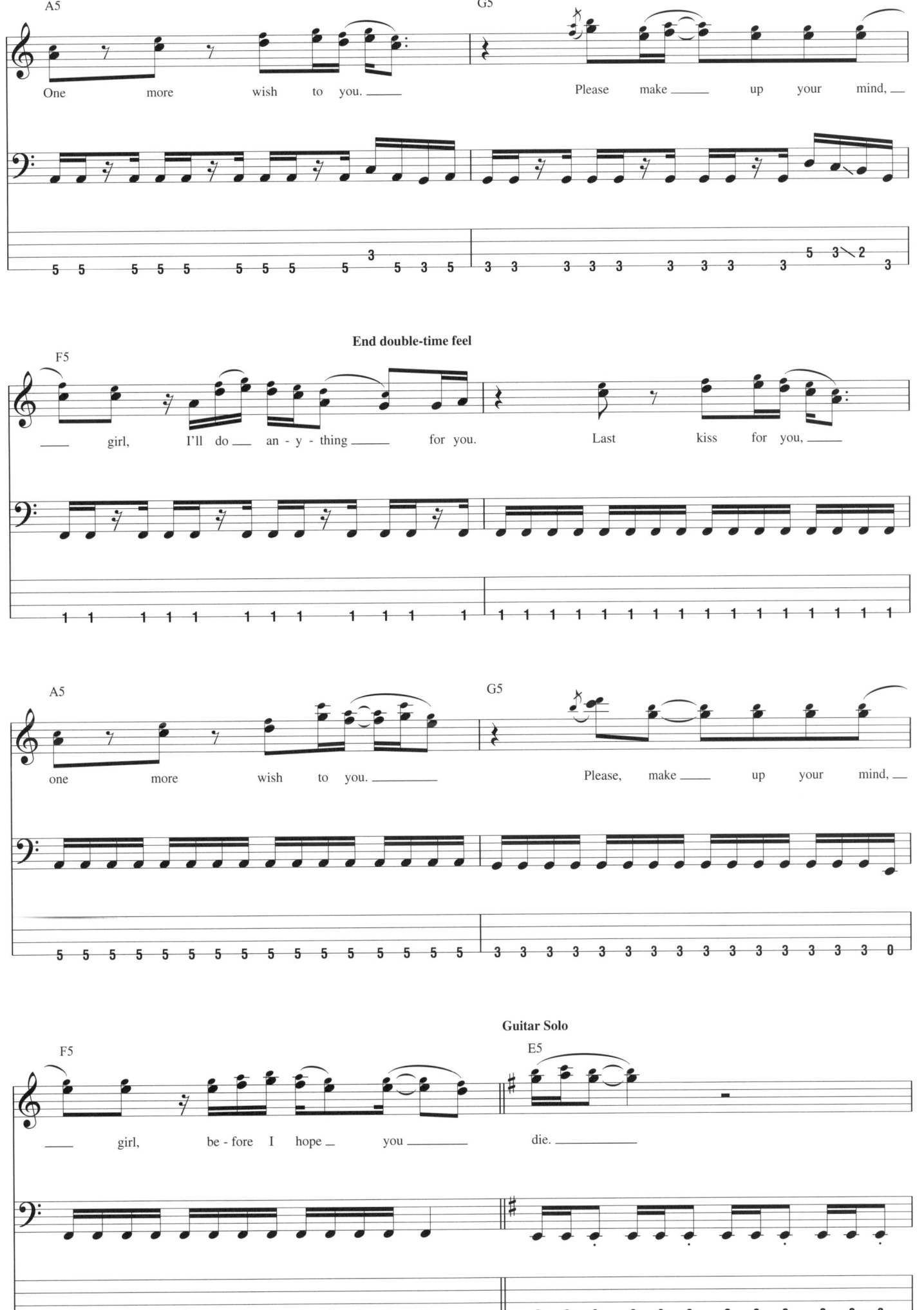

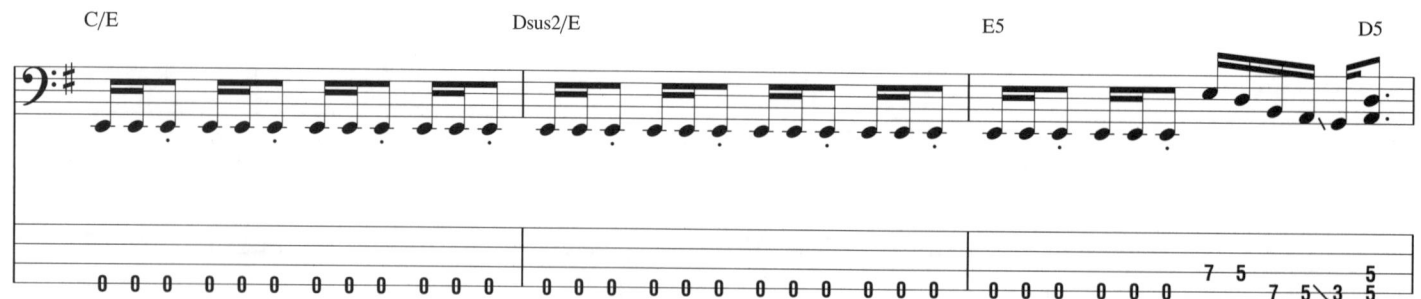

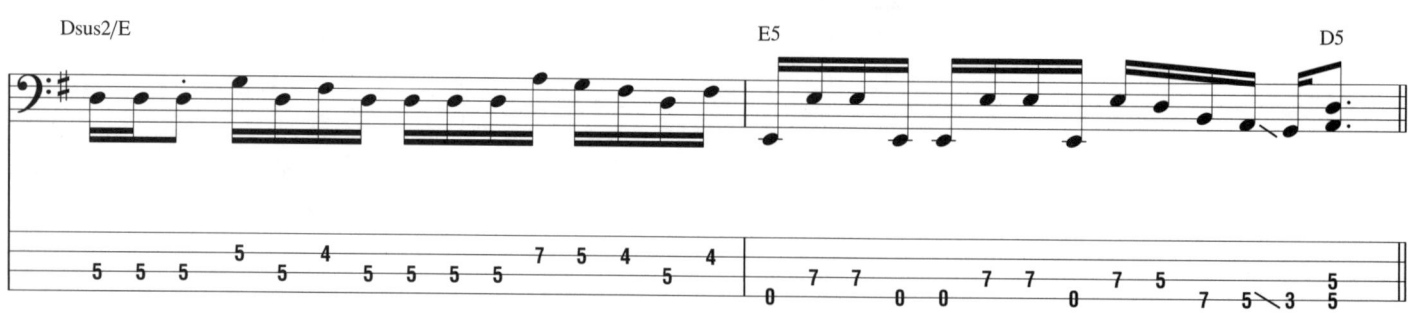

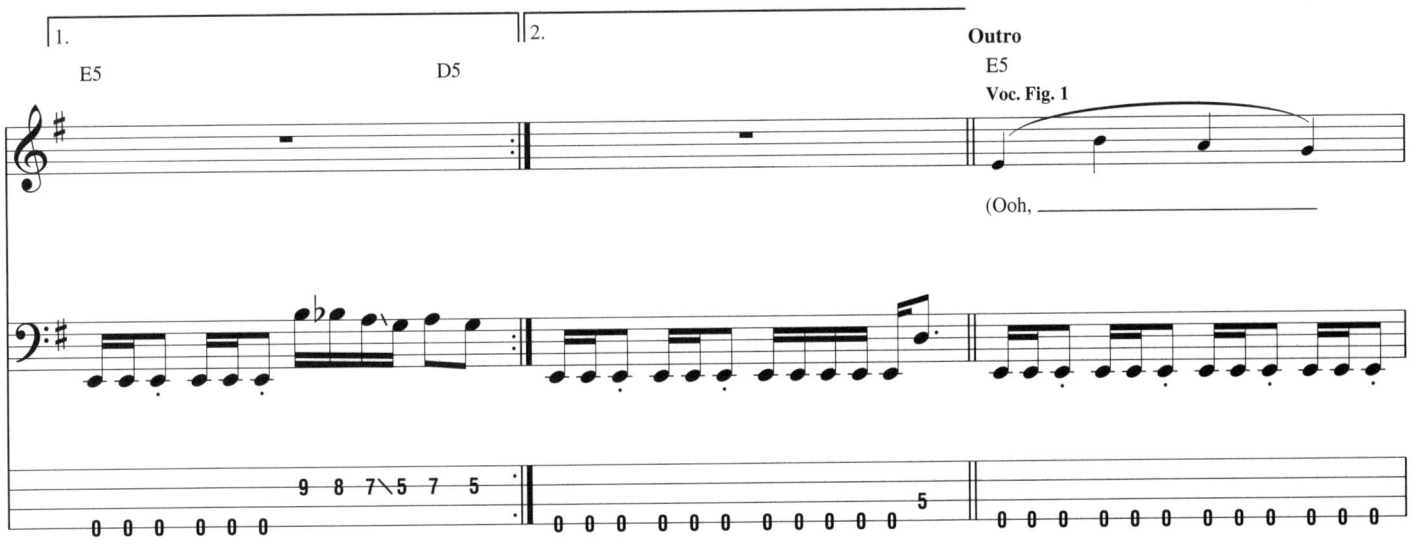

(Ooh, _____

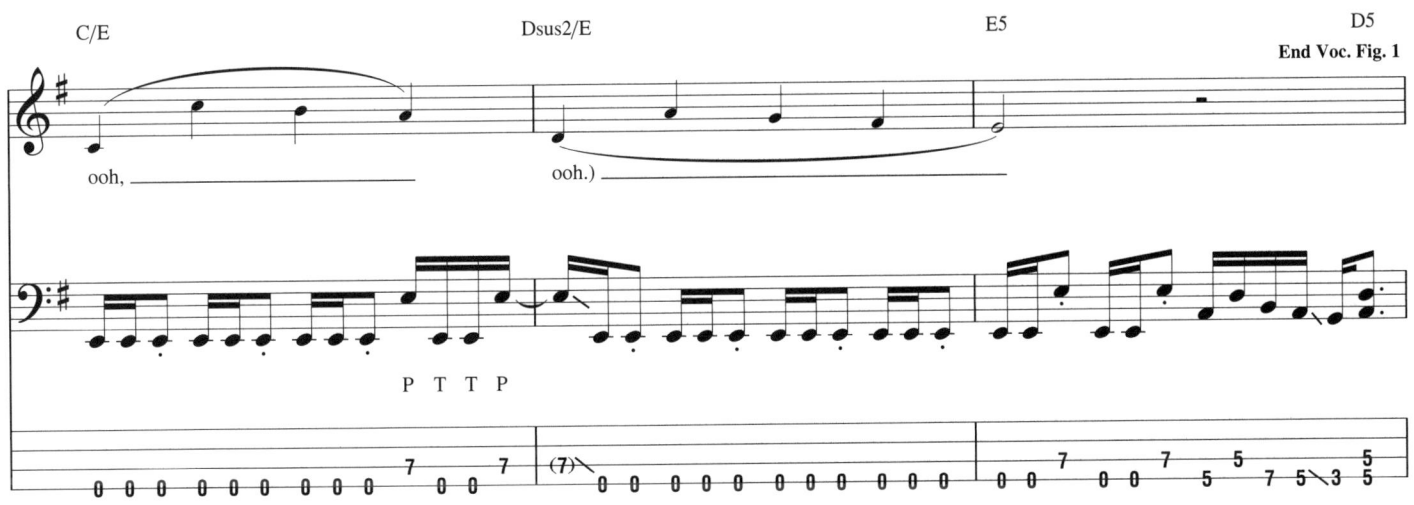

ooh, _____   ooh.) _____

Bkgd. Voc.: w/ Voc. Fig. 1 (till fade)

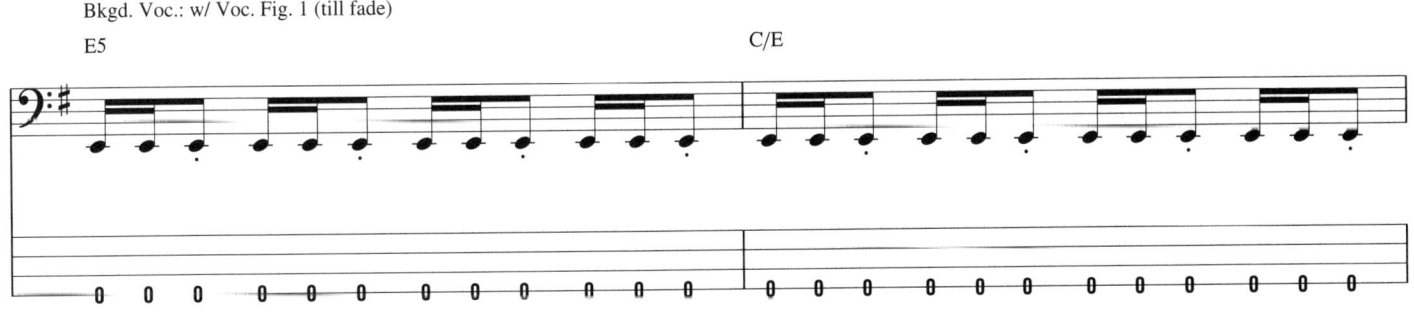

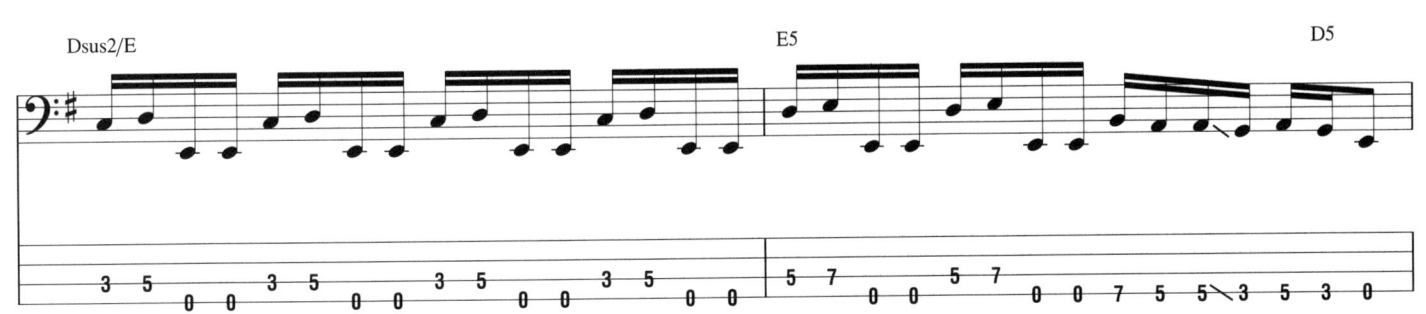

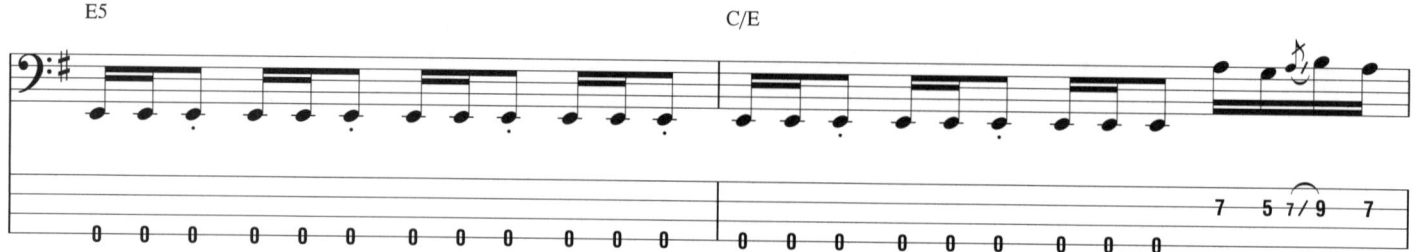

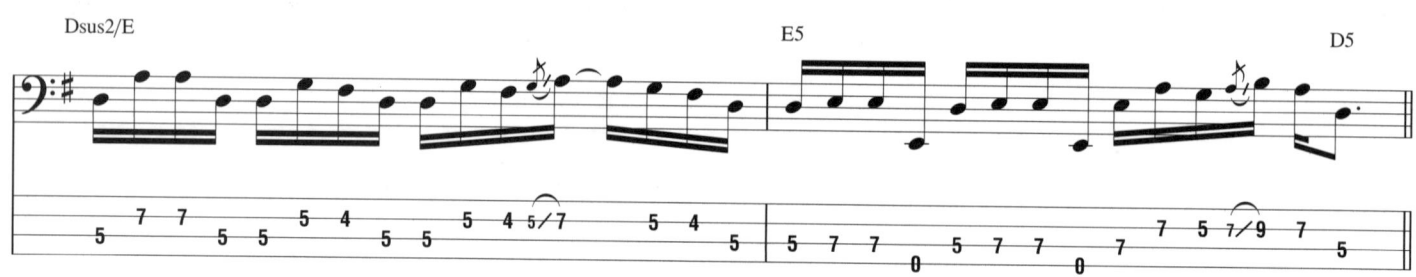

*2nd time, **Begin fade**

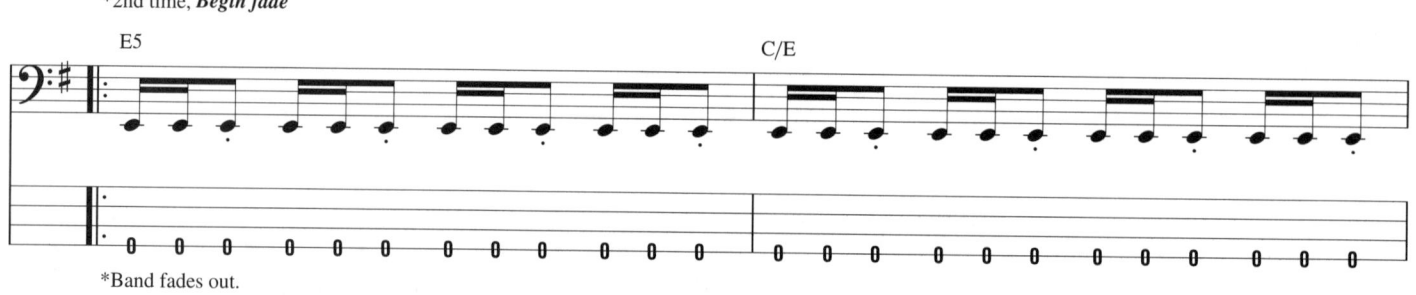

*Band fades out.

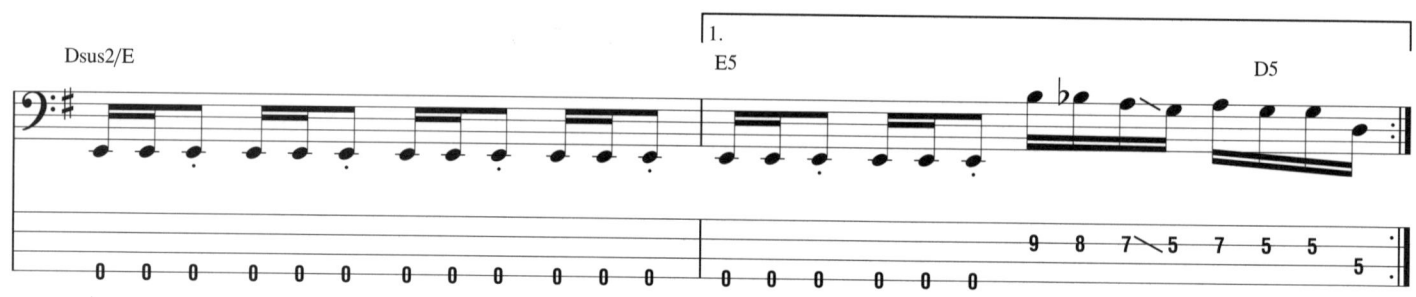

Bass: w/ Bass Fig. 1 (till fade)

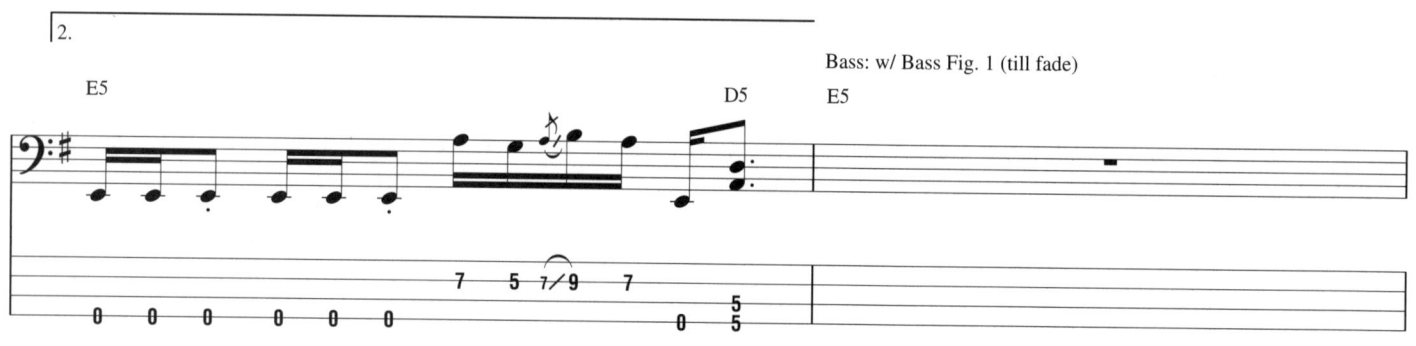

When You Were Young

Words and Music by Brandon Flowers, Dave Keuning, Mark Stoermer and Ronnie Vannucci

Tune down 1/2 step:
(low to high) E♭-A♭-D♭-G♭

Intro
Moderately fast ♩ = 130

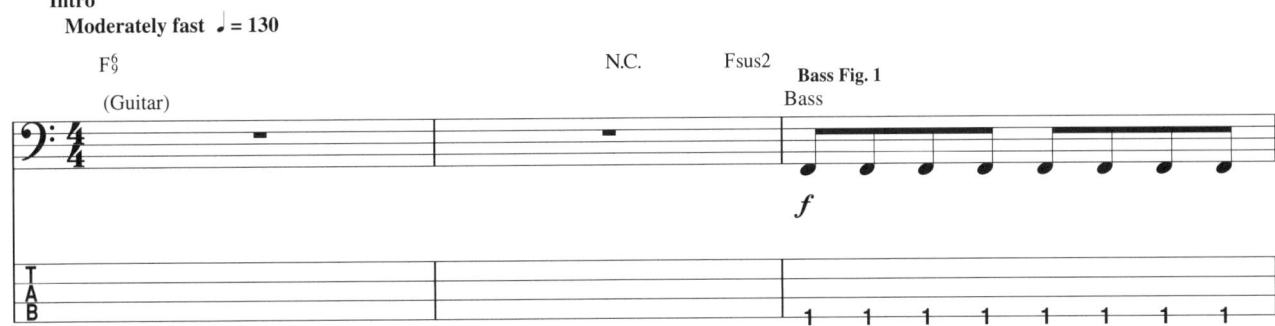

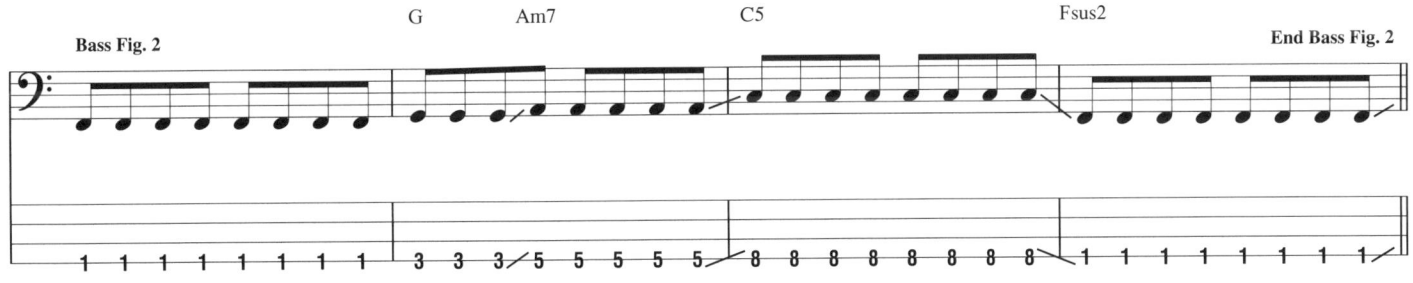

Verse

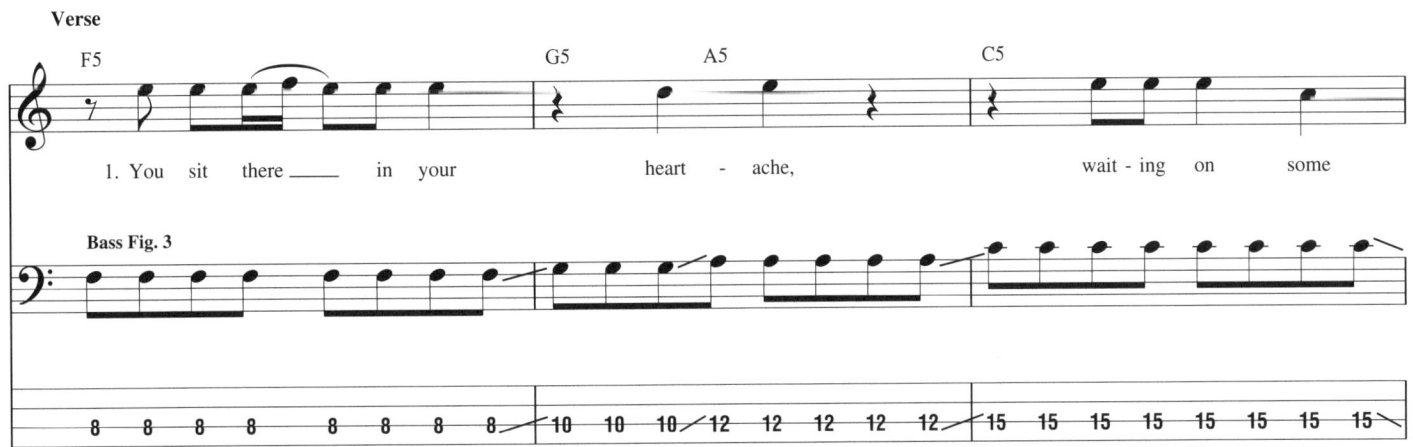

1. You sit there ____ in your heart-ache, wait-ing on some

beau - ti - ful boy ___ to, ___ to save you ___ from your ___ old ways.

Chorus
Bass: w/ Bass Fig. 1

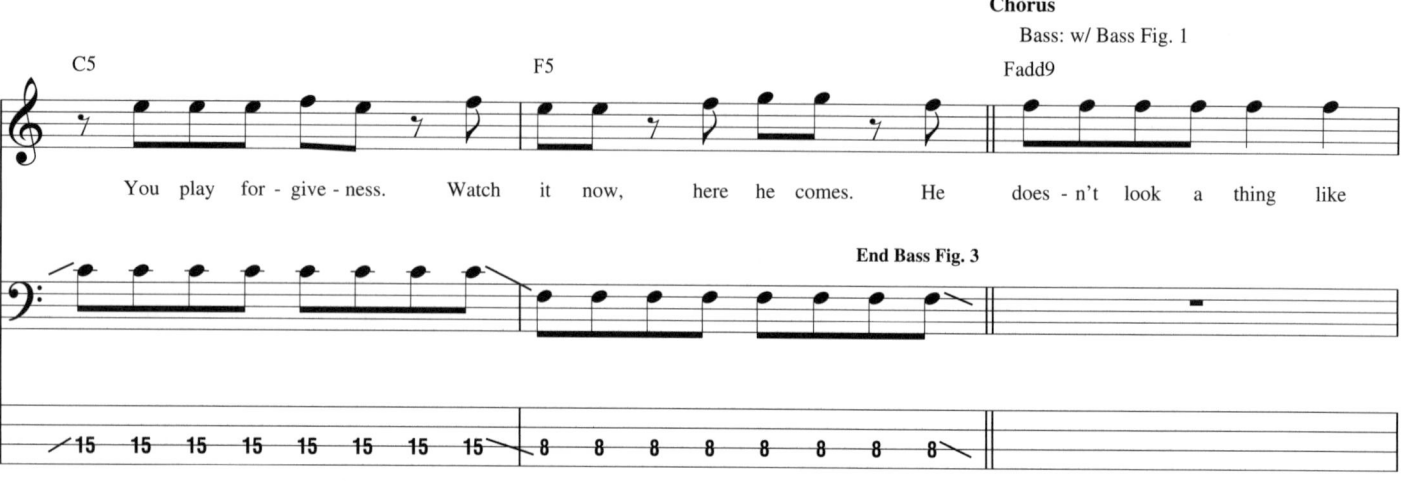

You play for - give - ness. Watch it now, here he comes. He does - n't look a thing like

End Bass Fig. 3

Je - sus ___ but he talks like a gen - tle - man, like you i - mag - ined when you ___

Bass: w/ Bass Fig. 2

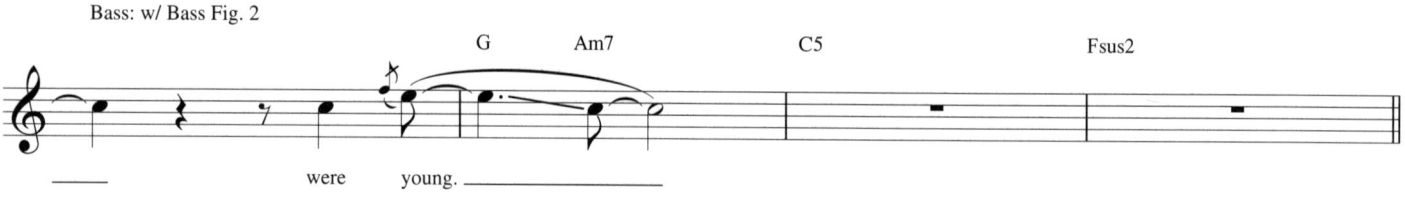

___ were young. ___

Verse
Bass: w/ Bass Fig. 3

2. Can we climb ___ this moun - tain? I don't know. High - er now ___ than ev -

Voc. Fig. 1

(Ah. ___

er be - fore, ___ I ___ know we can make it if we take it slow. ___

(Ah.)

Chorus
Bass: w/ Bass Fig. 1 (3 times)

Let's take it eas - y. Eas - y now, watch it go. We're burn - ing down the high - way

End Voc. Fig. 1

sky - line ___ on the back of a hur - ri - cane that start - ed turn - ing when you ___

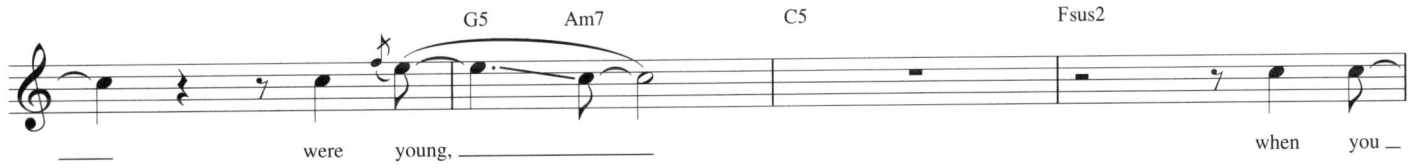

were young, _____ when you ___

were young. _____ And some -

Verse

- times you close your eyes ___ and see the place ___ where you used to live ___

163

when you ____ were young. ____

They say the

Dev - il's wa - ter, it ain't ____ so sweet. ____ You don't have to drink right now,

but you can dip your feet ____ ev - 'ry once and ____ a lit - tle while. ____

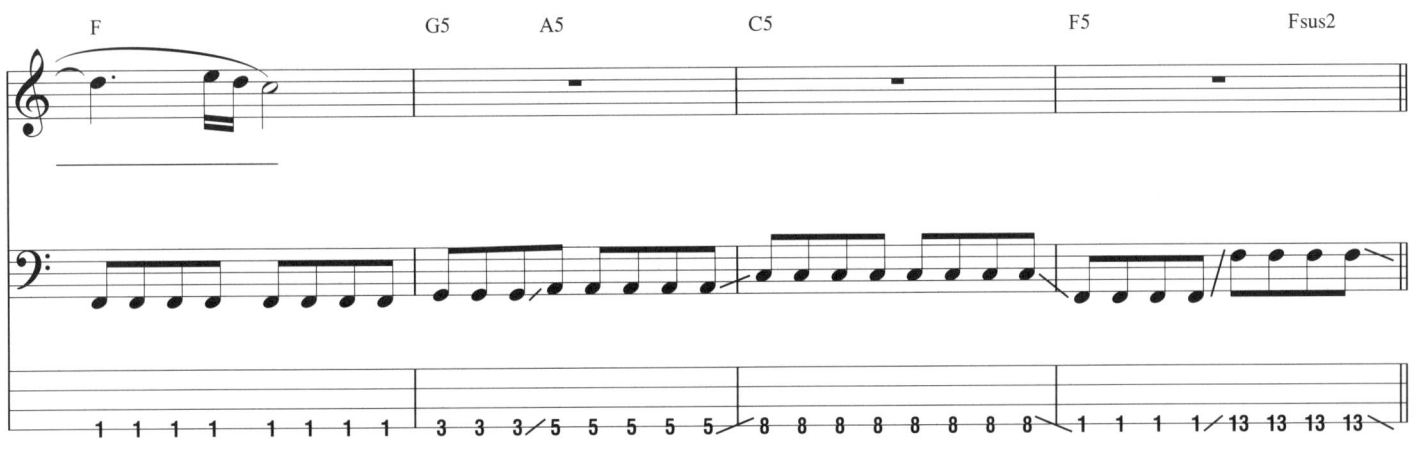

Interlude

Bass: w/ Bass Fig. 1 (2 times)

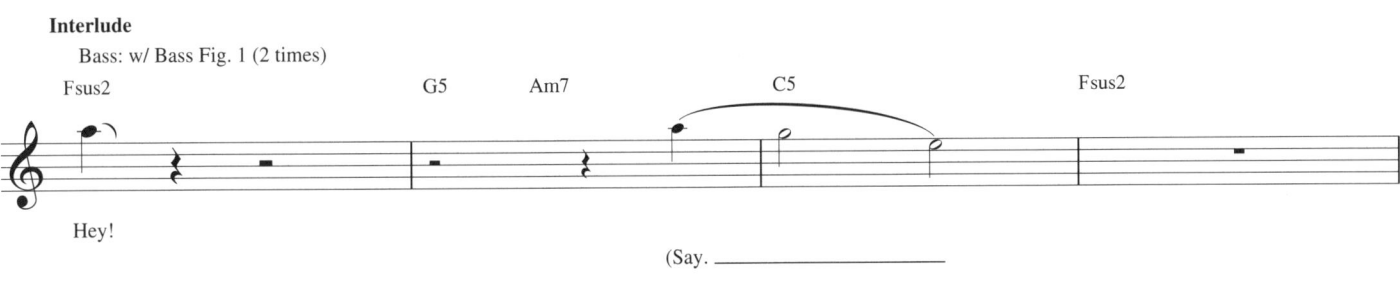

Hey!

(Say. _____

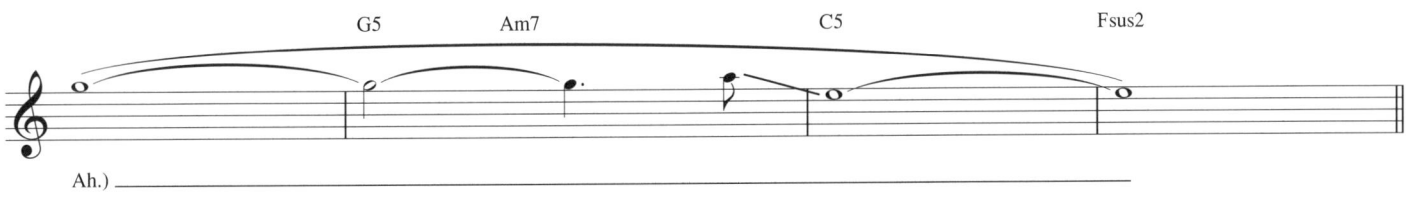

Ah.) _____

Verse

Bkgd. Voc.: w/ Voc. Fig. 1
Bass: w/ Bass Fig. 1 (1 1/2 times)

4. You sit there ___ in your heart - ache, wait - ing on ___ some

beau - ti - ful boy to, to save you from ___ your _____ old ways. ___

Outro-Chorus

You play for - give - ness. Watch it now, here he comes. He does - n't look a thing like

Won't Get Fooled Again

Words and Music by Pete Townshend

don't get fooled _ a - gain. _____

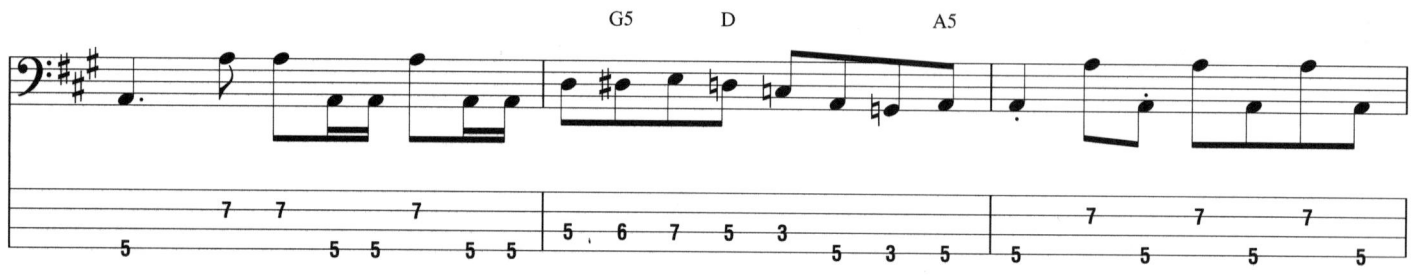

2. A

Verse

change, it had ___ to come. _____ We knew it all ___ a - long. ___

G5   D5   A5   D/A

A5   D/A   A5

I'll

Bridge
B5   E5

move my-self   and my fam-'ly a-side, _____   if we hap-pen to be

174

left half __ a - live. __ I'll get all my pa - pers and smile __ at the sky, oh, I

know __ that the hyp - no - tized nev - er lie.

Do ya?

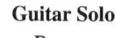

Guitar Solo

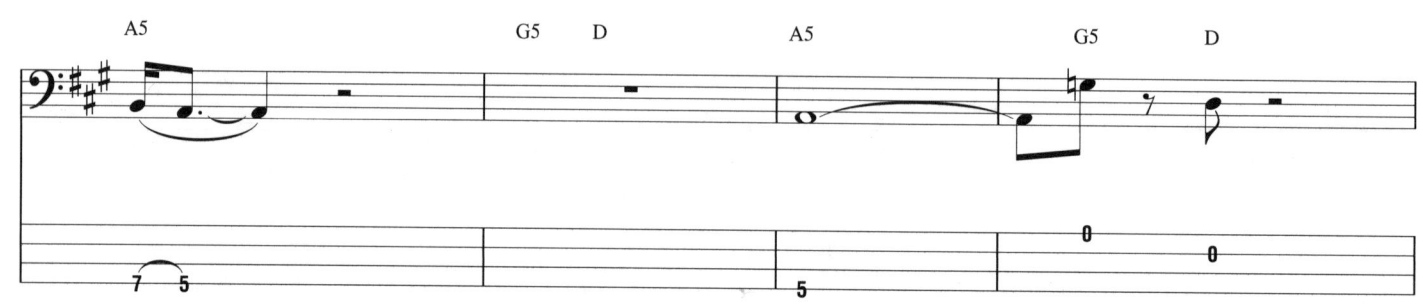

176

No, no!

N.C.(A)

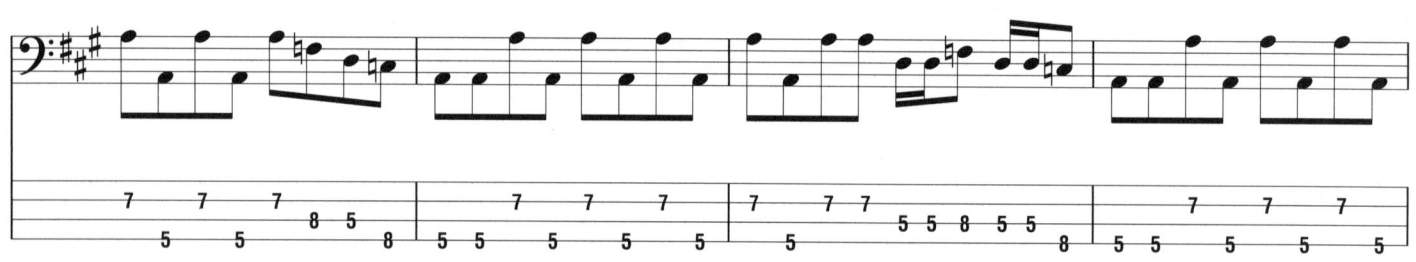

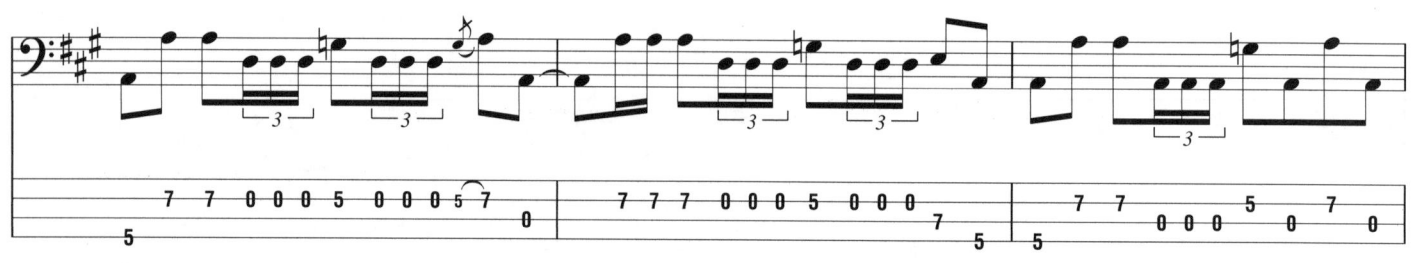

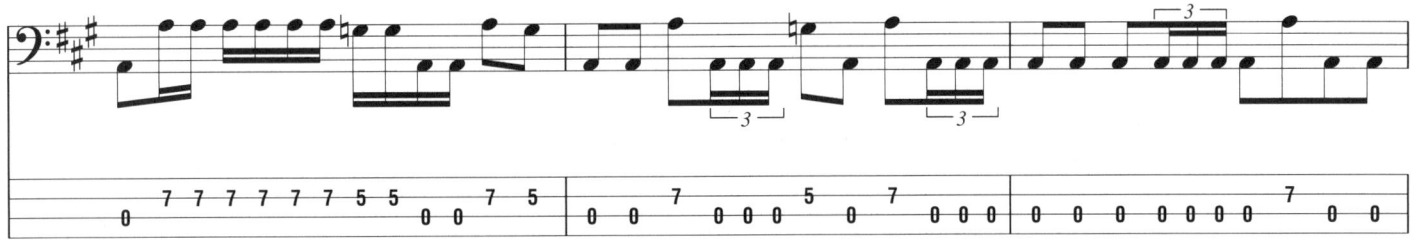

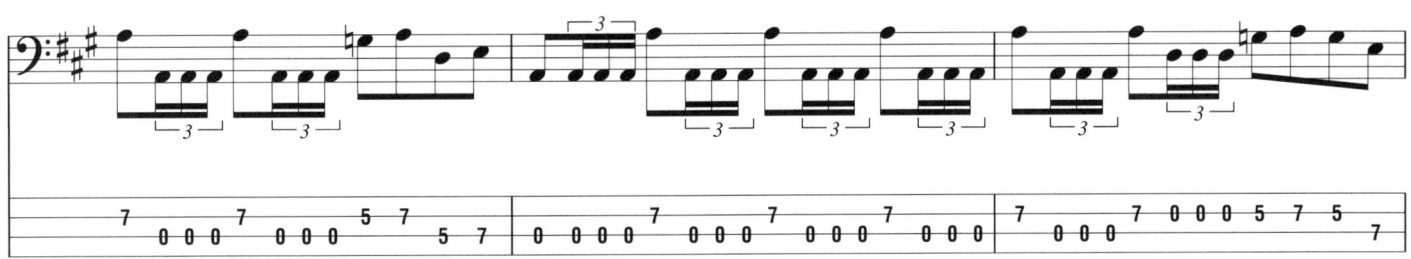

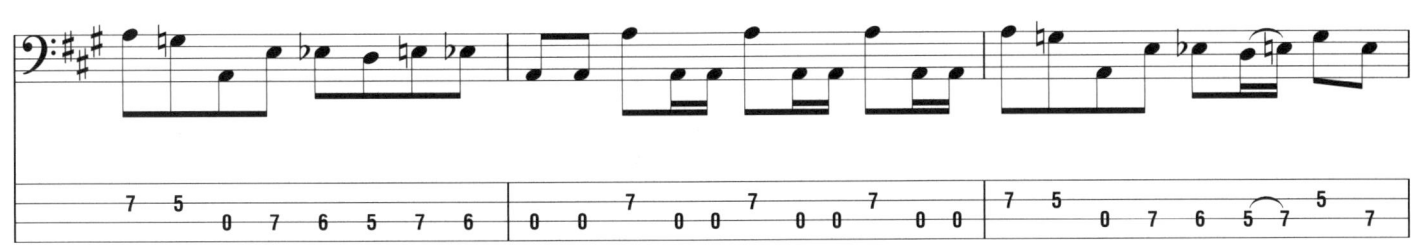

Interlude

Bass tacet

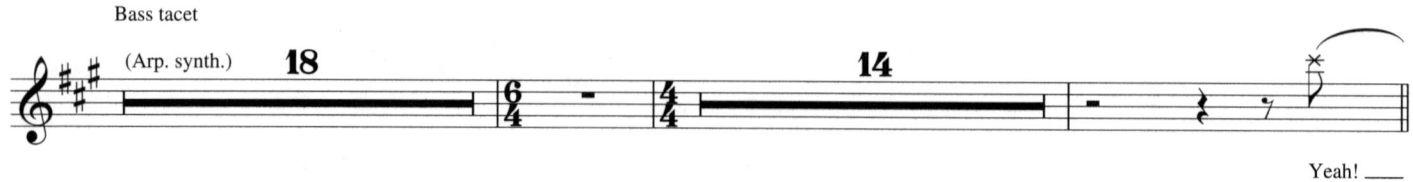

Yeah! ___

Outro

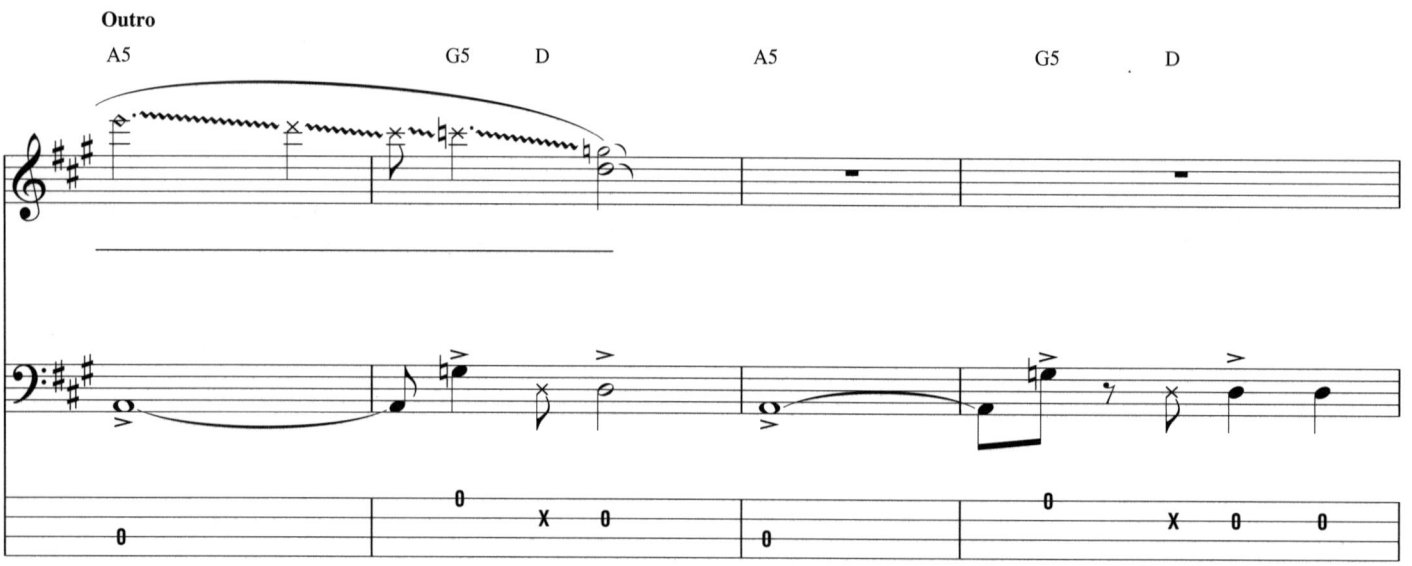

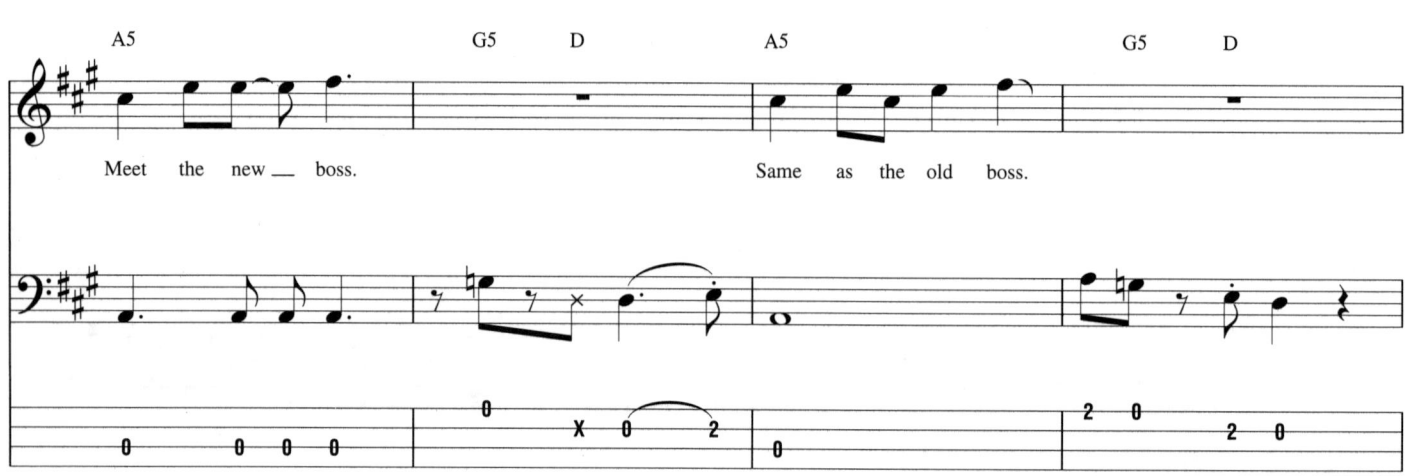

Meet the new ___ boss.   Same as the old boss.

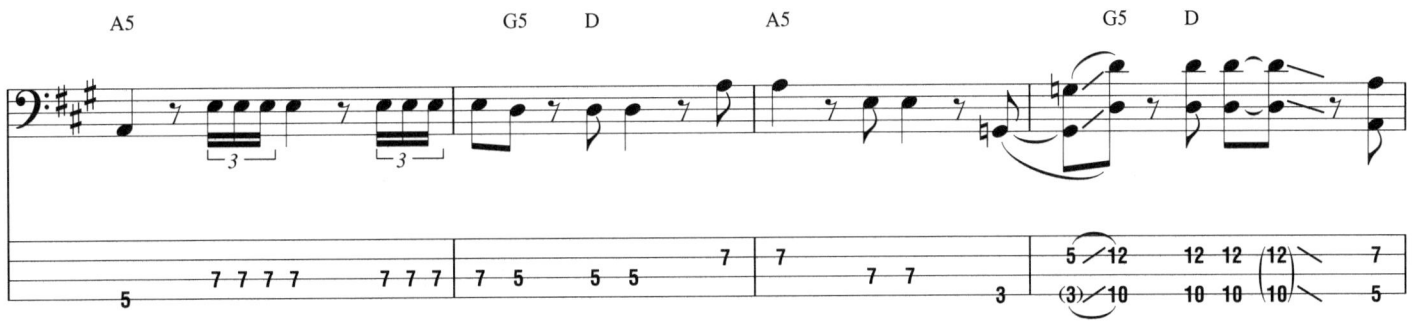

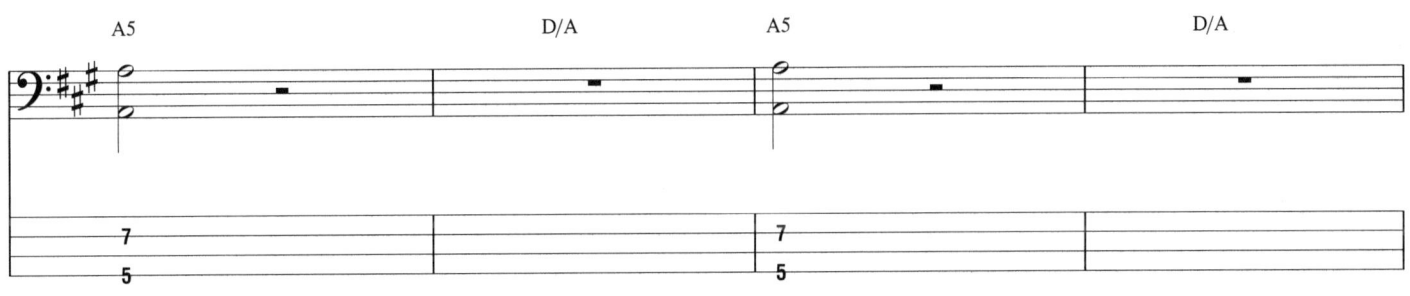

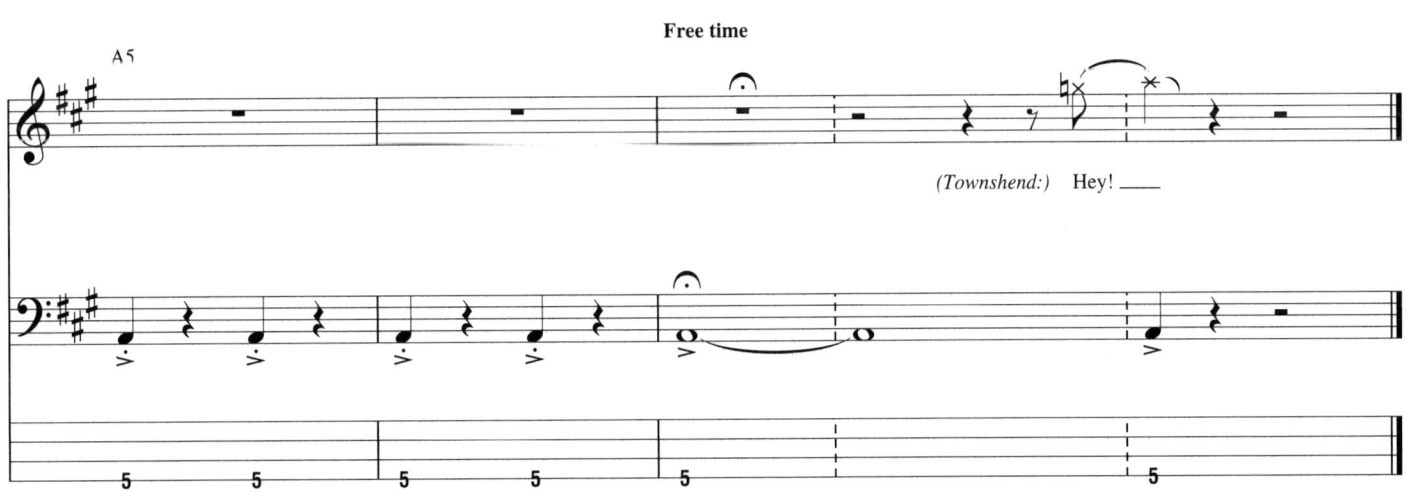

(Townshend:) Hey! ____

Bass Notation Legend

Bass music can be notated two different ways: on a *musical staff*, and in *tablature*.

THE MUSICAL STAFF shows pitches and rhythms and is divided by bar lines into measures. Pitches are named after the first seven letters of the alphabet.

TABLATURE graphically represents the bass fingerboard. Each horizontal line represents a string, and each number represents a fret.

Notes:

3rd string, open   2nd string, 2nd fret   1st & 2nd strings open, played together

HAMMER-ON: Strike the first (lower) note with one finger, then sound the higher note (on the same string) with another finger by fretting it without picking.

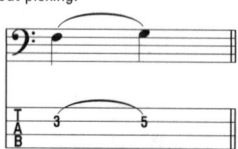

PULL-OFF: Place both fingers on the notes to be sounded. Strike the first note and without picking, pull the finger off to sound the second (lower) note.

LEGATO SLIDE: Strike the first note and then slide the same fret-hand finger up or down to the second note. The second note is not struck.

SHIFT SLIDE: Same as legato slide, except the second note is struck.

TRILL: Very rapidly alternate between the notes indicated by continuously hammering on and pulling off.

TREMOLO PICKING: The note is picked as rapidly and continuously as possible.

VIBRATO: The string is vibrated by rapidly bending and releasing the note with the fretting hand.

SHAKE: Using one finger, rapidly alternate between two notes on one string by sliding either a half-step above or below.

NATURAL HARMONIC: Strike the note while the fret hand lightly touches the string directly over the fret indicated.

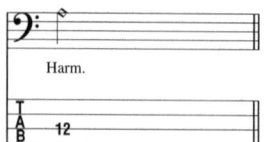

MUFFLED STRINGS: A percussive sound is produced by laying the fret hand across the string(s) without depressing them and striking them with the pick hand.

BEND: Strike the note and bend up the interval shown.

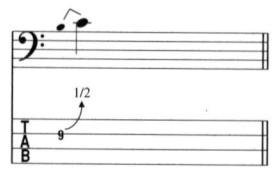

BEND AND RELEASE: Strike the note and bend up as indicated, then release back to the original note. Only the first note is struck.

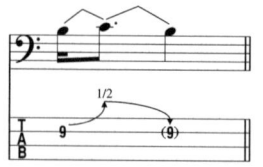

RIGHT-HAND TAP: Hammer ("tap") the fret indicated with the "pick-hand" index or middle finger and pull off to the note fretted by the fret hand.

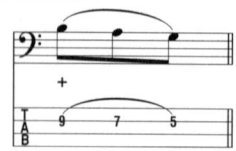

LEFT-HAND TAP: Hammer ("tap") the fret indicated with the "fret-hand" index or middle finger.

SLAP: Strike ("slap") string with right-hand thumb.

POP: Snap ("pop") string with right-hand index or middle finger.

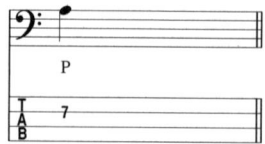

Additional Musical Definitions

 (accent) • Accentuate note (play it louder).

 (accent) • Accentuate note with great intensity.

(staccato) • Play the note short.

⊓ • Downstroke

V • Upstroke

D.S. al Coda • Go back to the sign (𝄋), then play until the measure marked "*To Coda*," then skip to the section labelled "**Coda**."

D.C. al Fine • Go back to the beginning of the song and play until the measure marked "*Fine*" (end).

Bass Fig. • Label used to recall a recurring pattern.

Fill • Label used to identify a brief melodic figure which is to be inserted into the arrangement.

tacet • Instrument is silent (drops out).

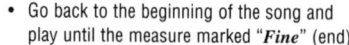 • Repeat measures between signs.

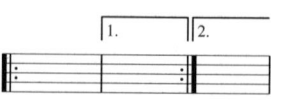 • When a repeated section has different endings, play the first ending only the first time and the second ending only the second time.

NOTE: Tablature numbers in parentheses mean:
1. The note is being sustained over a system (note in standard notation is tied), or
2. The note is sustained, but a new articulation (such as a hammer-on, pull-off, slide or vibrato) begins, or
3. The note is a barely audible "ghost" note (note in standard notation is also in parentheses).